COMMUNITY-BASED LEARNING AND SOCIAL MOVEMENTS
Popular Education in a Populist Age

Marjorie Mayo

First published in Great Britain in 2020 by

Policy Press
University of Bristol
1-9 Old Park Hill
Bristol
BS2 8BB
UK
t: +44 (0)117 954 5940
pp-info@bristol.ac.uk
www.policypress.co.uk

North America office:
Policy Press
c/o The University of Chicago Press
1427 East 60th Street
Chicago, IL 60637, USA
t: +1 773 702 7700
f: +1 773-702-9756
sales@press.uchicago.edu
www.press.uchicago.edu

© Policy Press 2020

British Library Cataloguing in Publication Data
A catalogue record for this book is available from the British Library

Library of Congress Cataloging-in-Publication Data
A catalog record for this book has been requested

978-1-4473-4325-7 hardback
978-1-4473-4327-1 paperback
978-1-4473-4326-4 ePdf
978-1-4473-4328-8 ePub

The right of Marjorie Mayo to be identified as author of this work has been asserted by her in accordance with the Copyright, Designs and Patents Act 1988.

All rights reserved: no part of this publication may be reproduced, stored in a retrieval system, or transmitted in any form or by any means, electronic, mechanical, photocopying, recording, or otherwise without the prior permission of Policy Press.

The statements and opinions contained within this publication are solely those of the author and not of the University of Bristol or Policy Press. The University of Bristol and Policy Press disclaim responsibility for any injury to persons or property resulting from any material published in this publication.

Policy Press works to counter discrimination on grounds of gender, race, disability, age and sexuality.

The cover image, 'Seeds of Change', was chosen as an image of hope for popular, community-based learning.
Cover design by Robin Hawes
Printed and bound in Great Britain by CMP, Poole
Policy Press uses environmentally responsible print partners

To my family and to the memory of Simon

Contents

List of figures		vi
Acknowledgements		vii
1	Popular education in a populist age	1
2	Popular education and its roots	19
3	Spaces and places for popular education and participatory action research	41
4	Principles and practice	57
5	Sharing understandings of varying histories and cultures	77
6	Making connections: linking issues and struggles across space and time	95
7	Power and power analysis	117
8	Community–university partnerships	137
9	Taking emotions into account	155
10	Looking backwards, looking forwards	175
References		187
Index		201

List of figures

3.1	The economy, civil society and the state as separate spheres	46
3.2	The economy, civil society and the state in the context of increasing marketisation	46
7.1	The power cube	124
7.2	Competing interests for the Holloway site (1)	127
7.3	Competing interests for the Holloway site (2)	128
7.4	Power and sympathy mapping grid	129

Acknowledgements

My appreciations and thanks to all those who have contributed in their varying ways, as family, friends, former colleagues and fellow activists. You have continued to provide – and challenge – so many of the ideas that are included here, contributing such a range of information and advice. Thank you all so much.

I should like to add very particular thanks to the following: Andy Bain, Charlie Clarke, John Gaventa, Morag Gillie, Emma Jackson, Meirian Jump, Budd Hall, Paul Hoggett, Susan Kelly, Roger McKenzie, Zoraida Mendiwelso-Bendek, Juliet Merrifield, John Page and Rajesh Tandon. Ines Newman read through earlier drafts in their entirety, providing extremely valuable, detailed feedback. My special thanks to her, as always, my frankest and most valued critic.

My thanks and appreciations to the Institute of Development Studies for permission to reproduce the power cube, in Chapter 7.

Colleagues at Policy Press have been unfailingly supportive, as always, too. My thanks to you all and to your readers for your very helpful feedback and suggestions. Any remaining errors are, of course, down to me, alone.

1

Popular education in a populist age

> Inescapably we live in both interesting and disturbing times.
> (Boffo et al. 2019: 247)

'Inequality is maintained by misleading the public', Danny Dorling has argued, with governments blaming their predecessors for the 2007–08 financial crisis (Dorling, 2018: 5). Adding insult to injury, he has continued, British governments have been attempting to justify the policies of austerity that have followed, shifting the costs onto the poorest and most deprived in contemporary Britain. It has been these most vulnerable groups who have then been held to blame, the so-called benefit scroungers, the immigrants, the refugees, the Muslims – anyone other than those who had actually caused and then benefited from the crisis in the first place. Symptomatically the Oxford dictionaries selected 'post-truth' as word of the year in 2016, defining this as shorthand for circumstances in which objective facts are less influential in shaping public opinion than appeals to emotion and personal belief. This has been about promoting the politics of misplaced blame and fear rather than the politics of reasoned democratic debate.

The UK is becoming increasingly polarised, not only economically, but also politically. Far Right politicians have been exploiting people's anxieties in this precarious climate, playing on popular feelings of alienation and distrust. This has been causing growing concern, both in Britain and elsewhere, with the rise of xenophobia (Fekete, 2009) and of White Supremacist movements in different contexts. The media – including social media – have the capacity to exacerbate such emotions, re-enforcing feelings of anxiety and resentment.

Meanwhile authoritarian populist governments have been coming to power, from Europe to Latin America and beyond, including India, where Far Right politicians have been associated with violent attacks on minority communities in the recent past. Such violent episodes characterise the behaviour of those at the most extreme end of the Far Right spectrum. But they serve as warnings about the possible outcomes of the politics of hatred.

While the Far Right has been spreading these toxic messages, others have been responding to the challenges of neoliberal austerity in very different ways, offering very different explanations of the causes of people's problems. Increasingly concerned about the causes of the rise of Far Right populism, racism, xenophobia, anti-Semitism, Islamophobia and violence, critics have been exploring alternative ways forward in differing international contexts. Hopeful rather than hateful futures can be promoted, building support for social justice agendas – with the active engagement of communities and social movements. But communities need to be critically informed if they are to make effective challenges to misleading populist claims about the causes of people's problems, just as they need to feel equipped to respond to populist appeals to destructive emotions and socially divisive beliefs and prejudices.

This is where popular educators have potentially significant contributions to make to the development of progressive movements for social justice and community solidarity. Working in partnership with communities and social movements, academics and community professionals have been developing new approaches to community-based learning, popular education (including social movement-based learning) and knowledge democracy, promoting less socially divisive and more hopeful strategies for active citizenship. This book aims to meet the growing interest in sharing these experiences and reflecting on such approaches to community-based learning and socially engaged research, building shared understandings about the causes of social problems, and developing collective support for strategies to promote social justice and community solidarity.

This chapter starts by exploring differing definitions and approaches to understanding Far Right populism and its emotional appeals. How has populism been variously understood? What have been the theoretical and ideological roots? How can we understand the growth of Far Right populism in contemporary contexts, taking account of the divisive effects of increasingly authoritarian forms of neoliberalism, continuing austerity, increasing inequalities and mounting insecurities on a global scale?

This sets the scene for reflecting on more constructive approaches in response, focusing on the development of strategies to promote popular education and participatory action research. Far from representing 'magic bullets', popular education and participatory action research have much more limited – but still valuable – contributions to make, in the context of these global challenges. Through shared understandings, active citizens, communities and social movements can develop alternative and less socially exclusive responses to their problems, problems that have been leading to such feelings of alienation and anger, especially but not only among those feeling left behind.

Subsequent chapters move on to explore differing definitions and varying approaches to popular education and participatory action research, both in theory and practice, taking account of their inherent tensions and challenges. How can communities and social movements be supported to develop alternative ways forward, as active citizens, analysing the underlying causes of their concerns, taking account of the power relationships that need to be considered both within and between communities and structures of governance? And how can they be supported in engaging with people's emotions to address people's anxieties and fears of the 'other' in more socially inclusive ways? The book concludes by reflecting on the implications for developing strategies and alliances for social solidarity and social justice – while recognising the continuing challenges for popular educators, for the future.

There has, of course, been a longstanding tradition of academic and professional interest in adult education and participatory action research, drawing on the work of Paulo Freire and others, in varying contexts internationally. This book draws on these debates as they have developed over time, as the following chapter explores in further detail. This sets the context for exploring the emergence of a wide range of initiatives in more recent times, promoting popular education (however defined) from the bottom up. As the call for papers for the Popular Education Network's (PEN) 2018 conference explained, 'Everyone seems to be doing "popular education" now – it's one of the latest trends', going on to add that:

> As the majority of people feel deeply the effects of climate change, global expansions of right wing and neo-colonial attitudes worsen the everyday life of working class and poor people. Meanwhile social activists and popular educators, located in various places and spaces, are resisting and working towards a radically different world.

Some of these initiatives have been developed by practitioners, with or without academic support, but many have been developed by social activists themselves, very often young activists, educating themselves and others about the issues that concern them most. The Occupy movement organised teach-ins and 'free universities', for instance. More recent examples range from workshops to tackle the causes of racism and xenophobia through to more academic sessions on Marxist explanations of the economy, with students questioning the basis for austerity policies, as they challenge the predominance of neoliberal economics within their universities more generally.

While I have been particularly struck by the emergence of popular education initiatives in the UK, I have also become more aware of a number of parallels in international contexts, from popular education events in response to the US presidential elections of 2016 through to the development of popular education and participatory action research projects as part of peace-building efforts in Colombia. These initiatives have set out to work with communities and social movements through popular education – community-based learning and research for social justice agendas. Rather than simply responding with the 'facts', these approaches have been aiming to offer more effective ways of addressing the underlying causes of the rise of populist movements of the Far Right and their emotional appeals, accompanied, as these have been, by increasing incidences of hate speech and violence.

Populism and the Far Right in context

Definitions of 'populism' have been, and continue to be, contested. Historically 'populism' has been applied to very different movements in Europe and elsewhere, including both Latin and North American countries (Lazaridis et al, 2016). There have been soft versions of populism and hard versions of populism, it has been argued, with populisms of the political left (Mouffe, 2018) as well as populisms of the political right, the term being applied to differing movements, ideologies and political practices (Laclau, 2005). Not all populists come from the Far Right, then, just as not all of those on the Far Right could be described as populists, far from it in fact. Despite the differences, however, populisms have tended to share a common approach to identifying the 'people' as against the elites (Lazaridis et al, 2016).

While recognising that fascist populisms in Europe have differed from each other, from Nazism in Germany, to Francoism in Spain, and that European populisms have differed from the populisms of Latin America in the 1930s and 1940s, Laclau has similarly identified a number of features that can be identified in particular historical situations. To summarise – and to simplify a far more complex set of arguments – populism tends to emerge in crises of representation, he suggests, when formal political processes fail to meet social demands. In such contexts a section of the community (the underdog) may then present itself as representing the whole community – the people versus the elite/the establishment.

Crick (2002) has described populism in similar terms as a 'style of politics and rhetoric that seeks to arouse a majority who are, have been or think themselves to be outside the polity, scorned and despised by an educated establishment', defining the 'us' of this despised majority in terms of their differences with the 'others', such as immigrants and Muslims, for example. These 'others' are then being defined as posing threats to the majority, threats that the elite/establishment is failing to address. The emergence of this type of populism symptomised wider shortcomings in representative democratic processes, in Crick's view, democratic deficits that he himself was keen to address through the promotion of active learning for active citizenship (as described in Chapter 3). Before moving on to focus on learning and popular education, though, the roots of populism need to be explored, together with the particular factors that have been associated with the growth of Far Right populism in the contemporary context, characterised by crises of representation as well as by increasing inequalities in the UK and elsewhere.

Populism has been associated with emotional appeals to notions of identity, such as national, ethnic or religious identities (including white nationalist identities), typically framed in terms of the contrasts between 'us' and the 'others'. The 'others' may be minority communities, including newcomers, such as migrants and refugees, especially those from different cultures and religions. And the 'others' may be elites, politicians, the plutocracy, or in the case of the US, the 'Washington insiders' (Panizza, 2005: 3).

Combatting such views with appeals to the 'facts' simply misses the point here. Especially if the 'facts' come from distrusted sources: 'They would say that, wouldn't they?' And who needs experts anyway? Myth-busting exercises about the impacts of immigration have been challenged for precisely such reasons. Those already opposed to immigration may simply refuse to believe the counter arguments, even when these arguments are supported by seemingly irrefutable facts. So where does such scepticism come from?

Populism's roots

There would seem to be theoretical roots to be traced from aspects of postmodernist thinking, approaches that became predominant in the last decades of the 20th century, challenging more structural approaches, including Marxist approaches, to the study of social issues. Although there were signs that the cultural hegemony of postmodernism was weakening, according to David Harvey, way back in 1990, postmodernist thinking had been and continued to be highly influential in a number of fields, in his view, including the arts as well as the social sciences. Harvey welcomed the contributions that postmodernism had been making to the study of contemporary capitalism (Harvey, 1990), in the context of neoliberal globalisation. He was appreciative of the radical potential of postmodernist critiques of previously accepted approaches. And he valued postmodernist emphases on the importance of addressing social divisions in terms of gender, sexuality and race, although he continued to locate these in relation to the centrality of class divisions in capitalist societies.

But these positive aspects of postmodernism had their downsides, in Harvey's view. Anti-authoritarian iconoclasm could be deployed for radical ends. Or conversely, deconstructionism could lead to the 'suspicion of any narrative that aspires to coherence' challenging all basic propositions and 'all consensual standards of truth and justice, of ethics and meaning' (Harvey, 1990: 350). This could lead to forms of nihilism, ironically preparing the way for charismatic politics 'and even more simplistic propositions than those that were deconstructed' (1990: 350). If nothing is to be believed, then anything goes? Other responses to the critique of metanarratives could include overemphasis on localism and competition between the fragments, he continued, with identity politics taking over from class politics, rather than enriching class politics with more complex understandings of the intersectionalities between class and other forms of discrimination and oppression. Harvey referred to the title of Andre Gorz's influential publication, *Farewell to the Working Class*, in this context, identifying this as symptomatic of the logic of postmodernism, potentially contributing to the growth of the politics of the Far Right, whatever the author's original intentions to the contrary.

There are significant elements here with resonance for subsequent discussions of Far Right populism. Postmodernist scepticism has paved the way for more general doubts about the very possibility of objective truth, it has been opined.

Such approaches have been linked with forms of anti-intellectualism that mark a return to pre-modernist or pre-Enlightenment thinking, others have also argued (Wodak, 2015: 2). If anything goes, then any interpretation is as valid as any other. So why fuss about the 'facts'? And if identity politics should come to supersede class politics, with identifications based on feelings and emotional attachments, where does that leave the working class and working class politics, Wodak questioned.

So what? Why would this matter if these were no more than academic debates? But what if such views had wider resonance, part of the mood music of the times? Postmodernism has been seen as having appeal beyond academia, fuelling the cynicism and the relativism which became fashionable among disenchanted sections of the left, towards the end of the last century (D'Ancona, 2017). How might such attitudes play into wider scepticism about truth claims or indeed about the relevance of arguments based on factual evidence at all? Davis's discussion of the context for 'post-truth' and 'fake news' explores similar connections, linking the spread of 'bullshit' with societies where relationships of trust break down, 'where people stop caring about the evidence and ask whose side the communicator is on' (Davis, 2017: xx). In fraught times, divisions between traditional left and right wing politics can give way to fragmentary forms of identity politics, Davis suggests, accompanied by more general feelings of anger at elites – potentially populist responses, in other words. Social media can have particular significance in such contexts, fanning the dissemination of 'alternative' truths.

The retreat from class politics has been identified as particularly relevant, in relation to the frustrations of the traditional white working class. The Runnymede Trust's report *Who Cares about the White Working Class?* (Sveinsson, 2009) explores the causes of these frustrations, set against the background of divisive forms of identity politics. The report challenges the media's focus on competition between different ethnic groups – with the white working class losing out to particular minority communities. This is set against the reality that the most disadvantaged in society are working class people of whatever ethnic background, the poorest fifth of the population who are increasingly separated from the most prosperous majority – rather than from each other – by inequalities of income, housing and education, among others. This is not, of course, how these divisions are necessarily perceived, however.

Meanwhile, 'middle class commentators may be happy to defend white working class interests against the onslaught of politically correct multiculturalism' in the Runnymede Trust report's view, but 'they will simultaneously deride and ridicule the feckless and undeserving poor, who have squandered the opportunities gracefully given to them by the welfare state, and can therefore rightfully be left to wallow in their own poverty' (Sveinsson, 2009: 5). The demonisation of the white working class has featured in a number of studies in recent years (Jones, 2012; McKenzie, 2015), demonisation processes that have been amplified on social media, along with television series portraying the 'underclass' as benefit scroungers at best, if not actually dangerous criminals.

There have been challenges to these demonisation processes, of course. Poverty porn has been resisted, as people at the sharp end of austerity have organised to make their voices heard. 'We don't have to accept this attack on our living standards, we don't have to accept the demonization of the various minorities, be they disabled, poor, single parents, immigrants or refugees,' a disabled activist explained (Sng, 2019). 'We can stand up, join forces, and support one another,' she argued:

> Little by little we are hopefully changing minds and opinions, and countering some of the lies spread by certain sections of the media. We are telling people there is a better way, that life doesn't have to be as hard as it is today, that austerity is a deliberate ideological choice designed to punish the poor for the deliberate actions of the rich, particularly the bankers. (Sng, 2019)

This account is just one among so many portraits of hope and resilience in contemporary Britain. But this is in no way to underestimate the extent of anger and resentment, and especially, although not only, within working class communities. And there is plenty of evidence to point to the existence of just such feelings. Vic Seidler, in his reflections on *Making Sense of Brexit*, described the vote to leave the European Union in 2016 as 'a scream of protest' (Seidler, 2018: xiv). He went on to draw parallels between the Brexit vote and Trump's election victory in the US in the same year. Both outcomes challenged the logic of neoliberal globalisation in his view, but negatively. They were expressing the frustrations of those who felt powerless, disenfranchised and alienated from the political system and 'the ways in which the economic logic was working against them' (Seidler, 2018: 14). There were layers of suppressed anger 'at being constantly patronised and talked down to', with feelings of enragement 'when it seemed that only the rich 1%, connected to corporate power, were really benefiting from globalised neocapitalism' (Seidler, 2018: 14). Seidler's reflections raise a number of interrelated factors here: the increasing inequalities that have been accompanying neoliberal globalisation, the perceived failures of political systems to address the resulting social problems, on both sides of the Atlantic, and the resentments of those who have felt marginalised, derided, victimised and blamed as a result, voters who were expressing 'a howl of rage against exclusion, alienation and remote authority' (Monbiot, quoted in Seidler, 2018: 143).

While such feelings may have been particularly identifiable within older de-industrialised working class communities, they have been by no means confined to these. Brexit slogans such as 'Take Back Control' have appealed to wider sections of the population too, chiming with feelings of nostalgia for a mythical golden age perhaps, an age when Britain – like America – was seen to have been great, when shared cultures were valued and communities were believed to have been strong. O'Toole has linked these types of feelings with mythologies about the Second World War and its aftermath, when plucky little Britain stood up for freedom and democracy, only to be denied its rightful place in the international order; feelings of resentment and self-pity as Britain lost its empire (O'Toole, 2018). Such emotional factors have been central to the growth of Far Right populism it has been argued, as well as the economic, political and social factors that have given rise to them in the first place.

Arlie Hochschild's study of 'Anger and Mourning on the American Right' explores the evidence for such a view, based on her fieldwork in Louisiana, US (Hochschild, 2016). She sets the scene in terms of the financial crash of 2008 and its aftermath, in the context of the politics of austerity, as interpreted by Far Right media, such as Fox News. People in the southern states, especially white people, felt frustrated by falling wages/declining incomes and other material concerns in her view, as they bore the brunt of governmental decisions to bail out the financial elite that had caused the crash in the first place. But southern whites also responded more emotionally, feeling alienated, pushed back by the liberal elites who despised them. 'Oh, liberals think that Bible-believing Southerners are ignorant, backward, rednecks, losers. They think we're racist, sexist, homophobic, and maybe fat (adding insult to insult)', she was told (Hochschild, 2016: 23). People felt 'strangers in their own land, afraid, resentful, displaced and dismissed by the very people who were, they felt, cutting the line' (cheating their way ahead of them; Hochschild, 2016: 218).

Powerful parallels emerge from a series of focus groups conducted by the Think Tank Demos, in 2017.[1] The participants were mostly older white British people in former industrial areas, places described as having had 'thousands of jobs, loads of different factories, ship yards, coal mines' but where 'now, there's nothing at all'. Unsurprisingly then, these focus groups revealed profound anxieties about economic precariousness, along with expressions of mistrust in politicians' capacity to improve people's lives. There were feelings of particular resentment, anger and hostility towards these politicians – described as robbers, lining their own pockets rather than addressing the concerns of those they were supposed to represent.

There was also evidence of nostalgia, the feeling that Britain had lost its sense of community and become progressively more selfish and individualistic. Political correctness was described as having gone too far, suppressing patriotism and the celebration of British cultural identity and Christian values. People wanted to take back control, to get their country back. 'It don't feel like our country any more.' This view was accompanied by some expressions of negativity towards immigrants more generally. Were immigrants scrounging on the welfare state? But there was also evidence of some acceptance of the need for controlled immigration. There were jobs that needed to be filled, after all. And there were different views about Brexit more generally, some nuances of feelings about the future as well as expressions of nostalgia for a mythical past.

Winlow, Hall and Treadwell's study of the Far Right English Defence League (EDL) identified a number of similar feelings, focusing this time, in contrast, on younger sections of the population. As this study explained, a growing number of people were very angry (Winlow et al, 2017), expressing pervasive cynicism about neoliberal realities. Those associated with the EDL, an amorphous set of groupings around the Far Right, were predominantly white, working class and disproportionately although not exclusively male. They were frustrated at the lack of economic opportunities, but by no means anti-capitalist. Rather they were resentful of those they thought were doing better than themselves, especially Muslims who were described as having 'the nice cars, the big houses' while 'ripping us off' (Winlow et al, 2017: 155).

The focus on Islam was at least in some part explained by the context for the research, the authors explained. The fieldwork had been carried out against a background of public concern about South Asian men who had been accused of grooming vulnerable white girls. This was quoted as exemplifying the problems with Muslims, portrayed as rapists as well as terrorists, scrounging on the welfare state while simultaneously taking over the only available jobs. While EDL supporters gave voice to such expressions of prejudice, however, they typically denied being racist per se. 'I'm not racist, not really', as one of them put this (Winlow et al, 2017: 97). The research did not identify widespread anti-Semitism, or indeed much homophobia, or prejudice about the rights of people with disabilities, as it turned out either. Nor was there much evidence of opposition to women's rights.

Copsey and Worley's collection of essays on the Far Right in Britain since 1967 identified similar ambiguities in relation to attitudes to gender (Copsey and Worley, 2018). Muslims were the focus of much of the anger of EDL supporters in Winlow et al's study. But EDL supporters' feelings of resentment were not just related to immigration or even focused on economic insecurity, important though these aspects evidently were. EDL supporters were also frustrated and angry about metropolitan liberalism and what they saw as its co-option of the political system.

Like white people in the southern states of America, they were expressing feelings of loss and grievance. The white working class was being ignored or demonised, they felt, their communities undermined by the forces of change. There were feelings of nostalgia for a past golden age, melancholia for a lost world of solidarity, security and belief. And for past glories – 'We used to have an Empire for fuck's sake. Now look' (Winlow et al, 2017: 125).

Identifying with Far Right organisations and groups was enabling their supporters to find a sense of community, defining themselves against the 'others', both Muslims in particular and liberal elites and politicians more generally. 'The politicians today are just money-grabbing bastards mate, fucking liars and cowards' (Winlow et al, 2017: 92). Liberals who criticised EDL supporters for being racist came in for special venom. 'The rich cunts in the City ... calling us racists. It's not their jobs on the line is it?' (2017: 95). Along with politicians of the left – 'posh white people who've taken over the Labour Party' (2017: 126) – these were the people who 'think everyone's a fucking vegan and shops at Waitrose' (2017: 126).

While support for the EDL may have tailed off or moved in different directions, taking new forms since the fieldwork for this particular research was completed, as the researchers themselves suggested, the frustrations that were giving rise to such feelings were still to be addressed, in their view. They concluded that the New Labour years had been 'an absolute disaster for the left', failing to offer convincing challenges to neoliberal globalisation, leaving so many people with feelings of abandonment as a result. Danny Dorling endorsed this view, describing *The Rise of the Far Right* as a 'fast moving novel take on how New Labour and the liberal left media created the circumstances in which the English Defence League would grow and of how UKIP and the EDL are linked' (Winlow et al, 2017: back cover). Support for the EDL had been most marked among working class people in declining industrial areas. But the politics of the 1%, 'the few', were impacting on far wider sections of the community, all those affected by precarious employment, unaffordable housing and public services under strain from a decade of austerity. The latter are 'the many' that New Labour's successors have been looking to represent, rather than continuing to support the policies that have been disproportionately benefiting the 'few'.

While the material roots of popular grievances need to be understood, set against the background of neoliberal globalisation compounded by the impacts of austerity over the past decade, such grievances do not seem to provide a total explanation, however. Far from it, in fact. Far Right ideologies have traction within more privileged sections of society as well as within less privileged sections, even if such ideas are expressed in other ways. The rise of Far Right populism needs to be understood more comprehensively as subsequent chapters will suggest, taking account of the range of historical, cultural and ideological factors and practices that popular education initiatives need to address.

Developing alternatives and the scope for popular education

While the increasing inequalities and frustrations that have been accompanying neoliberal austerity policies have been associated with the rise of Far Right populism, there have, of course, been very different responses. Politics have become increasingly polarised in response to these widening divisions, with the resurgence of progressive movements for social change, replacing the politics of hate with the politics of hope. As Vic Seidler reflected, one million people marched in the Women's March on Washington on the day after the Trump's inauguration in 2017. There were calls to resistance with enormous marches and rallies in different cities, chanting slogans such as 'Love not hate makes America great' (Seidler, 2018: 18). And there have been practical expressions of alternative approaches, challenging racism and xenophobia in action by providing sanctuary for refugees in USA, for example (Paik, 2017).

Alternative aspirations have also been manifested in more explicitly party political ways. So many young people have been attracted by the views of politicians such as Jeremy Corbyn and Bernie Sanders, politicians who have rejected the politics of austerity, arguing for more radical approaches to meeting the needs of the 'many not the few'. And so many older people have been re-engaging in party politics, with the prospect of campaigning for more progressive policies for social change.

This upsurge has also been associated with growing concerns with popular education, as subsequent chapters illustrate. Young people, but by no means only young people, have been participating in a range of activities to examine the political situations in which they find themselves as the basis for exploring the scope for developing alternatives. As Kenan Malik (2018) has been pointing out, 'there is growing backlash against the consequences of free market policies and a sense of alienation from mainstream institutions' as the lives of so many young people have been shaped 'by the financial crash of 2008, by the austerity policies that have followed and by the gross inequalities that disfigure the world'. They have been asking questions about the underlying causes of the financial crisis of 2008 and why so few economists saw this coming. Could Marxist approaches to the study of economics provide more convincing explanations? What else could have been done, subsequently, in response? And how might austerity policies be replaced with policies to promote environmentally and socially sustainable development, tackling inequalities of income, wealth and social opportunities?

The programmes for 'The World Transformed' (TWT), events that have been organised alongside Labour Party conferences since 2016, illustrate the range of topics that have been debated, in the context of such concerns. These events have attracted impressively large audiences, young people getting involved in politics for the first time and older people re-engaging as the parameters of political debate have been widening beyond the middle ground of the so-called Third Way. This focus on popular education has been seen as central to the construction of alternative approaches. The aim has been to develop a broad movement in support of transformative policies for 'the many not the few', as the 2017 Labour Party election manifesto expressed it (although TWT is not a party political organisation per se, being committed to engaging people and groups across the spectrum of transformative politics).

This inclusivity has been mirrored in TWT's events. Over 5,000 people attended the 2017 TWT programme. There were sessions on economic, social, political and environmental issues, along with a variety of cultural happenings. The programmes for 2018 and 2019 were described as offering a similarly wide and participatory set of events, attracting even greater numbers of participants, with four days of socialist politics, art exhibitions, and other forms of community and cultural activity. Jointly organised with Global Justice Now the focus was on international as well as more local issues, with grassroots activists exchanging experiences and views as well as hearing from well-known names. Chapter 6 discusses TWT's contributions in further detail.

The World Transformed is just one example, of course. There have been workshops, seminars, courses and informal events of similar ranges, including the self-education activities that have been accompanying social movements and social movement campaigns, depending on their particular focus. Second wave feminist groups in the 1970s typically began by members sharing their experiences and feelings, as a way of raising their collective consciousness, for example. When tenants and other housing activists developed their responses to what became the Housing and Planning Act 2016, they also started by educating themselves on the issues involved, going through the proposed legislation in detail, working out the likely implications, identifying the most significant aspects on which to mount their campaign. Subsequent chapters provide a range of illustrations, exploring a variety of ways in which social movement activists have been learning together, in the pursuit of social change agendas. There have been community-based initiatives, rooted in localities, addressing their common concerns, and there have been popular education initiatives on wider scales, developing participatory action research in partnerships with universities and colleges, as subsequent chapters go on to illustrate.

Popular education offers no magic bullet, as it has already been suggested. On the contrary, popular education has its own inherent tensions and challenges. But despite the limitations, popular education can still contribute to the development of social justice agendas, it will be argued – enabling people to develop more critical understandings of the issues that concern them most, sharing strategies to address these collectively. The legacies of Paulo Freire and others have relevance here, emphasising the importance of starting from people's own priorities, actively engaging individuals and communities in participative ways. So many of the principles have continuing relevance, particularly the importance of listening to people and taking their concerns – and their feelings – seriously, rather than attempting to persuade people by simply bombarding them with the facts.

Before moving on to focus on varying approaches to popular education and their histories in subsequent chapters, this chapter concludes by summarising the chapters that follow.

The chapters that follow

Chapter 2 starts by summarising definitions of the contested notion of popular education (Crowther et al, 1999). This leads into the discussion of popular education's roots in the UK and elsewhere, including approaches developed by Freire in Latin America (1972) and Horton in the US (Bell et al, 1990). Having outlined these different approaches, the chapter focuses on participatory action research and learning for active citizenship and democratic social change within social movements more generally. The chapter concludes with a brief summary of more recent approaches towards the promotion of knowledge democracy, active citizenship and participatory action research – including approaches developed via community–university partnerships (Tandon, 2005; Schuller and Watson, 2009; Fryer, 2010; Hall et al, 2012a; English and Irving, 2015).

Chapter 3 focuses on the varying contexts in which popular education and participatory action research partnerships have been taking place, the contested spaces and places for popular education in practice. Adult educators have faced challenges when promoting popular education and participatory action research from within university bases. And community and youth workers have faced their own challenges, as this chapter goes on to explain, along with the challenges faced by community outreach staff including those based in museums, galleries and libraries. Meanwhile, social movements have been promoting 'popular education' for themselves, in a variety of spaces and places. This chapter concludes with examples from feminist and anti-racist movements, trade union and labour movements, and political mobilisations such as Hope Not Hate.

Chapter 4 looks more specifically at varying approaches to the principles, value bases and practices of learning for active citizenship and social change. UK approaches will be summarised from the Workers' Educational Association (WEA) onwards, together with more recent approaches such as those developed through the Take Part learning programme for active citizenship (Mayo and Annette, 2010; Mayo et al, 2013). Other examples include a range of initiatives developed via the arts (Clover and Sanford, 2013; Rooke, 2013) both in the UK and internationally. The chapter concludes by focusing on a number of such approaches, including those being promoted in Latin America.

Chapter 5 moves on to explore ways of developing popular education approaches for specific contexts, taking account of their particular histories and cultures. Although there have been commonalities, there have also been significant differences both within and between communities and social movements, differences that need to be understood if popular education programmes are to be tailored to take account of these differing experiences and needs. The arts can stimulate such discussions, exploring the strengths – as well as the limitations – of previous approaches, providing the basis for shared learning about the most effective ways of building alliances between different types of organisations and social movements in contemporary contexts, including campaigns for housing and planning to meet social needs.

Having explored ways of working across differences, Chapter 6 focuses on working around the commonalities, making the links between people's immediate concerns, pursuing the connections between jobs, health and the environment, for example, along with the links between housing and planning, education and health. The first part of this chapter looks back to previous experiences of organising in solidarity across international borders, campaigning to address people's health and environmental concerns. This is followed by reflections on experiences of popular education and participatory research in response to urban regeneration initiatives, involving a range of interrelated planning issues and challenges. The chapter concludes with a focus on building connections between popular education initiatives in Britain in the contemporary context, identifying ways of developing mutual support systems.

Chapter 7 concentrates on sharing understandings of the underlying structures that need to be addressed, analysing the power structures that impact on communities at local levels and beyond, taking account of differing definitions and varying perspectives on power and empowerment. Having explored ways of analysing and then mapping such power structures, the chapter moves on to investigate ways of understanding power relationships *within* communities, such as power differentials based on gender, class, ethnicity and age. The chapter concludes by posing questions about the potential implications of such power differentials for community–university research partnerships, striving to build alliances in the pursuit of social justice agendas.

Chapter 8 takes up the potential contributions of community–university partnerships more specifically. Community-based research and the co-production of knowledge have been threads running through previous chapters. This chapter focuses more specifically on ways of developing partnerships for co-producing 'really useful knowledge' while taking account of the differing interests *within* and *between* universities and communities and the challenges involved in working with these differences. Despite the pressures from marketisation within universities in so many contemporary contexts, there are examples of very different – and more cooperative – approaches being developed. The chapter draws on different examples, co-producing knowledge for development and community solidarity.

Although centrally important, structural analyses and evidence-based research need to be complemented by popular education strategies that take account of people's emotions. These concerns run throughout the book, but with more specific focus in Chapter 9. The roots of Far Right populism, racism and xenophobia need to be understood and addressed; simply appealing to the facts can be counterproductive. Popular educators and participatory action researchers have experiences to share here, exploring ways of engaging with people's emotions, including emotions of fear and hatred of the 'other', addressing the prejudices that further disempower the most disadvantaged. There are international examples of community-based learning strategies to engage with such feelings and prejudices, together with more local initiatives to tackle hate crime, such as via 'Hope not Hate' workshops in Britain, along with strategies to tackle racism, anti-Semitism, xenophobia and other forms of prejudice via the arts and sport.

The final chapter reflects on the implications in terms of the theoretical underpinnings involved. How can these enable popular educators to respond to the challenges of the contemporary context most effectively? And how might popular educators and participatory action researchers contribute towards the development of wider movements for social transformation while taking account of the continuing challenges?

Note
[1] www.demos.co.uk/project/citizens-voices/

2

Popular education and its roots

This chapter identifies popular education's definitions and roots in the UK and elsewhere, exploring competing approaches to popular education and participatory action research, both in theory and in practice. This summary includes the approaches developed by Paulo Freire in Brazil (1972), Myles Horton in the US (Bell et al, 1990) and Orlando Fals Borda in Colombia (1985), approaches that have had their own roots in wider debates in educational theory and practice, internationally, over time. Having identified the varying strands of popular education in their economic, political and social contexts, the chapter concludes with a brief summary of the development of participatory action research, knowledge democracy and active citizenship – including approaches being developed via community–university partnerships (Tandon, 2005; Fryer, 2010; Hall et al, 2012a; English and Irving, 2015).

What do we mean by 'popular education' anyway?

The Popular Education Network (PEN) is an international network of university-based teachers and researchers who share concerns with popular education and participatory action research. PEN has defined 'popular education' as follows.

> Popular education is understood to be popular, as distinct from merely populist, in the sense that it is:
> - rooted in the real interests and struggles of ordinary people
> - overtly political and critical of the status quo
> - committed to progressive social change. (Crowther et al, 2005a: 2)

In other words, 'popular education' is far from being neutral. On the contrary: popular education is aligned with wider efforts to promote a more socially just social order through democratic change processes, based on a clear analysis of the underlying causes of social inequality, exploitation and oppression, and the power relationships that underpin them. In this sense, popular education is profoundly political, although not party political per se (whereas the more directly *party* political approaches are described as being 'popular political education' in the chapters that follow).

This broad alignment with wider movements for transformative social change implies the need for democratic, participatory approaches to teaching and learning in practice, in PEN's view. As Crowther, Galloway and Martin continue, the process of popular education

> has the following general characteristics:
> - its curriculum comes out of the concrete experience and material interests of people in communities of resistance and struggle
> - its pedagogy is collective, focused primarily on group as distinct from individual learning and development
> - it attempts, wherever possible, to forge a direct link between education and social action. (Crowther et al, 2005a: 2)

This emphasis on the links between learning and social action distinguishes popular education from community-based education more generally, Crowther et al argue. Education as a process consists of contradictory interests and intentions, they point out, citing Paulo Freire's view that education 'embodies simultaneously the potential both for "liberation" and domestication, transformation and reproduction' (Crowther et al, 2005a: 3). People can learn to 'know their place', thereby reproducing existing social relations, learning to cope as best as possible, to be 'tooled up' and resilient, whatever structural inequalities they face. Whereas popular education

> starts from the real and systematic inequalities and injustices that currently exclude many people from anything but a nominal notion of citizenship ... listening to and articulating those voices which have been silenced and excluded from the public business of civic and political life. (2005: 3)

This is described as a 'bottom-up' process, starting from people's own interests, aspirations and lived experiences. 'Learning is essentially about making knowledge that makes sense of their world and helps them to act upon it, collectively, in order to change it for the better' (Crowther et al, 2005a: 4).

Like so many contested definitions and approaches, this raises further questions and tensions that will reappear in varying ways, as it will be suggested subsequently. In reality, as Liam Kane explains in the same collection of papers, '"popular education" is interpreted in a myriad of ways', diverse and sometimes contradictory understandings that need to be confronted, in his view (Kane, 2005: 32). Most importantly, this definition has inherent tensions and challenges. Who exactly are the 'ordinary people' that Crowther and others refer to as the target for popular education? And do these 'ordinary people' have real interests in common? Who is to define these interests, and how to take account of differences within as well as between communities and social movements?

The very notion of 'education' itself been challenged in some contexts too, taken to imply unacceptably hierarchical relationships between the educators on the one hand and those that are to be educated on the other. In Colombia, for example, those who have been directly involved in community–university partnerships have preferred to use the term 'learning' instead, thereby signifying a more democratic relationship between academics and their partners in communities. This could be signalling an alternative approach with wider applications – except that 'learning' is a potentially contested term as well. Critics have located this within the context of neoliberal approaches more generally, individualising educational provision, presenting this as an investment good, offering varying returns on individuals' learning – to be calculated in terms of the future earnings to be anticipated (Collini, 2012, 2017). Chapter 8 explores these debates in further detail.

There are fundamentally problematic notions and contested terminologies inherent in the very concept of popular education. But PEN's definition and approach do still offer a starting point for discussing popular education in different economic, political and social contexts, taking account of varying relationships with social movements over time. Popular education is not just about political education in general, however important that may be; this is about education for social change (another notion that needs further unpacking, to take account of varying approaches in practice).

Although PEN itself has been bringing university-based teachers and researchers with interests and commitments to popular education together, their approach has resonance more generally too, including for those directly engaged in popular education as social movement activists themselves. As Jack Jones, a leading trade unionist, reflected on his own experiences in the trade union movement, for instance, he had been learning by doing. Educational 'teach-ins' had played quite a part in his own involvement in the motor car and aircraft industries, with shop steward discussions and classes engaged in 'workers teaching each other' (Jones, 1992: 8). Even if they had been over-concentrating on the practical problems that they faced, he concluded, 'trade union organisation and democratic participation was immensely strengthened thereby' (1992: 8). They could be further strengthened by educational initiatives to promote wider critical analysis, in his view, valuing the contributions of previous pioneers. The scope for developing such collaborations between academics and social movements represents a continuing theme in subsequent chapters, along with the potential tensions involved.

Roots and tensions

As PEN's definition explains, popular education has been distinguished in terms of its overall purpose as well as in terms of its approach to educational methods. Both of these distinguishing features have roots in the past, whether or not they have been explicitly linked. Educational theorists have argued the case for starting from learners' own interests and concerns as a general principle. And educational theorists and activists have made the case for social purpose education, more specifically focusing on the importance of promoting 'really useful knowledge' – knowledge to 'enable people to make sense of the causes of hardship and oppression … with a view to challenging them' (Hughes, 1995: 99) – as this term has been summarised. There is not the space to explore the history of these varying educational debates in detail in this particular book. Rather, the aim is simply to identify some of the approaches that have had the most influence on those involved in popular education from the past through to more recent times.

This history can be traced back through the centuries, as Tom Steele (2010) among others has argued. But the real flowering of debates emerged from the Scientific Revolution of the 17th century and the Enlightenment of the 18th, both in Britain and elsewhere, debates that were 'generated in the belief that knowledge could be harnessed to political change' (Steele, 2010: 107). 'Knowledge is power' emerged as a slogan from way back then, whether this was knowledge and power to manage social change from the top-down, or whether, conversely, this was knowledge and power to promote social change for social justice agendas from the bottom-up. Steele's study provides a guide to these varying developments across Europe, with their differing orientations and approaches, from folk high schools and study circles in Denmark and other Nordic countries through to popular education and nationalist movements in the Habsburg regions of the Austro-Hungarian Empire. This was the wider – and varied – context for developments within Britain.

Education could be used as a means of training and maybe domesticating the emerging working class, as employers began to need better educated and more disciplined workforces to meet the requirements of the industrial revolution. Roger Fieldhouse and Associates' history of adult education in Britain traces the roots of these types of approach in terms of employers' responses to the need for more skilled workers – together with many workers' interests in gaining increased skills to improve their prospects for employment, to get better jobs and so lift themselves out of poverty (Fieldhouse, 1998). Mechanics Institutes developed across the country during the 19th century, for example, described as 'a mixture of autonomous working-class enterprise and paternalistic middle-class provision' (Fieldhouse, 1998: 23). This was to promote what has been described as 'useful knowledge' to enable people to cope with rapid economic and social change. But this was without implying that it was within the power of workers to change the existing economic order, as Engels (2009) reflected, writing about the British working class in the mid-19th century.

There were more radical approaches though, linked to campaigns for political reform, including approaches that were developed via corresponding societies, secular Sunday schools and co-operative societies, many of which established libraries, reading rooms and lecture rooms to widen access to learning and critical thinking more generally. The focus here was on the promotion of 'really useful knowledge', knowledge to enable people to analyse their situations in order to promote democratic change for social justice. These were bottom-up initiatives with links to the Chartist Movement in the first part of the 19th century, for instance, aiming to prepare people for political action, campaigning for the vote as a step towards democratic participation as active citizens. These types of initiatives could be seen as representing the roots of popular education for the future.

There is not the space for further detail here. This summary simply highlights some of the tensions that have been running through debates on adult education and popular education over time. These differing approaches have frequently been in tension with each other as a top-down instrument of control and/or as a bottom-up instrument of social emancipation.

But not always, as it will be suggested in more detail subsequently. There have been those who have rejected the notion that these are 'either/or' choices, rather than 'both/and' choices to be made. This more nuanced view applies to the tensions between individual empowerment on the one hand and collective empowerment on the other, for example. The personal and the political can and should be joined, it has been argued (von Kotze et al, 2016). And people may choose to acquire specific knowledge and skills, for the short term, while also learning to develop strategies for the longer term, alongside social movements for democratic change. Or not. People may choose not to engage in wider agendas for social change, preferring to focus on their more immediate concerns, as subsequent chapters illustrate (Recknagel with Holland, 2013). There are inherent tensions here for popular educators committed to learner-centred approaches, tensions that emerge in varying situations and guises.

But this doesn't mean that popular educators should be ambivalent as to which side they are on. While recognising the tensions involved for individuals and communities, as well as the tensions between individuals and communities on the one hand and those in power on the other, in the South African context, Astrid von Kotze and her colleagues quote a popular educator's conclusion. 'As a radical educator,' she argued, 'you actually do have to take political responsibility for your own position' (von Kotze et al, 2016: 104).

There are potential implications here when it comes to deciding how to engage with the structures of power and influence. Governments have provided, and to varying extents continue to provide, resources and other forms of support, and so have universities and colleges, among other institutions. There have been continuing debates about the implications. To what extent can popular education benefit from state support without losing sight of popular education's longer-term aims and objectives? What about the risk of becoming co-opted? And what about the risk of becoming dominated by academics – experts on top rather than experts on tap? People can and do learn for themselves, reflecting on their experiences in social movements (Foley, 1999; Merrifield, 2010). So where does this leave the role of the popular educator? These debates have been taking varying forms in different contexts, as the thinking and the experiences of Paulo Freire, the Brazilian popular educator, will illustrate in more detail subsequently.

Ruskin College Oxford and the Workers' Educational Association: tensions and debates in 20th-century Britain

The experiences of Ruskin College Oxford and the Workers' Educational Association (WEA) illustrate some of these debates in 20th-century Britain, debates with continuing resonance in more recent times. The potential implications of state funding have been hotly debated, as the history of the WEA illustrates. And so have the implications of working in partnership with universities and colleges as the history of Ruskin College Oxford also illustrates. There have been very different views on both these questions. And there have been more nuanced approaches. As a member of the WEA and a former tutor at Ruskin, I have interests to declare here (and personal insights perhaps, having been directly involved in some of these debates in more recent times).

To summarise these histories, the WEA was founded by Albert Mansbridge in 1903 (Alfred, 1987) with the aim of making university education available to working class adults who had no other opportunities to access higher education at that time (Simon, 1992a; Mayo, 1997; Fieldhouse, 1998). The project had roots in the university extension movement, developed to make university level learning more widely available. This was strongly backed by Christian Socialists (Mansbridge himself was a Christian Socialist). And the project enjoyed the support of prominent figures in public life – an initiative from the top down, in other words.

But this was also an initiative that was firmly rooted in democratic principles and approaches to learning, approaches that underpinned the development of the WEA. It was WEA members themselves who were to say 'how, why, what or when they wish to study' (Alfred, 1987: 25). So it was the students themselves who chose the subjects for study, exploring the selected topics in tutorial classes, led by academics and educationalists, including leading socialist thinkers such as R.H. Tawney, the author of a number of well-known publications including a seminal book on equality (Tawney, 1964). By the 1920s the WEA had developed classes across the country, with over 20,000 members, along with trade union and international links. The Workers' Education Trade Union Committee was also a major force, providing classes for 84,000 trade unionists by the late 1950s (Corfield, 1969).

While this approach prefigured aspects of popular education from the turn of the 20th century, the WEA was not without its critics. There were some who were suspicious of university experts (Simon, 1992a), along with some who questioned the WEA's approach to objectivity – exploring issues from different perspectives rather than focusing on teaching Marxist economics and socialist thought. These critics included the National Council of Labour Colleges, an initiative that had emerged from the parallel differences that had rocked Ruskin, with the tensions coming to a head in 1909.

Ruskin had been set up at the turn of the century to provide opportunities for working class people to study in a residential setting (Pollins, 1984; Simon, 1992a). From its early days Ruskin was a centre for lively discussions and differing approaches. There were debates about the extent to which the college should cooperate with the university, for example. Would such cooperation strengthen the college academically, widening opportunities for its students as a result? Or would the university connection act as a brake on the college's radical mission?

There were arguments in parallel about the college's main purpose. Was this 'to equip its students to challenge the existing order and work to transform it, or to prepare students to function within the limitations set by existing social relations?' (Simon, 1992a). Was this about enabling individuals to obtain qualifications, preparing them for leadership positions? Or should Ruskin be more concerned with developing collective, class-based understandings, as the basis for building movements for progressive change?

There was a major split along these lines in 1909, following a student strike. The predominantly Marxist 'Plebs League' then broke away to set up the rival Central Labour College (Craik, 1964), an initiative that led to the formation of the National Council of Labour Colleges (NCLC), alternative providers of learning for a number of decades from the first part of the 20th century (subsequently merging within the Trades Union Congress's educational provision in 1964).

From the start the NCLC criticised Ruskin – and the WEA – for their neutral approach to learning. This was seen as effectively supporting the status quo. And the NCLC's approach was criticised for being 'mere class-war propaganda and not education at all' (Pollins, 1984: 19).

These debates have continued subsequently, albeit in varying ways, taking account of differing economic, political and social policy contexts. To what extent should Ruskin be 'the Eton of the working-class' (as I have heard it described), preparing individuals for leadership roles? Or to what extent should the college be focusing on more collective, labour and progressive movement learning for social change? How could we be mainstreaming gender and race equality struggles, and community struggles, in the process (Andrews et al, 1999)? And how could we maintain our commitments to learning for social change against the background of neoliberal policy developments, targeting public funding in educationally narrower and increasingly instrumental ways?

These dilemmas have been highlighted in recent times with restructuring, due to what have been described as cruel cuts, posing new challenges for Ruskin's role and reputation (Ledwith, 2019: 7). Ruskin has been described as having been 'a force across the international labour movement' (Ledwith, 2019: 7). But this was no longer the case in Ledwith's view. Cuts and redundancies had led to a drain on knowhow and experience, inflicting severe damage as a result, in the view of a former director of Ruskin programmes in trade union and women's studies (Ledwith, 2019).

Meanwhile the WEA was facing comparable challenges. There were similar pressures to focus on more instrumental approaches to learning as the price of continued public funding. And there have been similar pressures to demonstrate impacts – in terms of learners going on to improve their employability, for example, pressures that have been affecting universities and colleges in parallel. Despite these challenges, I have also been impressed by the ways in which WEA initiatives have supported popular campaigns for social justice, including social movements campaigning against racism, discrimination against refugees (Hartley, 2010) and discrimination against people with disabilities (Recknagel with Holland, 2013), as subsequent chapters consider in further detail.

While celebrating these achievements, I am only too aware of this wider policy context. As Fieldhouse, Simon and others have also recognised, governments have become increasingly focused on far more instrumental approaches to education and training, approaches to lifelong learning that have been impacting on the provision of trade union education (McIlroy, 1992) just as these pressures have been impacting on universities and colleges in their turn. How to work with structures of governance while enabling people to develop alternatives as active citizens campaigning for social justice agendas then? How to be both 'in and against the state', to borrow a phrase from earlier debates about similar dilemmas in the past (LEWRG, 1979)?

These dilemmas have been playing out in varying ways over time, as it has already been suggested, depending on the wider economic, political and social contexts. Public policies have been centrally important here, offering greater – or lesser – scope for developing agendas for popular education for social change. But social movements have been centrally important too. When they have been relatively strong, they have been able to make so much more impact, and vice versa. These interrelationships between social movements and structures of governance represent a continuing theme in the chapters to come.

More of these tensions and dilemmas later. But before moving on to more recent times, a pause to summarise the contributions of some of the theorists who have made particular impacts on the development of popular education and participatory action research.

Previous thinkers who have had an influence: from Dewey, Lindeman and Mezirow to more recent times

Just as popular education has historical roots, both in Britain and beyond, so has the thinking that has underpinned popular education practices. The contributions of British educationalists and thinkers such as Albert Mansbridge (1876–1952) and R.H. Tawney (1880–1962) have already been mentioned. Although they differed in their approaches to social reform, both were firmly committed to learning for citizenship and democracy (Alfred, 1987; Elsey, 1987). Meanwhile, different approaches to lifelong learning and active citizenship were being developed in the US. Although he has been most renowned for his contributions to debates on child-centred education, John Dewey (1859–1952) was also concerned with education and human growth throughout the life cycle (Cross-Durant, 1987). His ideas about problem-solving approaches to learning and democracy have been widely influential, impacting on subsequent thinking and educational practices. Popular educationalists have embraced the notion of active learning, rather than learning by rote, focusing on the potential implications for developing active citizenship and democratic social change.

Dewey's occasional collaborator and friend, Eduard Lindeman, has been noted for his applications of Dewey's approach to adult learning, starting from adults' needs to adjust to new situations and challenges, attempting to make sense of their realities at work and in their communities (Brookfield, 1987a). Again there are implications here for the subsequent development of popular education approaches (although focusing less on *adjusting* and more on *changing* those realities, perhaps).

From the last quarter of the 20th century, Jack Mezirow's writing on the transformative dimensions of adult learning has added a further influential strand, this time focusing on the processes by which 'the frames through which we view and interpret our experience are changed and transformed' (Mezirow, 1991: xii). He was concerned with exploring how people were constructing their realities and how reflective learning could transform these frames in empowering ways. Mezirow described how he had developed his approach, reflecting on his own wife's empowerment as a result of engaging in adult learning – an account that has resonated with my own experiences at Ruskin and subsequently elsewhere, seeing how learners can be, and so often are, empowered – and how their perspectives and aspirations can be transformed in the process.

Mezirow has been criticised for being too prescriptive about the stages of these processes (Newman, 2014) and for being too focused on the development of the individual. But he did also recognise that there were implications for learning and social transformation in groups and social movements, including the Civil Rights Movement in the US, making references to the work of Myles Horton at the Highlander Research and Education Center.

This whistle-stop tour is, of course, no substitute for more systematic study. Rather than trying to provide a more comprehensive account, the above summary simply highlights some of the key influences on the development of popular education into more recent times (Jarvis, 1987; Simon, 1992a). Which brings the discussion to the specific contributions of Paulo Freire, Orlando Fals Borda and others.

Paulo Freire (1921–97)

So far the discussion has focused on popular education's roots in the UK, with passing references to experiences and movements elsewhere in Europe (Steele, 2010) and to theorists from North America, including the contributions of Dewey, Lindeman and Mezirow. Some of the most significant contributions in more recent times have wider international roots, from the global 'South'. Latin American countries have particularly rich histories in these respects, including the contributions of Carlos Nunez, Carlos Torres and Francisco Vio Grossi (Austin, 1999). Rather than attempting to explore these southern roots in further detail, this chapter simply focuses on the particular contributions of Paulo Freire and Orlando Fals Borda, along with the contributions of participatory action research theorists from elsewhere.

Paulo Freire is probably the best known of these popular educators; internationally quoted and misquoted, his ideas have been applied and misapplied in so many contexts. He was born in North East Brazil, developing his particular approach to popular education through his work with illiterate peasants in the region – until the military coup in 1964. After a brief spell in prison following the coup, he went into exile in Chile, before working in the US and then in Geneva as special education advisor to the World Council of Churches. With the return of democracy, Paulo Freire returned to Brazil in 1980 and joined the Workers Party, developing literacy programmes in São Paulo, where he was appointed Secretary of Education. He was working for government in this position, he explained, while also maintaining his work with social movements, working both in and against the state, depending on the context and the scope – or lack of scope – for developing progressive educational programmes for social change.

Much has been written about Paulo Freire and the influences on his work in contemporary times (P. Mayo, 2004; Borg and Mayo, 2006). These publications provide key guides. Readers are also encouraged to go to Freire's own writings from his early publications (Freire, 1972) through to his later reflections on his life and work (de Figueiredo-Cowen and Gastaldo, 1995) including *Pedagogy of Hope* (Freire, 1996b). As Freire has explained, he was very influenced by his early experiences of poverty and hunger (although he came from a middle class family, there were hard times during the depression years between the wars). From an early age he came to understand the links between poverty, social class and knowledge – or the lack of knowledge and power. As a teacher, and then as a university lecturer, he set about identifying ways of enabling the poor to acquire the knowledge, critical understanding and skills that they needed in order to develop effective strategies for social change.

Paulo Freire came from a Catholic background, influenced by the Liberation Theology movement that had been supporting progressive change in Latin America and elsewhere, at that time. He had also read and reflected on classical philosophers, as well as educational thinkers. And he acknowledged his debts to Marxists, including critical Marxist theorists, and anti-colonial thinkers such as Frantz Fanon (Freire, 1972). Later in life he was asked about the extent to which he had also been influenced by the Italian Marxist Antonio Gramsci, a thinker who was particularly concerned with education and cultural struggles, emphasising the importance of developing critical understandings of the underlying causes of poverty and inequality in capitalist society. Freire replied that he had only read Gramsci when he went into exile.

> I read Gramsci ... and I discovered that I had been greatly influenced by Gramsci long before I read him. It is fantastic when we discover that we had been influenced by someone's thought without even being introduced to their intellectual production. (de Figueiredo-Cowen and Gastaldo, 1995: 63–4)

So his was an eclectic approach, developed as a work in progress. He reflected: 'The eyes with which I review the past are not the same eyes with which I saw in the past' (Freire, 1996a: 3). While developing his approach over time, taking account of subsequent contributions and criticisms, he retained the strength of his commitment to the oppressed, determined to support them in liberating themselves and so regaining their full humanity.

This commitment has not been shared by some of those who have re-interpreted Freire's writings, applying his approach for very different ends. But he was philosophical about the way in which the political right had attempted to co-opt his work. This was only to be expected, in his view. And he was deeply critical of sectarianism more generally, whether this was from the right or indeed from the left of the political spectrum, both suffering from what he described as an 'absence of doubt' (Freire, 1972: 18).

So what have been the key features of Paulo Freire's approach that have made so much impact? While there are identifiable strands from the past, Paulo Freire brought these together in innovative ways, building on his own experiences and insights, together with his commitment to learning for social justice; starting from people's own experiences, issues and concerns, engaging in processes of dialogue to develop critical consciousness together, working towards empowerment and social transformation.

He started from a focus on human liberation, rather than simply focusing on the liberation of the most oppressed. Because, in his view, 'injustice, exploitation, oppression and the violence of the oppressor' (Freire, 1972: 20) were dehumanising for the oppressors as well as for the oppressed. Humanisation, in contrast, was affirmed by struggles for freedom and justice – for all. The oppressed were thereby recovering their lost humanity. But this was not about taking over the roles of their oppressors (becoming landowners for example, in the Brazilian context), thereby becoming potentially oppressive themselves. Rather the goal was to be social transformation – the fundamental transformation of social relationships overall.

Like both Fanon and Gramsci before him, Freire recognised the ways in which oppressors' thinking could be identified within the heads of the oppressed themselves ('colonized man' as Fanon (2001) had described this in the context of French colonialism). Oppressive social relationships could be seen as inevitable, unchangeable or even justifiable, the 'common sense' of the existing social order. The pedagogy of the oppressed was to change this. But this could only be achieved by working with, rather than for, the oppressed. It was for the oppressed to liberate themselves and then 'all *men* [sic]' (Fanon, 2001: 31). (Freire subsequently responded to feminist criticisms that he had failed to take sufficient account of women's specific oppressions, and that he had used sexist rather than more inclusive language, on occasion.)

Working *with* rather than *for* the oppressed was central to Freire's approach. He emphasised the importance of starting from people's own issues and concerns, using relevant images to engage learners' interest, for example, and then 'decoding' them, to unpack their meanings. Pictures of everyday situations could provide the trigger for exploring people's underlying problems, questioning previously taken for granted assumptions – and then reflecting on the implications for taking action.

Paulo Freire's particular approaches to teaching literacy in Brazil may or may not be readily transferable to very different contexts. But the underlying principles emphatically are. As Giroux has so clearly argued, the Freirean approach to critical pedagogy has continuing relevance as a way of promoting citizen participation and effective political action. In Giroux's view, this is central to 'the question of whether a democracy can survive without an educated (i.e. critically educated) citizenry' (Giroux, 2010: 115). There are resonances here with the particular concerns of this book, as Chapter 1 has already outlined, exploring responses to the rise of Far Right populism in different contexts, accompanied by rising concerns about fake news – in times of 'deceit', in a world which 'rests on fear not hope' in Giroux's words (2010).

Freire was convinced that popular education needs to be both relevant and actively engaging, proceeding through processes of dialogue. The traditional 'banking' approaches that he critiqued involved treating students as 'receptacles to be filled by the teacher' (Freire, 1972: 45). Rather than treating students as passive recipients of knowledge, students and teachers should both be learning from each other, simultaneously, he argued, recognising and valuing what each could bring to the process.

In later life Paulo Freire responded to the criticism that this approach devalued the role of the teacher. On the contrary, in his view. Although both learners and teachers were key to the process, he explained, this 'does not mean they are equal to each other' (Freire, 1996: 127). Teachers do have specialist knowledge – knowledge which they need to share with learners through processes of problem-posing dialogues.

Through such dialogical processes, learning could form part of cycles of reflection and action, developing critical consciousness for liberating forms of social change. 'Liberation is a praxis,' he pointed out, 'the action and reflection of men [sic – again!] upon their world in order to transform it.' The learning should involve the whole community, rather than simply focusing on training community leaders, leaving the rest of the community as vulnerable to manipulation and domination as before.

Feminist critiques

At this point the question of feminist critiques needs to be raised more explicitly. These critiques have not simply related to Freire's use of sexist language in his early writings, the use of 'he' and 'man', a terminology that potentially marginalises if not actually erases just over half the human race, it has been argued. Feminists have certainly raised questions about his use of masculine nouns and pronouns. But they have gone further too, challenging Freire's analysis in more fundamental ways. As Lynn Tett explained in her reflections on 'What Freire means to me', 'His analysis seems to me to focus too much on class alone, rather than showing how other factors such as race, gender, culture, language and ethnicity intersect with class to frame both oppressors and the oppressed in specific ways' (Tett, 2018: 46).

In contrast, Tett has argued, the writings of bell hooks have added a black feminist consciousness, building on Freire's concept of critical consciousness to take account of these gaps in his earlier thinking. These were important gaps, in Lynn Tett's view, 'valid criticisms' that reflected changes in socio-political understandings over time.

Freire recognised the importance of addressing these issues more explicitly in his later writings, as Lynn Tett and others have also appreciated. Concluding on his influence overall, she pointed out that he had made a 'huge impact on my thinking because it has provided both a vision of what education might achieve and a pedagogy of how it might be undertaken' (Tett, 2018: 48).

Other feminists have made similar criticisms – while similarly valuing his contributions overall, including a number of the contributors to the collection of essays on gender in popular education that Walters and Manicom (1996) edited. They too raised questions about his use of language, and about his analysis, more fundamentally. But feminists could also build on his methodology, in their view, starting from women's own experiences as the basis for engaging in critical conversations, linking their personal issues with the wider political context.

Christina McMellon has also described an encounter between bell hooks and Paulo Freire when he came to speak at the university where bell hooks was also speaking. While she was preparing to question him, other participants became anxious, not wanting feminist issues 'to intrude on this great educator' (quoted in McMellon, 2018: 53). Paulo Freire took a very different view, in contrast. He responded to these attempts to silence bell hooks 'by reminding his audience that learning happens when we ask difficult questions and, by implication, wrangle with difficult answers' (2018: 53). These debates run through subsequent discussions. Feminists have made such significant contributions both to the theory and to the practice of popular education and participatory action research, as subsequent chapters go on illustrate.

Meanwhile, rather than attempting to provide a fuller account of Paulo Freire's approach, readers are encouraged to read more of his writings for themselves, identifying the roots in previous thinking and experiences along with the contemporary relevance of his life's work. So much of his writings still resonate. The importance of developing critical consciousness is central to this book's concerns, in fact, challenging the causes of increasing inequalities, just as this is central to resisting populist forms of manipulation and domination, whether coming from the left or from the right of the political spectrum.

Paulo Freire and Myles Horton (1905–90): *Conversations on Education and Social Change*

Myles Horton has also been a key figure, developing popular education and research, working with the Civil Rights Movement and other movements for environmental and social justice in the US. Like Paulo Freire, his early influences were Christian, along with his own experiences of inequalities, growing up in Tennessee – developing a strong moral sense about injustice as a result (Peters and Bell, 1987). He met John Dewey and Eduard Lindeman as a young man, reading them and other theorists, including Marxists and others concerned with social justice issues. And he visited folk high schools in Denmark (community-based learning initiatives that had been developed in a number of Scandinavian contexts). Although he had mixed views about these as possible models he did draw on a number of their features.

Like Paulo Freire, Myles Horton came to the view that 'There is no such thing as neutrality. Neutrality is for the status quo' (Peters and Bell, 1987: 250). The implication was clear: to work with people and social movements struggling for social justice. Together with Don West, a divinity graduate who was similarly concerned with challenging social injustices, Myles Horton set up the Highlander Folk School in 1932. Although closed by the state of Tennessee to curb its progressive activities, Highlander was subsequently re-opened in 1961 as a result of these popular educators' undaunted determination – renamed as the Highlander Research and Education Center. Highlander organised educational schools with trade unions and other social movements, basing the learning on the learners' own experiences and issues.

As Myles Horton had quickly recognised, poor people 'weren't socialized to go through the formal school system as we [were]' (Peters and Bell, 1987: 251). It was important to teach within people's own experiences. And it was important to use a range of methods including improvisational drama, singing and song-writing.

Increasingly Highlander focused on black people's issues supporting the development of Citizenship Schools around the southern states, providing literacy training to enable black people to exercise the right to vote (a right that was restricted by literacy requirements at that time). This was central to the development of the Civil Rights Movement. One of the Center's best known students was the young trade union activist Rosa Parks, who sparked a historic protest by refusing to give up her seat on the bus to a white man in Montgomery Alabama, in the early days of Civil Rights campaigning. Her protest led to a bus boycott, led by, among others, Dr Martin Luther King.

In later years Highlander became involved in education and research with trade unions and communities tackling environmental issues, including the issue of controlling toxic waste. These had transnational implications – and collaborations – including collaborations in India and South Africa, as Chapter 6 considers in further detail. Myles Horton has been described as a 'citizen of the world' (Peters and Bell, 1987: 254), reflecting his view that education and social change had no boundaries.

It was not too surprising, then, that Myles Horton and Paulo Freire should meet and exchange experiences and views (Bell et al, 1990). They discussed Highlander's Citizenship Schools and the connections with voter registration and the Civil Rights Movement for example, comparing and contrasting this with Paulo Freire's literacy work in Brazil. Despite the differences, both were linking literacy and citizenship and both were working with the communities concerned, finding new ways of doing literacy based on their concepts of social change. And both approaches were based on the importance of treating learners with respect, focusing on what learners really needed to know, in terms of their own priorities. These represent continuing threads for those concerned with popular education in the contemporary context.

The significance of context was also highlighted in their discussions. Both recognised the problems with attempting to duplicate successful programmes from elsewhere, without taking account of the political situations in each place. There was scope for working with governments in some states of Brazil, in Paulo Freire's view, just as there was scope for working in some municipalities where 'we have very good people working seriously' (Bell et al, 1990: 93). But this was not always the case. Myles Horton also emphasised the importance of taking account of the context in relation to the strength of the social movements concerned and the levels of popular consciousness more generally, identifying pockets of hope with the potential for working for radical social change. These represent continuing issues.

So do their shared reflections on learning and organising for social change. As Paulo Freire explained, there was so much scope for learning through mobilising and organising for social change. But educating and organising were not the same thing, as Myles Horton also pointed out. Organisers could disempower people, if they simply brought in experts as educators to tell people what to do. 'You can learn from mobilizing,' he pointed out (Bell et al, 1990: 122), but although 'you can learn to educate people, you can learn to manipulate people' too.

These conversations have so many more reflections with relevance for those concerned with popular education today. There are continuing discussions about ideas and there are continuing discussions about educational practices, focusing on education for social change. There is not the space to go into further detail in this chapter. Before moving on though, there are the contributions of Orlando Fals Borda, Budd Hall and Rajesh Tandon to be taken into account, including the contributions of others involved in the development of participatory action research and knowledge democracy in the contemporary context.

Participatory action research and knowledge democracy

So far the discussion has focused on popular education and learning. But this still leaves questions to be explored in terms of the knowledge to be acquired, whose knowledge and who has the power to define this knowledge. Orlando Fals Borda (1925–2008), a Colombian sociologist and activist, has been associated with the development of participatory action research (PAR). In parallel with popular education, PAR starts by valuing what people know already, then enabling them to acquire research skills, creating new knowledge for social change. Speaking to academic sociologists in the US in 1995, Orlando Fals Borda expressed this as follows:

> Do not monopolise your knowledge nor impose arrogantly your techniques, but respect and combine your skills with the knowledge of the researched or grassroots communities, taking them as full partners and co-researcher. Do not trust elitist versions of history and science which respond to dominant interests, but be receptive to counter-narratives and try to recapture them. Do not depend solely on your culture to interpret facts, but recover local values, traits, beliefs, and arts for action by and with research organisations (Gott, 2008).

Orlando Fals Borda has been a major influence not only in Colombia but also elsewhere, as Budd Hall has reflected, starting from his own experiences developing adult education and action research in Tanzania. Engaging with Orlando in Colombia had been a powerful influence on his work, he explained. Orlando's vision had brought a number of distinct elements, arising from the work that he had developed with Andean peasants in the mountainous areas as well as with Afro-Colombians in the coastal areas of Colombia. He had wanted 'to challenge the political intellectuals of Latin America to consider a people-centred approach to knowledge creation as a critical tool for political and cultural action' (Hall and Tandon, 2017). 'In many ways,' Budd Hall continued, 'the vision of Orlando Fals Borda can be considered as a movement in the field of social science research parallel to that of Paulo Freire in the field of pedagogy' (Hall and Tandon, 2017).

Rajesh Tandon has identified similar connections with his own work, linking Orlando Fals Borda's work and the international networking that emerged as a result, with the development of the society for Participatory Research in Asia (PRIA). These international connections had included Myles Horton and John Gaventa of the Highlander Research and Education Center, as well as Orlando Fals-Borda himself, as they gathered at The First International Forum on Participatory Research, in what was then Yugoslavia, in 1980.

While based in India, PRIA has members in a number of other Asian countries. The organisation has been providing training for 35 years, as well as practising various forms of participatory research, 'articulating local knowledge about water, forest, land, construction workers and violence against women' (Hall and Tandon, 2017). More of this in subsequent chapters. PRIA has been working with academic institutions, to introduce training for both students and faculty, developing partnerships for participatory research and knowledge democracy more widely.

These reflections were shared at a gathering in Cartagena, Colombia, 2017, convened to pay tribute to Orlando Fals Borda and his work, echoing the inspirational international gathering with him in that same city, some 40 years previously. During a session with Budd Hall and Rajesh Tandon at this conference I invited Rajesh Tandon to reflect on his early influences. His reply was as follows.

> 'I got into this area of work in 1977 when I was doing field work in rural areas in India for my PhD dissertation. That one year of field work caused me a lot of difficulty and the need to rethink my own academic preparation. I had to accept that illiterate farmers can be knowledgeable. And more painfully I had to accept that the research methodology that had been taught to me was not working.'

Orlando Fals Borda's work had provided very helpful insights into the challenges that he had been facing, Rajesh went on to explain, along with the writings of Budd Hall.

Rajesh had subsequently met with Orlando Fals Borda in person in Caracas, Venezuela in 1978, along with a number of others concerned with the development of participatory research. At this gathering, he continued, they had shared ideas about taking the work forward. "We were, mostly naive, ... networking with other fellow crazies in other parts of the world" and "I took responsibility for Participatory Research in Asia". Since then, "I have had no other possible occupation other than to do this," he concluded.

Budd Hall has added further reflections on the origins of participatory research, based on his own experiences. He explained that "participatory research, as we called it in English, emerged from our work in Tanzania. This was influenced by the remarkable Finnish scholar Marja Liisa Swantz, by President Nyerere [of Tanzania] and by others, too." He added that the Chilean Francisco (Pancho) Vio Grossi was the first Latin American coordinator of the International Participatory Research Network (IPRN) which began early in 1977. "When I attended the 1977 Cartagena conference with Orlando Fals Borda," Budd went on to explain, "we found a huge and exciting new work of theory and practice that we wove into the IPRN."

Since 2012, Budd and Rajesh have been joint UNESCO Chairs in Community-Based Research and Social Responsibility in Higher Education. Through this position, they have been advocating for the co-construction of knowledge and respectful partnerships between communities, universities and governments.

Community–university partnerships are discussed further in subsequent chapters including Chapter 8, which focuses on their potential as well as some of their inherent dilemmas. As Paulo Freire had also recognised previously, universities should be embedded within their communities rather than simply focusing on serving elites. And most importantly they should do this without losing their academic rigour (Freire, 1996). There are parallels here with the role of the educator who needs to share their professional expertise as a teacher – but without being overly dominant, on the one hand, or simply passive, on the other. There are inherent tensions and challenges here, as subsequent chapters illustrate in further detail.

In summary

In summary, then, popular education and participatory action research share a number of common roots from past thinkers and from previous practices. There are interweaving histories and transnational influences to be traced. These need to be understood within their own economic, political, social and cultural contexts, rather than simply transplanted elsewhere in the contemporary context. But there are continuing threads interwoven through these histories, with recurring tensions, challenges and dilemmas, and with continuing debates that re-emerge in the chapters that follow.

3

Spaces and places for popular education and participatory action research

This book started from increasing concerns about the growth of Far Right populism, racism and violence, along with rising disquiet about 'fake news' in various international contexts. How might popular education and participatory action research contribute to the development of alternative approaches in response to these contemporary challenges, building support for more constructive ways forward? Although these concerns have become increasingly evident over the past couple of years or so, they have roots that date further back in the history of adult education more generally. According to Brookfield and Holst (adult educators who were shocked by the invasion of Iraq in 2003), adult education seemed to have lost its moorings, becoming 'uncoupled from its traditional, mainstream view of itself as a movement to create and build democracy' (Brookfield and Holst, 2011: 1). Adult education had traditionally been concerned with developing critical thinking, 'countering any process of brainwashing or ideological manipulation' (Brookfield and Holst, 2011: 2), they argued, promoting 'the health of participatory democracy'. How could such approaches to learning enable people to organise more effective resistance to contemporary challenges? Reflecting back on these developments in 2011, in the US context, this might seem hopelessly out of date, they acknowledged, given the policy emphasis on adult learning for 'skilling' or 'retooling' America's workforce to compete in the global economy. Were there still spaces and places for alternative approaches? Still, they argued, there were lessons to be drawn from earlier approaches, with relevance for those, like themselves, who were concerned 'with organizing education for and encouraging learning about the creation of democracy in political, cultural, and economic spheres' (Brookfield and Holst, 2011: 4). At the time of writing, a decade and a half on from the invasion of Iraq, these lessons would seem more relevant than ever.

Although Brookfield and Holst focused on adult education in general, their questions have particular relevance for popular education more specifically. First, Brookfield and Holst emphasised the importance of connecting adult learning with participatory democracy, raising questions about the political, cultural and economic spaces with which to engage. How might learning for participatory democracy fit in the wider framework of the changing relationships between the economy, civil society and the state? And second, what might be the implications, more specifically, in terms of the spaces and places for popular education and participatory action research in practice?

Having explored these questions, as they have been debated and addressed in the past, the chapter concludes with some examples from more recent experiences. These illustrate popular education and participatory action research initiatives in different contexts, including examples of working in partnership with formal institutions, in a variety of settings, along with examples of working from the outside in informal spaces and social movements.

Popular education, civil society and the state

The previous chapter described popular education as being aligned with wider efforts to promote a more socially just social order through democratic change processes, based on a clear analysis of the underlying causes of social inequality, exploitation and oppression. And this raises questions about popular education's relationships with the existing social order, the economy, the state and civil society, including social movements more specifically. These have been questions of concern to Paulo Freire among others (P. Mayo, 1999; English and Mayo, 2012). As the previous chapter also noted, Freire had acknowledged his debt to the theoretical contributions of the Italian early 20th century Marxist, Antonio Gramsci (de Figueiredo-Cowen and Gastaldo, 1995). Gramsci was a political educator as well as a theorist himself, before being imprisoned by Mussolini's Fascist government in 1926. Critical education was essential, in his view, if there were to be effective challenges to dominant ideas, the prevailing 'common sense' of existing (unequal) social relations. Gramsci (1968) described this 'common sense' as the hegemony of ruling class ideas, the ideas that seem so normal that they tend to be accepted without question. Neoliberal globalisation has been presented as being inevitable, for example, along with the view that there have been no alternatives to austerity, in response to the financial crisis of 2007–08. This has been about normalising austerity as the only game in town (Farnsworth and Irving, 2015).

Gramsci was also concerned with understanding how these dominant ideas were produced and reproduced, the oppressors' thinking in the heads of the oppressed, or 'colonized man', as Fanon (2001) described these processes in terms of their effects on popular consciousness. This is where Gramsci's writings on the structures of the state come in, along with his writings on the state's relationships with the structures of civil society (Gramsci, 1968). Rather than focusing on the state in terms of its repressive functions, Lenin's 'special bodies of armed men' (Lenin, 2014), Gramsci focused on the state's ideological functions, legitimising and reproducing the existing social relations of the status quo. He viewed education as being centrally important here, whether this was being provided by the state or by civil society organisations and structures (English and Mayo, 2012).

Far from being totally separate spheres, in fact, Gramsci envisaged civil society and the state as having overlapping – and competing – functions, providing much needed services on the one hand, while working within the framework of existing (capitalist) social relations on the other. Schools and universities prepare their students for the world of work, for instance, emphasising the importance of acquiring a disciplined work ethic as well as emphasising the importance of acquiring marketable skills. But schools and universities can promote critical thinking too, and so can civil society organisations and social movements. There are inherent tensions here, battles of ideas to be waged between competing approaches.

For Gramsci, these ideological struggles had central importance. In his view the transformation of exploitative and oppressive social relations would not simply be achieved by seizures of state power (seizures that he described as 'wars of manoeuvre'). Such changes of political and economic power needed to be preceded by changes through ideological struggles. And ideological and cultural changes required knowledge and critical understanding among the exploited and the oppressed and their allies in what Gramsci (1968) described as 'wars of position'.

By implication, civil society represents a contested space then, just as the state itself represents a site of contestation and struggle. Voluntary organisations, faith-based organisations and social movements can be more – or less – concerned with promoting social transformation, just as the state can be more – or less – concerned with meeting social needs rather than meeting the requirements of global capital. These tensions have been playing out in varying ways in different contexts depending on the balance of interests and forces at the time in question. The development of the welfare state in the UK after the Second World War, for example, resulted from progressive political mobilisations along with the impacts of ideological struggles (Miliband,

1972). And among others, these ideological influences included progressive demands arising from popular education initiatives in the armed forces during, and particularly towards the end of, the war, via the Army Bureau of Current Affairs (ABCA) and the Army School of Education. Reflecting on the 1945 Labour Election victory, the Conservative R.A. Butler wrote that 'the forces vote in particular had been virtually won over by the left wing influence of ABCA' (quoted in Denny, undated) thereby contributing to the Conservatives' defeat. Whether or not this was something of an exaggeration, this still offered some indication of ABCA's contributions to building a climate of support for progressive social change at that time. Through these initiatives there had been spaces for looking forwards for a better future, including better education for all.

Whatever the limitations of the welfare state's achievements in practice, as these have become increasingly evident over time, the contrasts between the post-war vision of 'winning the peace' and the policies of austerity are only too stark. Social inequality has been rising, in Dorling's view, as the welfare state's ideals are being eroded 'by five new tenets of injustice, that: elitism is efficient; exclusion is necessary; prejudice is natural; greed is good and despair in inevitable' (Dorling, 2010). Economic and political factors have been centrally important of course. But so have the ideological aspects that have been identified here. There has been a propaganda onslaught, blaming the poor for their own poverty, stigmatising them as work-shy scroungers, getting something for nothing, undeserving of popular sympathy (Shildrick, 2018). As Shildrick's study points out, media depictions of people experiencing poverty, such as the television series *Benefits Street*, reinforce individualised understandings of poverty 'and the idea that people are somehow culpable for their own predicament' (Shildrick, 2018: 24). And so the poor can come to internalise their exploitation and oppression. Meanwhile the underlying structural causes become obscured, thereby legitimising the processes of marketisation themselves. This is precisely why it has been so important to record alternative responses, portraits of hope and resilience, as people have been organising to stand together, join forces and support one another, as Chapter 1 has already referenced (Sng, 2019).

There have been related pressures on the voluntary and community sectors in more recent times, in parallel (Kenny et al, 2015). Critics have pointed to the ways in which marketisation agendas have been promoted through the voluntary and community sectors, pressuring them into becoming increasingly 'business like', adopting market mechanisms and thereby legitimising the erosion of public service approaches and values as a result (Milbourne, 2013; Milbourne and Murray, 2017). As Milbourne and Murray argue,

> Fundamental changes to British social policy have seen civil society organisations assume a significant role in welfare provision but chasing money and status have come at a price. What has happened to integrity and morality when many voluntary service organisations have become trapped in a gilded web of neo-liberal arrangements and a rapidly privatizing services industry? Why are they reinforcing the social, economic and political systems they were originally established to reform? (Milbourne and Murray, 2017: Cover).

The actual extent to which the Third Sector has already been co-opted in particular contexts has been a matter of debate (Taylor, 2011). But the significance of such processes has certainly been widely recognised – both within the voluntary and community sectors and within other sections of civil society and social movements.

Peter Mayo's reflections on faith-based organisations and movements point to similar contestations and struggles. The influence – and subsequent reduction in the influence – of Liberation Theology represents a case in point. Liberation Theology was a significant influence on social reformers in the second half of the 20th century, impacting on the thinking of progressive educationalists including Paulo Freire (P. Mayo, 1999), as identified in Chapter 2. Since then, the spaces for such approaches have been similarly challenged.

As the previous chapter has also pointed out, there have been parallel processes at work elsewhere. Trade union education has been similarly identified as a site of contestation and struggle, as public resources have been increasingly directed towards specific forms of training, eroding the space for more critical forms of education (McIlroy, 1992). But this by no means implies the end of the story, as subsequent chapters explore in further detail. There have been and continue to be significant interventions to promote popular education within and around the trade union movement. Both the state and civil society need to be seen as 'heterogeneous and mutually constitutive terrains of contestation', as Cornwall and Coelho (2007: 7) have expressed this more elegantly.

So there are parallels here with debates on the scope for working within the state itself – while maintaining a critical stance towards the impact of neoliberal globalisation. Public service providers have been engaging with these debates over past decades, as the publication of *In and Against the State* recognised in the 1970s (LEWRG, 1979). These form part of wider debates about the changing nature of relationships between civil society, the state and the economy, in more recent times in the context of neoliberal globalisation. Pressures from the market have been increasing, eroding public services while subsidising the bankers who precipitated the financial crisis of 2007–08. In this context, it has been argued, public service providers and civil society activists need to be *for*, as well as *in and against* the state (Shaw and Martin, 2008), claiming the spaces for promoting democratic change, in order to support the development of more appropriate and more effective forms of public provision.

Figure 3.1 illustrates the perception that the economy, civil society and the state operate as separate spheres.

Figure 3.1: The economy, civil society and the state as separate spheres

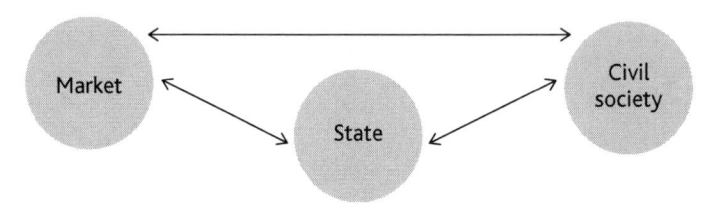

Figure 3.2, in contrast, illustrates the view that far from being separate spheres, the market has been increasingly dominant, extending greater and greater influence over civil society, as the state retreats in parallel.

Figure 3.2: The economy, civil society and the state in the context of increasing marketisation

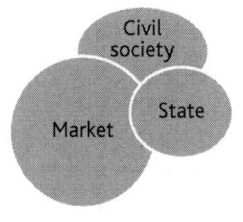

In summary then, these spaces have been under pressure, squeezed as a result of the ways in which neoliberal agendas have been impacting across sectors – including public services such as education and lifelong learning. Neither the public nor the voluntary/community sector

has been insulated from these pressures. So rather than focusing on whether to work from *within* or from *without*, it may be more helpful to focus on identifying the spaces within particular contexts more specifically.

There are analogies here with Cornwall's (2008) model of the spaces for participation and active citizenship in the context of international development work. In summary, she identifies these spaces as follows:

- *Closed spaces:* from which citizens are effectively excluded.
- *Invited spaces:* where citizens may be invited to participate – but on terms that have already been defined and limited.
- *Claimed spaces:* where citizens claim their right to participate and to put their issues on the agenda on their own terms.

If this approach were applied to adult education, this might be described as follows:

- *Closed spaces:* universities in the 19th century, when working class students and women were effectively excluded – the background to the establishment of Ruskin in Oxford, as outlined in Chapter 2.
- *Invited spaces:* the educational spaces that were opened up with specific agendas (to promote 'useful knowledge' to enable people to cope with rapid economic and social change).
- *Claimed spaces:* popular education initiatives and community–university partnerships established to work for socially transformative agendas.

How have these debates been emerging over time?

As the previous chapter has already outlined, the 1909 strike at Ruskin College followed debates on the extent to which there should be cooperation with the University of Oxford. Would Ruskin's 'claimed space' be effectively subverted? The university connection was seen as contentious, strengthening the College academically – or acting as a potential brake on the College's radical mission. So was the University of Oxford offering an 'invited space' with pre-set agendas? This connection could widen opportunities for students – but would those opportunities be strictly within the terms of established educational frameworks? Would such a connection prepare students to function within the limitations set by existing social relations (Simon, 1992a) rather than equipping them to challenge the existing order and work to transform it? Although the Plebs League broke away, bidding for independence in the move that led to the establishment of the rival National Council of Labour Colleges (Craik, 1964), debates continued as to which strategy was to be ultimately more effective.

The scope for building partnerships between civil society organisations and social movements on the one hand and formal institutions such as universities on the other remains contentious to this day. The outcomes have been various, as Chapter 2 suggested. Universities and civil society organisations and structures have been increasingly subjected to market pressures, in the contemporary context. They have also been experiencing their own internal pressures. Working in partnership with civil society organisations and social movements has been contentious within universities, for instance, and so has their engagement with action research. As the introduction to the history of Barnett House, University of Oxford from 1914 sets out, this illustrates 'how an academic institution which set out not just to study contemporary social issues but to promote reform' (Smith et al, 2014: 1) coped with the tensions inherent in such a mission. How to maintain academic rigour – demonstrating academic respectability – without being 'a set of detached voyeurs dissecting other people's miseries' (Smith et al, 2014)? These represented continuing tensions with the wider university as well as within Barnett House itself.

Such tensions continue in relation to participatory action research more widely. The spaces have been contested, and continue to be contested, within academia as well as from outside. Is this the type of research that really counts when it comes to academic promotions? Academics can feel pressured into focusing on publishing articles in prestigious academic journals, rather than putting time and energy into more 'alternative' types of research. But this by no means implies the complete elimination of spaces for popular education and participatory action research partnerships, as subsequent chapters explore more fully.

There would seem to be parallels here with debates on the extent to which civil society organisations and social movements could and should engage with the state itself – without losing sight of their missions and values. The WEA provides a case in point, as the previous chapter illustrated. State funding has enabled the WEA to continue to provide learning for over 50,000 students (2016–17), via some 8,000 classes, taught by some 2,000 tutors. Over the years, the WEA's provision has included popular education (WEA, 2018), working with trade unions and with social movements campaigning against racism and other forms of discrimination, facilitating campaigns for social justice as Chapter 2 also pointed out (Hartley, 2010; Recknagel with Holland, 2013). But the WEA has also had to contend with financial and other pressures, just as universities have had to contend with similar pressures within the context of neoliberal agendas more generally, as Chapter 8 considers in further detail.

Unsurprisingly then, key figures have come to different conclusions about the spaces for popular education and participatory action research depending on the particular contexts in question. Paulo Freire and Myles Horton were in agreement here (Bell et al, 1990). As Paulo Freire reflected, neither of their experiences happened 'in the air' (Bell et al, 1990: 92). He explained,

> In some states of Brazil today we have progressive governments, and in some municipalities all over we have very good people working seriously. In all these situations, it is possible to reorganize adult literacy, to reorganize education and health, lots of popular education. (Bell et al, 1990: 93)

He was helping as much as he could, he went on. But he did not see 'a possibility for a national campaign. The time is changed' (Bell et al, 1990). The spaces had to be identified in each specific context – and claimed.

The range of spaces has varied then, including spaces that have been claimed (if sometimes clandestinely) in the most apparently challenging contexts. Apartheid South Africa provides a case in point (von Kotze, 2005), where Paulo Freire's *Pedagogy of the Oppressed* was banned. Women have particular histories of creativity when it comes to finding and claiming spaces in such seemingly unpromising situations. Examples range from mobilising street dwellers and slum dwellers and providing access to literacy, numeracy, organising and consciousness raising in Indian cities (Patel, 1996) to engaging in educational work and participatory research with women working in factories with minimal rights in Malaysia (Chan, 1996).

More recent reflections include the following comments. As Crowther, Galloway and Martin pointed out in their collection of chapters on *Popular Education: Engaging the Academy*, the question was not whether but how to engage the academy. 'If education is understood as a dialectical process, it is also necessary to recognise that politically committed educators are dialectically positioned "in and against" it' (Crowther et al, 2005b: 4). This was particularly relevant, they continued, given that the academy, at least in the rich world, was 'a hotbed of market ideology orchestrated by the dictates of the new managerialism' where knowledge had become a commodity and the successful academic a 'trader in the educational marketplace' (Crowther et al, 2005b: 4). So *Popular Education: Engaging the Academy* set out to bring individuals within the academy together to 'suggest a variety of ways in which the contradictory positioning of university-based teachers and researchers can be harnessed to the politics of popular education through different kinds of social and political engagement' (Crowther et al, 2005b: 4). Other contributions provided examples, from Astrid von Kotze's account of popular education and the academy both before and after the end of the Apartheid regime in South Africa, to Liam Kane's reflections on his experiences of working both within and outside the academy in Brazil and in Scotland. The academic's role, in his view, was to use the spaces provided by the rhetoric of academic freedom to develop critical consciousness, thereby supporting popular education in the process (Kane, 2005).

Spaces and places in contemporary contexts

Given the previous discussion, the variety of the places involved in popular education and participatory action research may seem unsurprising. Spaces have been identified across institutions and sectors. The following examples offer a sample to provide illustrations of the range, rather than attempting to provide a more comprehensive account.

The first example spans the local and the global, engaging institutions of governance at different levels, including the international level, along with universities and colleges, working in partnership with a variety of civil society organisations and social movements. This is the Knowledge for Change (K4C) consortium for training in community-based research. K4C grew out of the University of Victoria–PRIA (Society for Participatory Research in Asia) agreement that supports the jointly held UNESCO Chairs in Community Based Research and Social Responsibility in Higher Education, Budd Hall from Canada and Rajesh Tandon from India. Drawing on their previous experiences of popular education and participatory action research Hall and Tandon set out 'to build a strong global partnership with shared goals, joint responsibility and a solid plan for building research capacity to address pressing local challenges, including UN (United Nations) Sustainable Development Goals (SDGs)' (K4C, undated). The initiative provides an 'international partnered training initiative between Higher Education Institutions (HEIs) and Civil Society Organisations (CSOs) for co-creation of knowledge academics and community groups working together in various training hubs around the world for addressing UN SDGs' – thereby reinforcing 'UNESCO Chairs' global leadership in the field of participatory approaches to research and community-university engagement' (K4C, undated).

Although this is a relatively new initiative, launched in 2017, hubs have already emerged in Canada, Colombia, Cuba, India, Indonesia, Ireland, Malaysia, Sardinia, South Africa, Tanzania and Uganda, building on previous partnership working so far. Mentor training began in January 2018, concluding with an international programme, bringing participants together for two weeks in March 2018. This marked the first phase of a programme to produce more than 1,300 community-based researchers and mentors over the coming five years, aiming to leave these as a legacy for the future of popular education and participatory action research – despite the pressures on the organisations and structures involved.

Community–university partnerships have their own history in the UK, as it has already been suggested. This was the model for programmes to promote learning for active citizenship under the New Labour governments (1997–2010), such as Action Learning for Active Citizenship (ALAC). The seven regional hubs that formed the first phase of the programme consisted of voluntary and community organisations with a history of providing popular education (based on Freirean principles) and supported by partner universities and colleges (Mayo and Annette, 2010). Subsequent phases included a number of local authorities too (Mayo et al, 2013). There were, of course, inherent tensions, as the publications that reflected on these experiences pointed out (Mayo et al, 2013). And these tensions increased over time, with pressure from public service modernisation agendas, pressures that impacted on the programmes themselves as well as on their constituent partners. 'Programmes to promote active citizenship began with an emphasis on active citizenship as participation and democratic engagement in the promotion of equalities, including space for campaigning on social justice issues', it was argued, but this was a focus 'that shifted over time, moving towards a narrower emphasis on citizen involvement in formal structures of governance' (that is, invited spaces; Mayo et al, 2013: 11). There was greater emphasis on the promotion of volunteering. And there was less emphasis on participatory action research and more emphasis on research to produce statistics: the numbers of those becoming school governors, for example, and the numbers of those enhancing their employability as a result of their involvement in the programme. But none of this is to suggest that there were no remaining spaces at all, whether in universities and colleges, voluntary and community sector organisations or indeed in structures of governance, in particular contexts.

Local government has its own history of providing spaces for popular education too. As Michael Newman (1979) pointed out, adult learning was taking place in many contexts, including local authority schools and adult education centres. The Inner London Education Authority supported the work that he described in *The Poor Cousin* (so-called because adult education was the 'poorest and most neglected sector of the education service') as a case in point (Newman, 1979: 3). This learning included both learning for leisure and what Michael Newman termed 'survival' learning; the list of courses included civil liberties, how to know your rights and how to access them, planning, housing, power and authority and community action. Each group of learners would pool their knowledge and skills, in the popular education approach, with the tutor acting as 'encourager, arbiter, adviser, questioner and group member as well as teacher' (Newman, 1979: 50).

Spaces and resources may have shrunk further since the 1970s, but the need for critical adult learning was more important than ever, Newman reflected, in the wake of the invasion of Iraq, as previously pointed out. Writing in 2006 he argued for teaching people 'how to make up their own minds, and how to take control of their moment' (Newman, 2006: 10). He emphasised the importance of learning how to listen and how to speak up, using both instrumental and more affective forms of communication (including the use of novels and drama) to enable people to explore the causes of their anger, analysing the nature of power and how to intervene most effectively.

Meanwhile, as Newman and others recognised, people have been doing it for themselves in a variety of settings. These have included formal institutions and public spaces, such as libraries and even prisons, as exemplified by the history of prisoners' self-organised political education initiatives in South Africa during the Apartheid regime and in Northern Ireland during the Troubles (Brookfield and Holst, 2011). And these spaces have included far more informal places such as people's front rooms – even the street.

Libraries have a particular history here, as spaces for adult education, both for individual auto-didacts and for groups and social movements. Local libraries can provide relatively warm, comfortable places for campaign groups to gather to inform themselves about the issues that concern them, issues such as proposed cuts to public services, for example. And libraries can provide places where groups can move on to develop their own strategies in response. Public libraries have been hosting a range of such gatherings, even if funding cuts have been impacting on library provision in too many parts of Britain in recent years.

In the US, meanwhile, a network of libraries has been established since the election of Donald Trump as president, in 2016. These libraries have been responding to popular demand for safe spaces in which to engage in political debate, how to make sense of the rise of Far Right populist politics and how to develop effective strategies in response. Following a seminar in 2017, bringing different libraries together, a group of such libraries formed a network, linked to international networks of libraries committed to facilitating popular education for active citizenship. So Community-Library Inter-Action (CLIA) was established to strengthen libraries' role as anchor institutions 'by working WITH, not just FOR communities, and supporting communities in acting collectively rather than alone'. The emphasis was to 'facilitate participatory dialogue and community action, contributing towards advancing justice, inclusion and equity', supporting movements towards social transformation and so to 'contribute to the collective action and impact of libraries worldwide to advance peaceful and sustainable communities' (Communication from Professor Clara Chu, Mortenson Centre for International Library Programs, University of Illinois, 9 May 2017).

CLIA has been building on the experiences of the University of Illinois Mortenson Center's work, supporting librarians worldwide, including via its 'Libraries for Peace' initiative. In addition CLIA has been drawing on international expertise, including the Take Part Learning Framework for Active Citizenship Learning. Making community–library collaboration the core strategy throughout May and June 2017, CLIA held two Co-Development laboratories with librarians and community members in the United States and in Colombia.[1] The following year, in 2018, CLIA received an Iberbibliotecas grant to take this work further, with a multi-national project called 'Interact with your community from the public library: Learning and advancing peace from the contexts of Colombia, Costa Rica and Peru'. This initiative involved workshops with around 100 librarians and community leaders in different types of localities in the three countries concerned. The project included 'community conversations' in some of these locations, community-based dialogues based on the principle that librarians need to learn to work *with* rather than *for* their communities. These conversations provided spaces for community members to meet each other around shared interests, as the basis for generating collective processes of local social change.

Meanwhile other libraries have organised themselves and their educational programmes independently in the voluntary sector. The Marx Memorial Library and Workers' School (MML) provides an example here. Marx House was established in London as a library and educational centre, founded in 1933 in response to Nazi book burning that year. The library was to take on the battle of ideas. MML's foundation was supported by communists, as well as by Labour Party activists and trade unionists who felt the need to promote working class political education at that time (Cohen, 1992). There were ten-week courses, longer courses in political economy (stretching over three terms) and one-off lectures, along with correspondence courses, summer schools, study groups and discussion circles. A sister Marx House was subsequently established in Manchester in 1934.

The Second World War disrupted these initiatives, however. Marx House, Manchester closed and Marx House, London was also temporarily closed in 1945, for repairs to war damage. MML was then re-opened in 1949, continuing to organise educational programmes alongside its archive and library functions, providing an invaluable archive of trade union and progressive movement records, including the archives of the International Brigade of the Spanish Civil War. As a trustee I have an interest to declare here, before I summarise the current range of educational activities in progress.

Over the past few years MML has been engaging with the recent upsurge of interest in popular education in general and political education more specifically. For example, lectures on political economy and the causes of the 2007–08 financial crisis have attracted new audiences of young people, keen to understand the current socioeconomic and political context as the basis for campaigning for more progressive alternatives. MML has been providing a range of such lectures and courses, together with a variety of seminars and international conferences, addressing the concerns of labour and progressive movement organisations including community organisations and groups (such as groups of housing activists). Streaming is being developed to share these learning experiences more widely and learning materials are made available online. The programmes offer both relatively formal forms of learning, such as lectures and seminars, and less formal learning activities, including the performance of plays and film showings, followed by discussion sessions. There have also been outreach initiatives such as exhibitions at labour movement events, taking these discussions out to wider audiences.

In addition to these educational activities, MML is currently working in partnership with trade unionists to develop a programme of participatory action research. Working together in regional teams, trade unionists are being supported to explore their own histories, examining past records and compiling oral histories, identifying issues and debates with continuing relevance for the contemporary context. The aim here is to produce a range of learning materials, both written and accessible online materials, for educational purposes.

While focusing on providing learning opportunities and learning materials for labour and progressive movement organisations and groups, MML is a charity, independent of any particular political party. This independence has been important from the outset. The library is committed to facilitating critical learning and reflection, rather than simply promoting party political propaganda.

Such political independence is characteristic of many other providers of popular and political education too. As Chapter 1 outlined, The World Transformed (TWT) has been one of, if not the largest, initiative to blossom over the past few years: the four-day long festivals of socialist politics, art, community and cultural events have been scheduled to take place alongside – but separate from – official Labour Party conferences. TWT has clearly made its mark on the political scene. But it has achieved this without becoming captive to any specific party political agenda. The aim has been to preserve and develop the space for critical reflection within as well as outside these mobilisations for social change.

Political parties do have their own histories of providing political education, however. Brookfield and Holst include references to the educational initiatives of the Communist Party in the US, as well as those of the Civil Rights movements, including the work of Highlander at that period (Brookfield and Holst, 2011). And Boughton (2005) references the work of 'The Workers' University', Australia's Marx schools, educational initiatives that linked political education with progressive social movement struggles. There had been networks of socialist and community party schools, both in Australia and elsewhere, internationally, from the 1920s onwards, a tradition that became effectively invisible subsequently, in the Cold War period and beyond, he argued.

Like other educational initiatives, party political interventions can and do take a variety of forms. These range from relatively formal conferences and workshops, through to far less formal popular education style discussion groups, the local branches that invite speakers to open discussions on topics of particular local concern – with a view to planning effective campaigning in response. How to understand the reasons behind a proposed hospital closure, how to develop the case for social housing on a local development site or how to address traffic problems in order to reduce pollution and make cycling safer, just to refer to recent examples from my own experience.

These types of discussions can take place in a variety of locations, from members' homes through to local community centres. And they can take place in the street. Guided walks can provide vivid ways of exploring particular issues, drawing out the lessons from previous experiences and struggles. As part of a Labour Party political education programme in 2018, for example, a guided walk in East London was organised around Brick Lane, an area that has been described as having been a battleground of the 1970s, in terms of challenging racist violence. The walk started from the Altab Ali Park in Whitechapel, so named after a young Bengali who was murdered by racists on his way home from work in 1978. The political education walk set out to tell Altab Ali's story and to explore the responses to racism that resulted, including the contributions of cultural activists such as the musicians who became involved in organising musical events to 'Rock Against Racism'. The lessons about building alliances to promote equality remain all too relevant issues.

In summary

In summary then, popular education initiatives have been taking place in a wide variety of places, from front rooms to public buildings of varying types. And they have been organised across sectors, whether they have been supported by structures of governance, universities and colleges or whether they have been self-organised via civil society organisations (CSOs) and social movements campaigning for transformative change. The spaces for popular education have been shrinking in many ways, trends that have been impacting across sectors in the wake of neoliberal globalisation. But there are still spaces to be identified and claimed, despite these wider challenges, whether these spaces are to be found in the public, voluntary or community sectors; or found in some forms of cross-cutting partnerships, spanning CSOs, social movements and the state.

Note
[1] http://librariesforpeace.org/projects/clia/

4

Principles and practice

Previous chapters have referred to the principles that underpin popular education in differing economic, political, social and cultural contexts. This chapter summarises these before exploring some of the varying ways in which popular educators have been identifying with these principles and developing strategies to apply them in practice. These examples include the discussion of relatively formal approaches to learning as well as less formal creative practices along with the discussion of mixed approaches, learning programmes that have been offering a range of methods and tools.

Values and principles as these have been developed

Popular education has been defined as being popular but not populist (Crowther et al, 2005b), as previous chapters have already outlined – and subsequent chapters explore in further detail. There are inherent tensions and challenges here. Popular education may involve challenging people's beliefs, engaging in processes of dialogue to explore the underlying reasons for racist, sexist, xenophobic, anti-Semitic or Islamophobic views, for example.

Popular education has also been defined as being political and overtly critical of the status quo (Crowther et al, 2005b). Here too previous chapters have already outlined different ways of interpreting this aspect. Being overtly 'political' does not necessarily imply being 'party political'. On the contrary, in fact. Political parties can and do engage in popular education of course, as Chapter 3 has illustrated. But this needs to be distinguished from the promotion of political propaganda. Popular education is committed to facilitating critical reflection, rather than necessarily following any particular political 'line'. And this includes the commitment to facilitate critical reflections on the nature of power and how to challenge inequalities of power and resources, in whichever context or structure they impinge (including political parties' own structures), along with challenging inequalities of power and resources within and between communities and social movements.

Finally popular education has been defined as being committed to progressive social change. This distinguishes it from political education and adult education more generally, where the focus may be on learning for a wider variety of purposes, including the purpose of learning for its own sake. Popular education is about learning in order to promote social justice agendas, facilitating critical understandings of the underlying causes of increasing inequalities and social deprivation, along with the causes of social conflicts and hate crimes.

The processes and practices of popular education have also been associated with the following characteristics (Crowther et al, 2005b).

- The curriculum emerges from people's interests, experiences and concerns, actively engaging learners in the process, respecting the knowledge that they bring to the learning encounter – while recognising the potential limits.
- The approach to learning is collective, emphasising the importance of group learning as well as the importance of learning for individuals.
- Popular education strategies include the use of participatory action research to promote knowledge democracy, co-producing 'really useful' knowledge for social change.
- Popular education aims to contribute to the development of strategies for social action, whether these links have direct implications for the present or less immediate implications, focusing on building capacities more broadly, for the future.

The values and principles of popular education have wide resonance in debates on adult education and active citizenship more generally. Fryer's study of citizenship, belonging and lifelong learning makes similar points, for instance, emphasising the importance of starting from learners' interests, needs and priorities, together with their own experiences, embracing all modes and forms of learning, formal, informal and incidental (Fryer, 2010). He also emphasises the importance of critical dialogue, quoting Brookfield (1987b) and Giroux (1997), both of them writing on the importance of critical thinking, challenging accepted ideas and developing alternatives as the basis for taking action, rooted in values of equity and social justice (Fryer, 2010). While these values and principles have been widely quoted, however, this by no means implies that their application has been unproblematic – on the contrary, as subsequent illustrations demonstrate.

Previous chapters have already identified some of popular education's potential tensions. Learners may – or may not – opt to engage in developing strategies for progressive social change, for instance, as previous examples have already suggested. The realities of people's lives may leave little if any time or energy for this– particularly if they feel sceptical about the likelihood of being heard by those with the power to respond, in any case. People may continue to define their interests in relatively exclusive or even divisive ways, whatever the aims of the learning initiative in question. Access to resources may be expected to be increasingly problematic in the current policy context, raising questions about whose agendas may be expected to become predominant in practice, whether these resources are being sought from the public, private/charitable and/or voluntary sectors.

So how have these values and principles been applied in practice? As the previous chapter has also suggested, popular education can be promoted in a variety of spaces and places. Popular education can take varying forms, taking account of such different contexts. And, as educationalists have long since noted, learning is absolutely not compulsory for adults. So the learning needs to be engaging. Otherwise adults can – and do – vote with their feet. Whether this implies that teaching adults is totally different from teaching children is a moot point (Knowles, 1970; Tight,1983). But there clearly are differences as well as similarities between the two. Popular education can be more flexible just as it can be less formal, taking account of the needs and concerns of the learners in question, as the following examples from a relatively recent UK initiative illustrate.

'Take Part': active learning for active citizenship

The initiative to promote 'Active Learning for Active Citizenship' (ALAC) set out to apply Freirean approaches to community-based learning for active citizenship. This was part of the UK government's 'Together We Can' and 'Take Part' programmes (2003–10). The aim was to promote learning for active citizenship and community engagement, based on the values of social justice, equality and respect for diversity, emphasising mutuality, cooperation and social solidarity. The programme set out to empower communities while encouraging the relevant structures of governance to learn to listen and to respond, working both sides of the equation 'to build a more active and engaged civil society and a more responsive and effective state that can deliver needed public services', as an early report summarised these objectives (ALAC, 2006).

The learning was to be delivered via community–university/college partnerships, based in seven regional hubs. These were to start from people's own experiences and interests, critically reflecting on these as the basis for developing effective strategies for change (Mayo et al,

2019). They were to provide pathways for individuals as well as for communities to move forward, whether by gaining qualifications to facilitate progression to further study and/or enhanced employment prospects or whether via taking up civic responsibilities such as becoming a school governor or a magistrate.

The ALAC approach encompassed a similarly wide range of delivery mechanisms. These ranged from one-off workshops and teach-ins through to more structured sessions, courses running over weeks or even months. The mechanisms in question varied, depending on the needs and the interests of the communities in question, and the barriers to be overcome in order to address them.

Monitoring and evaluation systems were developed as ongoing processes between the external evaluators and the hubs. The hubs were already well used to the need to account for their activities, including the use of systems for tracking individual learners' progression. These aspects were relatively straightforward to evaluate. The evaluation of the initiative's wider impacts proved far more challenging, however.

Between them the hubs and the external evaluators developed a shared framework, including participative ways of recording and evaluating ALAC's impact, such as the use of logs, diaries, photographs and videos. Once developed, the evaluation framework was then road-tested with participants from the different hubs, to share their perspectives, trying to capture the wider effects within communities and families as well the effects for the individuals concerned (Mayo and Rooke, 2006), the more specific and the more readily quantifiable evidence of progression that particularly appealed to policy makers. While there were inherent tensions here, there were still spaces for differing approaches, within a relatively flexible framework, nationally, including spaces for campaigning on social justice issues.

If government funding for community-based learning and participatory action research from the bottom up had sounded too good to be true, then it was. There were, of course, inherent tensions, as some of the original proponents recognised at the time. Val Woodward, the author of the report that laid the groundwork for ALAC, identified some of these inherent tensions right from the start (Woodward, 2004, 2010). The approach was contentious, yet strongly advocated, she pointed out, but 'with hindsight, there was insufficient opportunity for in-depth reflection and debate during the project's life' (Woodward, 2010: 101). This was to be a people-centred policy and programme of action, based on the notion that a healthy democracy depends on active citizenship, promoted via adult education – a notion that she referenced back to the founding principles of the

Workers' Educational Association (WEA) since 1903. And this was to be delivered as a joint project between government and the voluntary and community sectors, supported by universities and other learning providers. This was a complex structure, she noted, 'recognising that the state is likely to incorporate such projects primarily to legitimise its actions', hence 'the emphasis on grass roots control and attempts to alter power relationships in favour of the less powerful' (Woodward, 2010: 105).

As Val Woodward concluded subsequently, however, 'Encouraging local autonomy inevitably creates tensions for overall paths of development and does not easily mesh with central policy development ... The synergy and tensions between policy development, radical thinking and concrete action proved difficult' (2010: 119). Such tensions proved challenging enough for New Labour governments, attempting to manage the impacts of neoliberal globalisation via the compromises of the so-called 'Third Way' (promoting social justice agendas without fundamentally challenging neoliberal globalisation, in practice). More fundamental approaches to tackling structural inequalities could be expected to pose correspondingly greater challenges.

There were competing perspectives, and varying definitions of key concepts, including the notion of active citizenship itself. Was this about encouraging individuals to volunteer, for example (one of the official objectives)? And/or was this about individuals and communities learning how to engage more effectively with service providers and other structures of governance (a generally shared objective)? Or was it *also* about empowering citizens to work together to develop their own agendas for equalities and social justice, combining individual fulfilment with 'the larger demands of solidarity and concern for the public good', as Ralph Miliband (1994: 56) had previously written about this approach to citizenship? While all three types of definition had their place, this last was the one that resonated most closely with popular education agendas for social justice and democratic social change.

Still this was a very good try, in Woodward's view, ALAC having succeeded in showcasing ways of strengthening democracy, providing empowering education and fighting inequalities, as Miliband had also argued, exploiting contemporary spaces in government and civil society sectors of society to promote just such incremental change for the longer term (Miliband, 1994: 120).

This links back to the previous chapter's discussion of the spaces and places for popular education. The spaces for the Take Part approach were already shrinking, with increasing emphasis on the achievement of numerical targets – working towards more limited goals – even before the changes in national government policies that followed from the 2010 election onwards. 'Take Part' initiatives have been criticised for pursuing a narrower focus on citizen involvement, subsequently, emphasising volunteering and engagement in formal structures of governance (becoming a school governor for example) – with correspondingly less emphasis on advocacy and campaigning (Mayo et al, 2013). Even here though, it was argued, 'there turned out to have been some space still for advocacy and campaigning, for example around young people's issues' (Mayo et al, 2013: 14).

The points to emphasise then are simply these: that spaces were identified – and occupied creatively; and that elements of the approach survived to live another day, despite the loss of central government funding.

Active Learning for Active Citizenship: 'Taking Part' in practice

Although there were varying perspectives within and between the seven regional hubs, there was general agreement about the underlying principles and practices of adult learning that were to be applied, building on previous experiences of working with communities and establishing relationships of trust. These relationships were to be developed and sustained over time, rather than being confined to particular, one-off interventions. ALAC was to be distinguished from the types of projects that were being parachuted into communities at that time, only to be withdrawn when the funding ran out. And the learning was to be both 'useful and fun' (Woodward, 2004: 7), requirements that necessitated a flexible learning framework – despite spasmodic government interventions that were proposing the development of a national curriculum (proposals that were consistently and eventually successfully rejected).

So what did this all mean, in practice, in the regional hubs? Some of the methods seemed relatively surprising for the officials involved apparently; some 'found it difficult to accept that a lively participative dance, where, for example, some even took their shoes off, was a legitimate activity for a government sponsored project' (Woodward, 2010: 115). But although there were some such 'surprises', many of the methods were considerably more established, as learning practices. And many such established methods were combined with more participative approaches, providing a mixture of methods and practices.

Looking back over my experiences via the evaluation processes, I recall flip charts and sticky notes galore, trees and river of life diagrams, lines of identification and human sculptures – a whole range of participative tools, drawn from popular education and participative action research experiences both in the UK and beyond in international development contexts. We encouraged groups to use such tools as mechanisms for providing qualitative feedback, monitoring and evaluating their experiences of ALAC initiatives in practice. The evaluation report from the first phase included illustrations of flip chart diagrams of brainstorms, power diagrams, art making activities and a drumming group, for example, demonstrating the use of participative tools for learning as well as for evaluating that learning (Mayo and Rooke, 2006). But reading over some of the hubs' reports, I am reminded that these only represented part of the ALAC story. The range of methods was actually wider still. This was not about privileging any particular delivery method per se then, but about facilitating learning, aiming to identify the most appropriate ways, or the most appropriate mix of ways, in order to enable people to address their concerns together more effectively.

In the East Midlands hub, for instance, spaces were opened up for what were described as 'constructed conversations' – dialogues between adults and young people, as well as active citizenship learning for immigrants and for mental health service users and carers, working both sides of the equation. The aim was to support groups through these constructed conversations, providing spaces for reflection linked to social action, addressing the issues and injustices that were facing people in their communities in different settings. A range of specific learning activities was on offer too, including workshops, conferences and celebration events, as well as a number of semi-formal classroom-based activities such as IT sessions, English language classes and the exploration of citizenship concerns through music composition classes and community radio production workshops. Given the rural, relatively dispersed nature of the surrounding area, and the lack of public transport, there were activities that were taken out to learners in their localities as well as being provided in the city and the partner organisation, the University of Lincoln.

Mixed approaches were characteristic of other hubs' activities too. In the West Midlands, for example, the hub focused on working with women, aiming to address the barriers that affect women's abilities to be involved in decision making, in their family lives and in the public sphere. Rather than seeing these as being either/or choices, the view was that

> Women are generally not active in the wider world until they are active in their own life and so we can liken this to a journey to influence, starting with becoming influential in your own life and then moving on to becoming influential in other spheres. (Bedford et al, 2010: 195)

The IMPACT approach that the West Midlands hub applied started from a focus on 'valuing your own skills', then 'knowing yourself through and with others', 'knowing how the external world operates' and 'choosing where you want to be and finally knowing when to go to get what you want'. The IMPACT programme provided safe, women-only spaces to explore these issues collectively. There were workshops, residential events with Fircroft Residential College, field visits (to Westminster and to Brussels) and weekly sessions on Saturdays over a 6–9 month period. This learning programme was also accredited (with the Open College Network).

The issue of accreditation had been contested. Among popular educators formal accreditation requirements had been viewed as potentially offputting, especially for those without previous qualifications. Accreditation could have presented barriers, it had been feared, turning potential learners off. Despite funders' interests in accreditation – as a readily measurable indicator of progress – the hubs generally preferred for this to remain optional, opening opportunities for those who wished to pursue these, while respecting the choices of those who preferred not to do so.

Similar arguments applied to progression routes in terms of increasing engagement in civic roles and structures of governance. The IMPACT programme did result in a number of the women becoming involved in formal structures such as a Women's Enterprise Development Agency, a primary care trust, a community forum, a school governing board, a safety partnership board, a community empowerment network, a local environmental group and other agencies. But this was only part of the story. Participants could – and did – choose the nature and extent of their involvement for themselves. However much popular educators may have set out to encourage learners to become more actively involved, whether as volunteers, civic representatives or community activists, it was, in practice, for the learners to make their own decisions. And, as it turned out, they did not necessarily decide to progress as either the funders or, indeed, the popular educators might have preferred. This is the logic of learner-centred approaches after all, the tensions inherent in popular education for social change, as previous chapters have already identified.

Far from being relatively passive as facilitators, though, the hubs were prepared to engage with challenging issues. The South Yorkshire hub is a case in point. The hub was based in Sheffield, set up as a partnership between the WEA and Northern College, an adult residential college near Barnsley. Both organisations had long established track records of working with communities and social movements, including long experiences of focusing on international as well as on more local issues and concerns. And both were geared up to responding to local organisations and groups at short notice, as needs arose and as issues came to the fore.

This was an area that had been changing rapidly, as Ted Hartley (2010) from the WEA explained in his reflections on his experiences in South Yorkshire. There had been widespread social and economic atomisation, following the loss of jobs in mining and other industries. He associated these processes of atomisation with first Conservative and then New Labour free market led policy approaches, accompanied as these had been by shifts and changes in major services, as a result of privatisation.

Meanwhile, between 2001 and 2006, Sheffield's black and minority ethnic communities had increased from 8% to 30% of Sheffield's total population. There were refugees and asylum seekers. And there were economic migrants from the A8 EU countries (the countries that were joining the EU and so gaining the right to work in the UK), including Poland, Slovakia and the Baltic states. Hartley described local feelings, in this changing context, with 'the sudden impact of work migration, the equally sudden arrival of refugees and asylum seekers into their communities', changes that were bringing new uncertainties and added social strains (Hartley, 2010: 145). Meanwhile, in addition, terror attacks had been fuelling anti-Islamic feelings, with rising xenophobia in general and increasing Islamophobia, more specifically.

The rationale for the South Yorkshire's response to these challenges was outlined as follows. Rapid change, due to privatisation and the continued loss of manufacturing jobs was creating a climate of insecurity and fear, compounded by changes in the labour market with rapidly increased migration flows. The migrant and the asylum seeker were being demonised as the 'root of social ills' (Grayson, 2010: 157), 'the asylum seeker at the gate and the shadowy Muslim within' (Sivanandum, 2006). This climate, together with the accompanying growth of support for extreme right political parties (Grayson, 2010: 157), had to be challenged, along with the public policies that were exacerbating the problems. So this was to be an overtly anti-racist approach, developing courses to build solidarity and alliances 'around working-class issues across ethnic divides' (Grayson, 2010: 162).

> We set out to work in solidarity with anti-racist community organisations and social movements of refugees and migrant workers, organising around local anti-racist campaigning ... Our practice was aimed at developing critical consciousness and providing 'really useful knowledge', linking to political action in a traditional popular education way. (Grayson, 2010: 162)

So how did this approach work out in practice? Among other interventions, the College organised weekly teach-ins on 'Issues that Matter' (Rooke, 2010) – unpacking a range of issues of both local and wider concern. The 'teach-in' may have been a relatively well-established method of teaching, a method which appealed to Northern College's students on longer-term study programmes. But these events did also appeal to local organisations and groups. They had the additional advantage of introducing local activists to the College, offering taster events that could stimulate potential interest in learning for the future.

Other learning events that were directly supported by the hub included residential courses. Like teach-ins, residential courses have a well-established history, including a well-established history in popular education. The residential colleges, such as Northern College, were already providing short courses to support community groups, trade unions and other social movements, coming together for concentrated periods of collective learning, focused on issues of shared concern. This was a format that was taken up by other hubs too, providing practical support, such as transport and childcare costs, in order to enable the participants to engage, if only for a weekend, without the everyday pressures that generally encompassed their lives. As other hubs' experiences similarly demonstrated, these practical forms of support were particularly important for women with domestic responsibilities.

The point was not that residentials were necessarily more – or less – participative per se, rather that these residentials were specifically organised to explore the issues and experiences that concerned people most. They were organised for longer-established communities and those working with them. And they were organised to meet the needs of more recent arrivals – in each case using a mix of learning methods and tools, including methods and tools to promote anti-racist agendas.

The residentials that were organised at Northern College included courses on 'Combating Racism'. These were two- to three-day events 'to discuss and develop our approaches with workers and activists in voluntary and community organisations', as John Grayson, the Northern College tutor explained (Grayson, 2010: 162). The focus was on promoting anti-racism, resourcing anti-racist organisations 'to develop anti-racist working, solidarity and strategy' (2010: 162). There were sessions on 'Kicking Out Racism in Your Community', 'Challenging Racism for Community Trainers' and 'Divided We Fall; Resolving Conflict in Communities'.

Meanwhile, there were also residentials for asylum seekers and refugees including 'Living in the UK'. There was a course for Refugee Community Organisations (RCOs), 'How to Organise RCOs'. And there were residentials that brought different groups together, to explore their issues and experiences collectively. Examples included the sessions that the College and the WEA organised on 'Migration and Europe', which included a focus on the rise of Far Right sentiments across the continent (of continuing relevance).

This particular learning programme on 'Migration and Europe' consisted of a package of mixed methods, with a series of evening sessions in Sheffield (to make them accessible locally), together with a two-night residential at the College and a study visit to Glokala, a people's high school in Malmö, Sweden. The South Yorkshire participants came from refugee organisations, the local racial equality council, school support workers and officers from a primary care trust and a local housing provider (working 'both sides of the equation' with service providers as well as with local organisations and groups) to explore the issues and develop proposals for addressing them, back home in South Yorkshire. This study visit included opportunities to meet and share experiences with refugees and asylum seekers as well as with local community projects in Sweden, sharing experiences of how to take equalities agendas forward.

In addition to teach-ins and residentials, the South Yorkshire hub also provided a number of courses with weekly sessions, drawing on the WEA's experiences of providing tutors/invited speakers' inputs, followed by group discussions to explore the content collectively. There were courses for women refugees, for instance, meeting their practical information needs (including information about women's health issues such as contraception). And there were short courses for mixed groups, including a short course on the history of migration in Britain. Entitled 'Bloody Foreigners'; this course looked at the contributions made by people from all over the world. There was interest in Jewish, Irish and African immigration from the past, along with the history of those who had arrived with the MV Empire Windrush, after the Second World War. And there was interest in the stories of subsequent arrivals, from Pakistan and the Yemen and more recent arrivals from newly expanded European Union, along with refugees from elsewhere including Liberia and the Ivory Coast.

Like the course on 'Migration and Europe', this course also included study visits. The group visited Westminster as part of their study of the UK democratic system, a visit that included sitting in on 'Question Time'. This enabled them to learn how to approach their local MP to try to persuade him to put a question on the issue of their lack of primary identification documents (another issue of continuing contemporary relevance). And the group visited Liverpool's black community, and the Museum of Slavery.

Study visits featured in the South Yorkshire hub's work with other groups too, including the Roma. A group of Roma and Travellers and those working with them went to Hungary in 2006, for instance, linking up with popular educators at the Kunbabony Civil College. Together they gathered information and ideas for further action, taking up citizenship issues back in the UK, along with issues relating to employment and cultural programmes (Rooke, 2010). These study visits formed part of ongoing programmes, building on these different approaches to learning, tailored to the needs of particular groups. Yet again, the contemporary relevance of such initiatives is only too striking.

Although the South Yorkshire hub shared ALAC's wider commitment to working with communities consistently, building mutual trust over time, this did not exclude the provision of one-off learning events, either. On the contrary, in fact, the need for such one-off events emerged from these ongoing relationships. For example, a workshop was organised to provide information technology training for Somali communities. These groups were geographically spread around the area, presenting communication difficulties as a result. The IT training enabled the groups to tackle these challenges. IT training may not seem particularly participative per se, but this was popular education in practice, in the sense that this was providing communities with the specific tools that they needed, collectively.

The methods and tools were varied then, including both overtly participative and more conventionally established ways of learning. It was the overall approach to anti-racist work that was potentially more challenging. This emerged particularly clearly during the final evaluation sessions. A small minority of participants expressed reservations about taking such a direct approach. Unsurprisingly perhaps, given the findings from research elsewhere, these participants had come from an area that had experienced far less migration – expressing their anxieties about the unfamiliar? This potentially re-enforces rather than refutes the case for addressing such issues directly, unpacking the underlying causes, exploring areas of common interest within and between communities while being mindful of potentially divisive anxieties and fears. The South Yorkshire hub took these issues head on, rather than avoiding such contentious subjects in the hope that they would somehow disappear if you didn't talk about them publicly.

Reflecting on the range of the South Yorkshire hub's work with such inherent challenges, Ted Hartley concluded that one of the key findings was the importance of 'safe space where people can get together, with a skilled tutor, to discuss the difficult issues of the day' (Hartley, 2010: 153). This was particularly relevant when it came to the discussion of emotive issues. The Israeli-Palestine conflict had been a case in point, he suggested, illustrating the importance of people; being 'able to say what they felt without getting into debates about anti-Semitism, or racism' and the importance of working 'through the issues with people at their own pace and levels of understanding' (Hartley, 2010: 153). People who had been 'turned off' by formal politics in the past had changed their attitudes, with learners saying that they felt less disengaged and more prepared to keep connected and involved in the issues of the day, as a result of their learning experiences with ALAC, he concluded.

The work was continuing, he went on, including via WEA initiatives with European Social Fund support. The ALAC hubs had also formed their own network to promote adult learning for active citizenship. But the future was uncertain. Residentials and study visits come with costs, for instance, including the costs of providing transport and childcare, thereby necessitating support at both local and national levels. The key issue, he continued, was the political will to make the necessary resources available.

That was then, however. Subsequent governments have taken different approaches, with narrower educational parameters, approaches and challenges that have already been outlined. Despite shrinking spaces and diminishing resources, there have still been continuing struggles for survival. Some of these have been the subject of participatory action research, bringing universities and community-based organisations together, as part of a national programme to promote research capacity in the Third Sector.

For example, the Manchester hub continued to provide short courses, based on Freirean approaches via the University of Manchester. A school of participation, with participatory research and community leadership training, led to the development of the Refugee Charter for Manchester, for instance, covering basic rights, healthcare, housing, education and employment. Another such research partnership initiative addressed 'Practices and Alliances with Asylum seeking and refugee women'. And a third such initiative focused on research with small voluntary and community organisations and groups, identifying how they were being impacted by the economic climate and public expenditure cuts, exploring ways of promoting resilience and sustainability across the sector. But this has been easier said than done.

Writing in 2018, Carol Packham reflected that the

> legacy of the Manchester ALAC programme and its successors has become increasingly threatened by the university's failure to appreciate the mutual benefits of community engagement in general and short informal education courses in particular.

'Research and knowledge exchange initiatives have become increasingly focused on narrower approaches to students' employability,' she continued, along with 'partnerships geared towards income generation, in this period of continuing austerity' (Mayo et al, 2019).

The spaces for Freirean-based approaches to learning for active citizenship were becoming correspondingly reduced, in her view, posing new challenges for popular educators in the coming period.

Before moving on to more recent times, though, there remains the legacy of popular education and the arts. So far the discussion has focused on learning to acquire knowledge, critical understanding and skills. These are essential if communities are to pursue social justice agendas effectively. But so is the ability to relate to people's emotions, including anxiety, fear and hate, as previous chapters have already suggested. The arts have particular contributions to make in this respect.

Reaching the parts that other methods miss: popular education and the arts

Just as spaces have been shrinking in general, so have the spaces for the arts more specifically, in UK policy contexts. There had been growing unease, it has been argued, as the UK arts community had been 'finding itself delivering policy rather than providing what David Edgar calls "the voice of criticism, provocation and dissent" (Edgar, 2004)' (Tiller, 2013: 133). There had been increasing insistence on measurable outputs and outcomes. And this was before the impact of austerity policies from 2010 onwards, which has exacerbated these tendencies.

Despite such challenges, the role of the arts has also been recognised, being well placed to stimulate community action for social change. The Third Sector–university research partnerships that followed on from Take Part included case studies of community arts organisations' contributions, illustrating ways in which community theatre could engage communities across generations for example (Rooke, 2013). Community theatre has a long history, ranging from relatively didactic theatre, such as Agitprop – giving audiences very clear messages – through to more participative approaches such as role play and the use of forum theatre – involving audiences directly in co-producing the drama in question (Boal, 1979, 1995, 1998; Etmanski, 2007), providing safe spaces for audiences to experiment with new ways of being and new ways of challenging oppressive relationships and structures.

In this particular case, the London Bubble Theatre Company, the organisation in question, was well established locally, having built relationships of trust over previous decades. As a result London Bubble was able to engage local children and their elders in researching local experiences of the Blitz as an intergenerational project. This research formed the basis for the play that was then produced and performed locally, with participative workshops stimulating discussion of the issues involved – urban destruction and renewal in the past during the Second World War, along with urban redevelopment and gentrification in more recent times.

London Bubble has been described as an 'open and dialogical space' (Rooke, 2013: 159), flexible and welcoming, enabling participants to engage at whatever level(s) they found most comfortable, a continuing presence rather than the type of transient intervention that have been the subject of criticism in relation to so many one-off community arts initiatives. The research identified this openness and flexibility as central to London Bubble's impact in terms of participants' learning, especially young people's learning and their subsequent involvements as active citizens. Wider implications re-emerge in subsequent chapters, exploring some of the tensions involved in meeting funders' requirements for accountability while promoting collaborative research and critical reflective practice.

London Bubble is just one illustration among so many examples of community arts and popular education, including community arts based approaches to participative action research, encompassing poetry, song and dance, video, film and other forms of visual art. The arts can offer such creative ways of learning, as well as offering enjoyable experiences per se. And they can be more – or less – directly participative. The audience can be spectators (in the traditional sense) and they can be 'spectactors' in Boal's terminology, with direct audience participation in the drama, proposing and acting out alternative scenarios, testing different approaches and challenges in the safe spaces of forum theatre.

There are so many examples of the use of drama, 'the power of theatre to create dialogic spaces', moving participants from spectator to 'spectactor' (Butterwick, 2012), and so many uses of traditional forms of drama on which to build. Lissard's (2012) account of the uses of drama in Lesotho provides a case in point, illustrating the potential tensions but also the potential learning opportunities inherent in producing a play that raised issues about both colonialism and misogyny.

The art of quilting provides another example of an art form with particular relevance for feminist popular educators, committed to challenging 'women's multiple oppressions with the aim of promoting empowerment, transformation, justice and change' (Clover, 2012: 194). It is not just that quilting has generally been perceived as being a feminine skill, rather than a masculine skill (as would seem to have been the case in Canada, for example), but quilting also has the advantage of being able to combine individual creativity with collective forms of production. In the case study from Victoria Island, Canada, that Darlene Clover has described, women mobilised against the siting of a gas-fired power plant, developing a quilting project to express their feelings in a public way. The women produced individual squares which were then brought together to form a collective work of protest art (Clover, 2012) – creativity in the process of moving from the 'I' to the 'We'.

As Jane Thompson's Foreword to *The Arts and Social Justice* has emphasised in parallel, the arts have the power 'to stimulate radical learning and strengthen cultural democracy', providing a 'welcome escape from the dreary, instrumental, and increasingly coercive, preoccupation with skills for work and crowd control that so much routine practice in "Western" countries has now become', in her view (Thompson, 2007: xi). This particular collection of essays includes accounts of learning through 'singing, weaving, performance, quilt-making, embroidery, literature, poetry, banner-making, and rebel-clowning' (Thompson, 2007: xi) from a variety of international contexts. Their main purpose, she continued, was not to teach an artistic skill for individual gain, or for recreational purposes, although both of these outcomes could also result. Rather, the aim, in terms of popular education outcomes, was 'to address complex contemporary issues such as violence against women, gender discrimination, cultural imperialism, racism, poverty and other economic imbalances; as well as becoming producers and communicators, as distinct from passive consumers of culture' (Thompson, 2007: xi–xii).

As the editors of *The Arts and Social Justice* explain, 'engaging the aesthetic dimension enhances, or has the potential to enhance, transformative, democratic and emancipatory objectives of adult education' highlighting the role of the imagination (Clover and Stalker, 2007). Through artistic processes of working and learning, cultural identities could be re-positioned, 'strengthening cultural democracy and community leadership, enhancing people's abilities to challenge processes and practices that exclude, marginalise and disempower and (developing) new paradigms which foster social action' (Clover and Stalker, 2007). Most importantly too, for the concerns of this particular book, the arts can reach the emotions, enabling people to gain new senses of themselves and new understandings of others, developing ways of building social solidarity for the future.

There is not the space to go into further detail here. The arts offer such varieties of methods and approaches, centrally relevant for the values and practices of popular education and participatory action research, sustaining the democratic imagination in 'lean and mean times' (Meade and Shaw, 2010: 65). The point is simply to highlight these possibilities – hopefully encouraging readers to explore them further, for themselves.

In conclusion

The principles of popular education have their roots in progressive approaches to adult learning from way back, including those developed by the WEA and others in the UK and elsewhere, especially in international development contexts. There have been parallels here with the roots of participatory action research, including their application in the context of community arts based initiatives. These underpinning principles have then been applied in a variety of ways in practice, to meet the varying needs of differing communities and social movements over time – with a variety of outcomes, as subsequent chapters will consider in more detail.

Take Part exemplified these principles, while illustrating some of their inherent tensions in practice. There were potential tensions inherent in any such government-led attempt to promote initiatives from the bottom up. But there were also potential tensions between popular educators' agendas for social justice on the one hand, and their commitments to learner-led approaches on the other – continuing issues and dilemmas for popular education in practice.

Meanwhile, Take Part no longer benefits from government funding. But the principles and approaches continue to be applied in different contexts in UK and elsewhere, including Colombia, the birthplace of Orlando Fals Borda, a key figure in the development of participatory action research. Contemporary examples have included community–university projects to tackle very practical issues such as local energy systems and access to clean water and sanitation, for instance. And they have included initiatives to support those who have been displaced as a result of violence and human rights abuses, promoting inclusive community-based learning and research to support peace building processes in areas that have been ravaged by so many years of civil conflict.

While the underlying principles have been and continue to be similar, despite some inherent tensions and challenges, the range of teaching and methods and tools has been more varied. Looking back over Take Part's approaches, for instance, I have been struck by the range and mixtures of practices, combining different methods and tools, from relatively formal sessions through to more informal types of learning, including learning from study visits and community exchanges. More recent popular education initiatives, such as The World Transformed, provide a similar variety of learning experiences, from formal lectures and teach-ins through to workshops and community arts experiences. Rather than making a fetish of any particular method or tool, this is about tailoring learning practices most effectively, in order to meet people's learning needs.

While methods have been mixed, however, there have also been continuing themes. The importance of learning through dialogue has been particularly central, as Paulo Freire emphasised. In his view, critical consciousness could be developed through such processes of dialogue.

But there have also been continuing challenges, including the challenges involved in tackling some of the most emotive issues of the day – addressing racism, xenophobia and Islamophobia via anti-racist popular education. Chapter 9 explores the role of emotions in popular education further, while recognising the inherent challenges. But subsequent studies also demonstrate the problems with ignoring such uncomfortable emotive issues – in the hope that this will somehow magic them away (Fekete, 2018).

There would seem to be significant implications here for the contemporary context, with lessons from the past, in terms of the values, principles and practices of popular education. The popular educator's role involves facilitating processes of dialogue, respecting people's existing knowledge and experiences while 'making clear a reality darkened by the dominant ideology' (as expressed by Paulo Freire; de Figueiredo-Cowen and Gastaldo, 1995: 9); and so 'through a serious and proper political analysis, to unveil the possibilities for hope' (1995: 10).

5

Sharing understandings of varying histories and cultures

The previous chapter emphasised the importance of tailoring popular education approaches and practices, engaging with varying interests and learning needs within and between communities and social movements. How then to understand these different interests and needs, as these have been developing over time? And how then to facilitate shared understandings of varied histories, cultures and interests *within as well as between* communities and social movements – as the basis for building solidarity for the future?

While I was thinking about writing this chapter, I participated in a documentary film showing, part of a series showing films about the history of industrial struggles. The aim was to stimulate discussion – popular political education via the use of film, in other words. And stimulate discussion it most certainly did, if not quite as I had anticipated. Far from engaging with the substance of the dispute in question, younger participants expressed amazement at the activists' gender and ethnicity. How could they have been so predominantly male and so exclusively white? 'Pale, male and stale'? Before we could begin to reflect on the dispute itself, let alone consider its potential implications in terms of the interrelations between trade unionists, their employers and the state, we needed to take a step back. How and why had trade unions developed as they had, in different industrial contexts, in the past? How had they organised? Why had particular occupations been predominantly the preserve of men – despite the fact that women had shown themselves well capable of doing the jobs in question, as demonstrated during both First and Second World Wars? And how had struggles for women's equality and campaigns for race equality been waged in different trade unions and labour movement organisations, over the years?

This takes the discussion back to the tensions and challenges inherent in the very definition of popular education itself. As previous chapters have already noted, 'the real interests and struggles of ordinary people' have been and are being understood and expressed in *diverse* ways, within and between communities and social movements, including social movement organisations such as the trade union movement.

The first part of this chapter summarises these types of differences, together with some of the ways in which such differences have been impacting on varying approaches to learning. This sets the scene for discussing experiences of developing shared understandings in practice, providing the basis for building understanding across differing histories and organisational cultures, as these have been emerging from the past.

The slippery concept of 'community'

Much has been written about the contested concept of community, over past decades (Stacey, 1969; Popple, 2015). Rather than repeat previous definitions and their contestations in detail here, the points to emphasise are simply these. 'Community' has had different meanings in various contexts over time. And communities have contained and continue to contain differing interests and agendas. Recognising these differences is central, in fact, if *popular* education is to be distinguished from *populist* propaganda: propaganda that puts people and communities together as one; united in their differences from 'the other', however this 'other' is defined, politicians for example, purveyors of so-called 'fake news' perhaps, newcomers, minority communities, people of different faiths – 'enemies of the people'.

In the past, the term 'community' has actually been used in somewhat similar ways – to refer to the 'common people', as distinct from people of rank or indeed from the state (Williams, 1976). While usages have changed since then, elements of such potentially populist associations linger, the 'community' as 'the people'/'the ordinary people', rather than the 'suits and frocks', the bureaucrats and baddies versus the goodies from the 'grass roots' (Mayo, 2017). But communities can be formed around a variety of interests:

- based on neighbourhoods (communities of locality), for instance;
- expressing identities, such as those of race and ethnicity (communities of identity); or
- based around shared interests and concerns (such as mutual support groups; Popple, 2015).

And most importantly, communities, including transnational communities, can and do contain differences of interest and culture *within* as well as *between* them. They may be divided by differences of social class and caste (from socially mixed neighbourhoods in global cities through to socially divided villages in rural India). They may be divided by differences of gender, sexuality, age, ability and faith (whether living in the same neighbourhoods and/or sharing identities of race and ethnicity). And they may have very different interests when it comes to environmental sustainability – workers in environmentally polluting occupations fearing the loss of their livelihoods if others campaign for greater environmental protection (as with anti-asbestos campaigns in South Africa and India, for example; Waldman, 2010). There are challenges here, although unity *can* be built, including unity around environmental justice campaigns, identifying shared interests and bringing trade unions and communities together around these common concerns, as the story of environmental justice around the Ilva steel plant in Taranto (Apulia, Italy) illustrates (Barca and Leonardi, 2016). The second part of this chapter explores this and other examples of ways of addressing such challenges in further detail.

Writers have also suggested that 'community' has been used as a warmly persuasive term, with echoes of nostalgia for the imagined communities of a bygone past (Williams, 1976), expressing people's search for safety in an insecure world (Bauman, 2001). This would be consistent with contemporary populist appeals, calling for returns to golden pasts – to make America, or indeed to make Britain, great again. But 'community' has a darker side, as others have increasingly emphasised. Communities can be stigmatised in deeply damaging ways, whole neighbourhoods defined by their poverty, written off as dens of drug dealing and crime (Tyler, 2013; Shildrick, 2018). And communities can have exclusive cultures, banding together to exclude the 'other', whether these others are newcomers, such as migrants and refugees, or whether these others are simply different, as in terms of race, ethnicity, culture or faith (Kenny et al, 2015).

This makes it all the more important to recognise the differences that exist within as well as between communities, along with the differences *within* their own individual members. People have intersecting interests and identities, which can and do shift over time and space. Stuart Hall expressed this so clearly when he pointed out that identities are never completed, never finished: 'they are always, as subjectivity itself is, in process' (Hall, 1991: 47).

As Dhaliwal and Yuval-Davis have gone on to explain, 'Class cannot be experienced or lived outside of "race", gender, sexuality and the same is true of other categories', such as age or faith (Dhaliwal and Yuval-Davis, 2014: 35). And these categories can vary in terms of their significance, depending on the context, with her faith-based identity upfront for a Muslim woman faced with the threat of hate crime, for example, even if she is more concerned with her social class interests as a precarious employee in the world of work. She may identify with the concerns of her neighbourhood, when faced with the threat of displacement as a result of urban regeneration. And she may identify with her transnational community, when it comes to campaigning around foreign policy interventions and their impacts, internationally as well as more locally, here in Britain. Popular educators need to be aware of such complexities, within as well as between communities, if learning programmes are to be tailored to people's varying interests and priorities.

Social movements: just as contested?

If communities are diverse, so too are social movements, with a wide range of competing definitions and approaches, varying over time and space. Social movements have been theorised in a variety of ways in Europe and in the Americas, North and South, taking account of their differing histories and cultures (Foweraker, 1995; Della Porta and Diani, 1999; Crossley, 2002). Without suggesting that Della Porta and Diani provide an ultimately comprehensive solution, their definition does offer a very useful starting point. In their view social movement scholars from varying theoretical and territorial backgrounds still share concerns with the following aspects:

- Social movements consist of social networks of individuals, groups and organisations, whether loosely or more tightly linked.
- These movements share (at least some) beliefs and some degree of solidarity (although these beliefs and values may need to be developed).
- They engage in collective action, potentially involving conflict/promoting social change.
- They include the use of protest, in their repertoires of collective action. (Della Porta and Diani, 1999)

These last points have been summed up by Tarrow in terms of the mobilisations that take place when people 'try to exert power by contentious means against national states or opponents' (Tarrow, 2011: 6).

So far, so good. These characteristics could be applied to older as well as to newer social movements alike – to trade unions as well to movements for environmental justice – rather than distinguishing between them, as authors such as Touraine (1981) and Melucci (1996) have suggested in the past. Except that such definitions have their own inherent problems too, not least the problem that social movements have their own internal differences and potential tensions, including differences and tensions in relation to each of the above characteristics.

Social movements can and do vary widely in terms of their organisational cultures and structures. These range from the relatively formal representative structures of the trade union movement through to the typically less formally organised networks of community-based groups or second wave and subsequent wave feminisms from the 1970s onwards. Such differences have been categorised as 'vertical' structures on the one hand, as exemplified by trade unions and political parties, as contrasted with the less structured approaches of the 'horizontals'. Except social movements may be coalitions of different types of organisations and groups, whether 'vertical' or 'horizontal' in their approaches and organisational cultures. The US Civil Rights Movement represents a case in point, bringing together both formally organised sections of civil society such as black churches and the National Association for the Advancement of Colored People and less formal networks of black activists, white students and others. More contemporary social movements share comparable levels of organisational diversity. This could be said to apply to environmental justice movements for example, with formal organisations operating internationally alongside less formal groupings of activists. More of such differences and their implications subsequently.

Meanwhile, to return to Della Porta and Diani's definitional characteristics, social movements do need to share beliefs – or at least to have some shared beliefs and goals. But they can and do contain differences of aims as well. Here again the US Civil Rights movement provides illustration, having been described as accommodating those committed to the relatively limited aim of obtaining the right – and the effective ability – to vote as well as accommodating activists with the broader, more transformational goals of racial equality and social justice (Tarrow, 2011).

Social movements may have vigorous debates about strategies and tactics too. These may include different views about the nature of the conflicts of interests that are to be addressed. And they may include vigorous discussions about the use of protest tactics – when to strike and when to settle for instance, when to demonstrate and when to negotiate, when to organise a sit-in and when to organise an online petition? Or with what combination of tactics should they move forward?

Differing political perspectives underpin so many of these debates. Authors such as Melucci and Touraine have already been quoted as examples of scholars focusing on the differences between social movements over time. Older movements such as the labour movement were inherently reformist, in their view, in contrast with the supposedly wider, more transformational demands of newer mobilisations, such as social movements based on people's identities. But this type of approach has been criticised on a number of grounds, as well as being seen as needing further theoretical development (Crossley, 2002; Della Porta and Tarrow, 2005). The assumed political divisions between older social movements and newer social movements have been questioned (Munck and Waterman, 1999; Della Porta and Diani, 1999; Crossley, 2002; Holst, 2002). And such supposed dichotomies fail to take account of the significance of differences *within* as well as between them. Older social movements, such as the trade union movement, have their own histories of struggle between more and less progressive political positions. And identity politics can be deeply divisive, as the discussion of intersectionality has already suggested, illustrated by competing views on transgender issues within feminist debates, just to cite one contemporary example. So rather than attempting to categorise social movements in terms of which is more – or less – transformative per se, popular educators might more usefully explore the varying ways in which political differences play out within as well as between them. This is the focus that needs to be emphasised, in relation to popular education, over time and space.

Differing approaches within the trade union movement

By far the largest social movement in the UK (with 6 million members), the trade union movement provides examples for illustration here. Chapter 2 has already outlined the contested history of trade union and popular education in Britain, with illustrations from the splits that followed the strike at Ruskin College in 1909 (Simon, 1992b; Corfield, 1969). While the National Council of Labour Colleges (NCLCs) emphasised the importance of teaching Marxist economics and political thought, others, including the Workers' Educational Association (WEA), emphasised the importance of more neutral approaches to learning. Was the aim to prepare students to work effectively within the existing social order? Or was the aim to develop collective, class-based understandings as the basis for building movements for progressive social change (Simon, 1992b)?

The way in which these differences have played out in practice has been the subject of continuing debate, as Chapter 2 went on to point out. In the interwar period the WEA used teaching materials prepared by Marxists, including Maurice Dobb, Palme Dutt and

Robin Page Arnot, for instance (Corfield, 1969). By the 1940s and 1950s, Simon (1992a) has suggested, Marxism may actually have been discussed more fully in the WEA and university extra-mural departments than in the NCLCs. But both sets of organisations have faced significant challenges in more recent times, including pressures to provide more limited and more instrumental forms of education and training, as previous chapters have also suggested. Earlier debates around the balance between wider political versus more industry-specific approaches, between political commitment versus objectivity and between state funding versus independence have been described as becoming less prominent, from the 1980s, a period described in terms of reaction and retrenchment (Holford, 1994). Even so there were positive developments too, however, including the development of courses supporting women and members of black and minority ethnic communities in their struggles for equality. Each trade union has its own organisational history and culture here, with differences within regions and industrial sectors to be taken into account, for good measure.

The history of trade union education in the Transport and General Workers Union (T and G) offers a case in point (Fisher, 2005). Formed in 1922, the T and G was the largest working class organisation in the UK for much of the 20th century, its influence extending 'beyond industry to help shape the broad social development of the country' (Murray, 2008: 7) with the largest educational programme among Trades Union Congress (TUC) affiliates (Fisher, 2005). Over the years the union has developed varying methods and approaches to learning, from differing political interests and perspectives.

In summary, the differences between the WEA and the NCLC were reflected in the union's educational debates in the 1920s, with arguments for and against each (although the T and G was generally seen as having been closer to the WEA/Workers' Educational Trade Union Committee, WETUC; Fisher, 2005). In practice though, local activists worked out their own ways forward, with activists in the North West taking both Labour College and WETUC courses in the interwar period. Weekend schools and summer schools were organised by both, along with summer schools and longer residential courses at Ruskin and the other residential colleges, also attended by T and G activists. As T and G's provision grew this included learning via correspondence courses. These could be supplemented by day schools and study groups, typically provided in the local district. Programmes were developed by and for women and for the promotion of equalities more generally. In summary, then, there were both formal and informal opportunities for learning, from scholarships to attend the longer residential courses through to one-off events focusing on the interests of particular industrial sectors and localities.

While provision was diverse though, similar debates re-occurred over time, reflecting wider political debates within the union and beyond, in the labour movement more generally. To what extent should this be about promoting an organising agenda, building activism via the shop stewards movement? And how far should the union be offering opportunities for higher and further education for individual members? What should be the priority given to the provision of very specific training, such as that required for health and safety representatives? And how far should the union provide its own independent education and training, rather than accessing government funding through accredited courses via the TUC and other providers? There have been increasing pressures in these latter respects from the Thatcher years onwards, although with regional differences as to the educational outcomes.

In summary then, there have been challenges in common. But trade union education and training has varied between trade unions as well as within trade unions over space and time. Rather than attempting to provide a comprehensive account here, the aim is simply to flag the importance of developing understanding as the basis for building solidarity and sharing learning across such differences of approach.

Varied approaches to learning within second wave feminism

Meanwhile, towards the less formally organised end of the social movement spectrum there have been variations of approach to learning as well. As Sheila Rowbottom's reflections on 'Women in Action' conclude,

> Real women are a complicated and argumentative lot. Instead of presenting 'women' as an abstract category, it is better to see 'women' as people, who within particular historical situations are continually making choices about how they see and align themselves. (Rowbottom, 1992: 313)

Women have desires that are frequently contradictory 'and consciousness shifts and moves elusively' (Rowbottom, 1992: 313). This has applied to how women have learned and communicated in the past, she continued, adding that 'Though books are valuable forms of communication, it would be a mistake to assume that the only individuals endowed with ideas about change have been those with access to publishers' (Rowbottom, 1992: 313).

This diversity – of feminisms and of learning within and about feminisms – emerges from Miriam David's (2016) reflections on her experiences within second wave feminism and beyond. As she explains, her own formation as a feminist academic and activist came from a variety of sources, starting from being a member of a Women's Liberation Movement consciousness raising group in the 1960s. Consciousness raising groups, where participants met to share their experiences and feelings, would have seemed informal, to say the least, as an educational/collective self-educational approach. But however important these processes were, in their own right, these were only part of women's learning through second wave feminism, including learning through engaging in collective action. As Miriam David continued, she and others were also taking part in meetings of the Women's Workshop, with talks by prominent feminists such as Juliet Mitchell, Selma James and many others. 'We went on demonstrations about "abortion on demand" in the light of the Abortion Act 1967, and wrote of our own experiences, editing an issue of *Shrew*, the London Women's Workshop magazine' (David, 2016: 63–4). And Miriam David read widely, acknowledging second wave feminism's debts to a range of feminist writers, Eva Figes, Shulamith Firestone, Adrienne Rich and Mary McIntosh, to name but a few.

To summarise so far

In summary, like communities, social movements have their own differences and their own varied organisational cultures. And these include very different – and often contested – approaches to learning, whether this is more or less formal or from which political perspective. Social movements can and do provide popular education as well as providing education and training for their members more generally – although not all do. This applies to popular education provided by social movements in Latin America, including the Landless People's Movement in Brazil, for example (Kane, 2001, 2012) just as it applies to the varied experiences of the trade union movement in Britain. And conversely, people can and do learn from their experiences of activism within social movements, as Griff Foley (1999) explained in his accounts of informal learning in social action. They learn about organising and they learn about the challenges involved, along with the pushbacks to be faced. Second wave feminism has provided similar examples. There are two-way processes at work here, what has been described as a 'rich interaction of education, learning, teaching and action; a world of social movement learning that builds on the ideas of all the movements and intellectuals who have gone before us in the pursuit of an engaged and democratic life' (Hall et al, 2012b: x).

Varying histories and cultures in practice

So how do these varying histories and cultures work together, taking account of their differences in practice? The first illustration concerns the story of working class communities' campaign around the Ilva steel plant in Taranto (Apulia, Italy). This has already been mentioned as an example of differing interests coming together around their concerns for environmental justice (Barca and Leonardi, 2016). The steel plant in question was huge, accounting for more than 30% of Italy's steel production. In 2012, when the plant's future came into question, it employed some 12,000 workers, including manual, clerical and managerial staff, along with a further 8,000 or so employed in associated services. And, as Barca and Leonardi went on to explain, its gigantic scale was mirrored by dramatic data concerning its pollution emissions, linked to higher death rates with disproportionate risks from a number of causes, including lung cancer, and cardiovascular and respiratory diseases – 'an industrial machine producing death' (Barca and Leonardi, 2016: 66). In summary then, the plant was the major employer and the major polluter in the area, facing the community with stark dilemmas: their jobs or their environment.

In 2012 matters were brought to a head when the judge at a local preliminary hearing ordered the closure of the plant on environmental grounds. This triggered an unprecedented conflict between environmental and community activists on the one hand and the company owners, backed by government support, on the other. So what about the workforce? Where did they stand?

In the period leading up to the events of 2012, the workforce had been weakened by privatisation, resulting in widespread acceptance of what has been described as 'job blackmailing' (Barca and Leonardi, 2016). But this culture of acceptance had begun to change. Cracks were beginning to emerge. A grassroots organisation started to bring citizens and workers together, deciding to 'break the chain of a miserable blackmail which forced us to choose between health and work' (Barca and Leonardi, 2016: 69). This was a wide coalition, engaging workers, the unemployed, inhabitants of particularly affected neighbourhoods, students and other civil society activists, including paediatricians, physicians and academics concerned about the environmental impacts and the effects on people's health and wellbeing. As the coalition developed, the campaign focused on the demand for state intervention to tackle these problems, including tackling them via involving the Ilva workforce in cleaning up the local environment.

By this time the left-wing section of the Metalworkers' Confederation was beginning to incorporate some of the campaign's demands as part of wider arguments for a more sustainable economic policy for the Italian steel sector. This was a significant development. Despite histories of trade union reservations about, if not downright opposition to, environmental justice campaigns in Italy, the authors suggested, these positions could be shifted through such broadly-based struggles. There were political arguments to be won. As one activist commented 'The political division here is not that between workers and environmentalists, but between capital and labour, which creates the job blackmail and also an extreme individualisation of struggles. But Taranto people want to reclaim their city and their destiny' (Barca and Leonardi, 2016: 71).

The coalition's struggles for environmental justice in Taranto would seem to have involved processes of informal learning, as people engaged in the campaign and reflected on the underlying causes of their problems. There were inputs from campaigns from other parts of Italy too, sharing information and experiences, supporting the movement in developing its approach, questioning the primacy of profit-making over social and ecological wellbeing. Overall, the authors concluded, a process of cultural and political reframing had been taking place, although this was complex, with uncertain outcomes for the future. But workers and community activists were coming together through these processes, shifting their perceptions of the issues in question, challenging the false dilemma that was involved in having to choose between their jobs and their environment.

While the learning seemed to have been relatively informal in this particular case, other environmental justice campaigns have involved more organised forms of learning too, including significant contributions to learning via participatory action research. As Barca and Leonardi reflected, a number of important struggles against polluting companies, especially in the petrochemical and asbestos sectors, had drawn on what they described as 'popular epidemiology', tracking evidence about workers' health to support their cases against the polluters (Barca and Leonardi, 2016: 63). There have, in addition, been examples of academic research findings being made available in very accessible forms, to enable workers and communities to fight such hazards, refusing to bargain wages against safety. The British Society for Social Responsibility in Science's publication on asbestos is a case in point, challenging the asbestos industry's own research, setting out the real dangers along with guidance as to how to fight back, drawing on activists' experiences from across the globe (Dalton, 1979).

None of this is to suggest that, by themselves, local campaigns make more than marginal impacts on the global environmental challenges of our times. But these examples do still suggest the potential relevance of popular education and research, particularly participatory action research, supporting people and communities in identifying common interests, despite their differences – and supporting them in developing alternative approaches and strategies for social change. Subsequent chapters discuss the contributions of participatory action research in further detail, along with the contributions of community–university partnerships, academics and activists co-producing knowledge for social change.

The second illustration comes from campaigning in the UK in the context of the contemporary housing crisis. Unlike the previous example, this case study draws on my own experiences of community-based engagement, working with different interests and structures. In summary the background to these experiences has been as follows.

Local trade unionists had come together with community-based activists in Islington, North London, in response to the policies of austerity from 2010 onwards. The local trades council had taken the initiative here, bringing trade unionists together with others to resist cuts in jobs and public services – via 'Islington Hands Off Our Public Services' (IHOOPS). There had been a successful campaign to save local hospital facilities, for example, with leaflets distributed, letters written to the press and lobbies organised. There had been mobilisations in support of wider regional and national campaigns. And there had been conferences, bringing trade unionists and local organisations and groups together to share information and exchange ideas about the most effective ways forward – popular education in practice, although that was not a term that was used to describe these events at the time.

Then came the Housing and Planning Bill in 2015, a bill that was subsequently enacted in part, but not in its entirety in 2016. The UK already had a housing crisis of epic proportions, from the visible evidence of increasing homelessness on our streets through to the hidden homelessness of 'sofa surfing' among Generation Rent. The proposed legislation threatened to make this crisis even worse (Bowie, 2017) by a number of provisions including:

- reducing the supply of genuinely affordable social rented housing via the Right to Buy (by enabling housing association tenants as well as council tenants to buy their homes – but without ensuring that the stock of socially rented homes would be increased to replace these losses);
- increasing rents to market levels for council tenants over particular income levels;
- reducing security of tenure for council tenants; and
- proposing planning changes including changes that would reduce the sites available for traveller communities.

Activists came together to 'Kill the Housing Bill', building a national alliance of housing organisations and activists including tenants of different tenures (housing association tenants as well as council tenants and private tenants), housing workers and their trade unions, traveller and canal groups, and sympathetic local authority councillors, with support from a number of MPs, including the Leader of the Opposition and the Shadow Chancellor. In addition, the campaign had support from organisations and groups with specialist knowledge of housing and planning, including academics as well as very experienced campaigning organisations and groups. This access to informed analysis was a significant factor, building the campaign both locally and nationally.

There were meetings in Parliament and there were meetings in different localities, including packed meetings in Islington, organised by IHOOPS and others. These were informative meetings, followed up with local campaigning activities, taking the information out to local communities, explaining the nature of the threats involved, making the case for getting involved in the campaign. This was effectively popular education in action again, if not necessarily seen as such at the time either.

In the event the campaign made significant gains nationally, delaying implementation of some of the most potentially damaging provisions. At the time of writing, some aspects of the legislation remain on the statute book, however, which means that they could be revived at some future time, if the government of the day were so to choose. Meanwhile the underlying causes of the housing crisis, the lack of secure social housing, have remained unaddressed. So campaigning has needed to continue, both locally and nationally, rebranding 'Axe the Act' as 'Homes for All' once the bill became law.

How then did the campaign achieve the gains that it did? In some ways the government itself contributed to building such a broad alliance – by posing threats to so many different groups at once. Tenants with different tenures came together as a result, along with housing workers and other trade unionists, not only those involved in the provision and/or management of housing directly but others less directly involved as well. These included teachers for instance, concerned about the impact of the housing crisis on their pupils as well as being concerned about their own prospects of finding secure, affordable housing for themselves.

But there were also differences of interest just as there were differences of organisational cultures and operational styles. IHOOPS had already built mutual understanding, at the local level, bridging the differences between more formal approaches, such as trade unions' decision-making procedures, and less formal processes, such as some of the community organisations' ways of working. This solidarity provided the basis for the next phase.

The next campaign that was launched in Islington was in response to the proposed closure of Holloway prison, which was announced in November 2015. Holloway was a women's prison with a past, having incarcerated a number of suffragettes, among other prominent women radicals, over the years. There were concerns about how to mark the prison's history in positive ways, celebrating the achievements of the suffragettes and others, while highlighting the importance of providing support services for women, addressing the problems that had led to their incarceration in the first place. There were concerns about the relocation of the current inmates (some women ended up being moved far away from their families and communities), and further concerns about what type of redevelopment would be taking place subsequently. This was a major site, comprising ten acres of land, offering massive development opportunities. The Ministry of Justice, the government body that owned the land, was aiming to raise as much money as possible from prison sales – in order to invest in other prison developments elsewhere. So would this mean that private developers would have the opportunity to build highly profitable, luxury homes on the site? Or would this be an opportunity to build more genuinely affordable social housing along with much needed facilities to meet community needs, including women's needs?

The campaign took off, involving IHOOPS/Islington Homes for All, along with a variety of others including faith-based organisations and women's organisations and groups, particularly those with interests in women and the criminal justice system, including Women in Prison. Trade unions who wanted their members to be able to live locally were involved, along with local people in need of council housing for themselves and for the next generation. Most importantly the local authority and the local MP (Jeremy Corbyn, then Leader of the Opposition) supported the case for developing the site for homes and facilities to meet community needs. The local authority's first step involved public consultations as the basis for producing their planning brief (the Supplementary Planning Document, SPD), a key document because this would set the framework for the future development of the site. Local authorities can still have significant leverage in this way, even within the restrictions of the current legislative framework.

Meanwhile the Centre for Crime and Justice Studies came onto the scene. With educational and research resources, as an affiliate of the Open University, the Centre for Crime and Justice Studies began to play a key role, working with IHOOPS/Islington Homes for All and others, supporting community consultations, bringing different interests and groupings together in the process, sharing information, enabling different voices to be heard. There were street stalls, door knockings and five public meetings between late 2016 and mid-2018. And there were petitions and demonstrations, letters to the local press and letters to the Mayor of London, just to mention some of the numerous activities that have taken place. Hundreds of local people have been actively involved.

The planning brief that finally emerged, the local authority's SPD, drew on the Community Plan for Holloway, a document that had been based on the responses to the survey that the Centre for Crime and Justice had facilitated with local organisations and groups, including 21 organisations as well as over 900 individuals. We knocked on doors and ran street stalls in shopping centres, going over the issues and encouraging people to express their views. The high response rate that was achieved as a result was something of a record in terms of engaging local people in public planning consultations.

The local authority's SPD reflected the community's concerns, as expressed in the Community Plan for Holloway, prioritising genuinely affordable housing, along with public spaces and community facilities, including a women's building. This has represented a major step forward. Developers have to take this SPD into account, thereby limiting their opportunities for filling the space with luxury flats to maximise their profits, rather than providing much needed homes and facilities to meet community needs. But developers have, of course, tried to do precisely this, in other contexts, illustrating the need for continuing community engagement.

Since then the site has been sold to a housing association that has committed to providing a minimum of 60% affordable housing along with the provision of a women's building, with a full programme of inclusive and wide-reaching community engagement. This outcome demonstrates the success of community-based campaigning, along with the need for continuing mobilisations over the coming months and years. So far, so good.

This continuing engagement could be expected to present future challenges though, especially when it involves working with organisations and groups with differing interests and varying organisational cultures and style. I remember realising the potential extent of such differences right from the start, at one of the early public meetings, as different individuals and groups articulated their own priorities for the site. 'This won't work,' someone muttered beside me as we left the meeting, 'too many competing interests and agendas'. But it has been working – at least so far. So how has this been achieved?

Understanding and trust had already been built between a number of the key organisations involved. There was shared commitment to working together, taking account of their differences. This background has been centrally important. There have, in addition, been a number of individuals with links across organisations and cultures including trade unionists with specialist professional knowledge of the issues involved as well as personal understanding of the different ways in which organisations and community groups operate. And there have been local councillors who have been prepared to come to meetings, listening to local priorities and concerns as well as putting forward the local authority's own positions as these have developed over time, taking account of the public consultation process. Mutual understanding has been strengthened as a result. Community activists can appreciate the reasons for local authority positions, even if they don't necessarily agree with them – and vice versa. They can also appreciate that local councils have their own decision-making structures along with their own forms of democratic accountability, just as local councillors and trade unionists can appreciate that community organisations can and do take decisions in much less formal ways at their meetings – on the spot.

The Centre for Crime and Justice Studies has been a significant source of support to local organisations and groups here. As a charity working in partnership with a university the Centre had clear limits on the extent of its operations. Its remit was to facilitate community engagement, supporting the broadest possible consultation process, ensuring that people had the information that they needed in order to express their preferences effectively. The Centre worked with local organisations, including IHOOPS/Islington Homes for All, leafleting, running street stalls and organising local meetings – supporting the provision of information, promoting understanding of the issues, and facilitating participatory action research as part of the development of the Community Plan.

The Centre for Crime and Justice Studies was not enabled to engage in campaigning directly, however. This was strictly out of bounds for an organisation with charitable status. Far from being a disadvantage in practice though, this could be seen as being, in some ways, a source of strength. The Centre's remit was to engage people as widely as possible. So the partnership group that it established included representatives from faith organisations and different political parties (though, perhaps unsurprisingly, not all political parties chose to accept the invitation to participate) as well as having representatives from the trade union movement along with community organisations and groups.

Different groupings collaborated when it came to public meetings and activities around the development of the Community Plan. But they did their own things too. Women's groups worked on their imaginative plan for the women's building, for instance, catering for a wide range of activities as well as providing the base for public services to meet social needs. And campaigning groups took the initiative in organising public demonstrations, including a temporary occupation on part of the site. These were not activities that the Centre for Crime and Justice Studies could organise, of course. But this limitation was understood. Rather than blaming others for not participating in particular actions, as has happened in some campaigns that I have been involved with in the past, people appreciated the fact that different types of organisation can play distinctive roles – and that these could be complementary roles, each making their own specific contribution rather than being in competitive relationships with each other.

To summarise the situation at the time of writing, much has been achieved so far. A clear planning framework has been agreed, reflecting the priorities of the Community Plan. The housing association that has acquired the site has committed to respecting these priorities. And the coalition has been establishing a structure to provide an effective framework for continuing engagement. But this is far from being the end of this particular story, which can be expected to unfold over the coming years. The coalition has built on the knowledge, understanding and trust that had already been established by previous campaigns. These qualities may continue to be needed in the future, along with similar levels of commitment to building solidarity across differences. And future mobilisations may similarly benefit from access to informal popular education and professional expertise along with participatory action research.

In conclusion

The above examples illustrate some of the ways in which popular political education and participatory action research have contributed to mobilisations involving different interests and organisational cultures and styles – whether such contributions were identified in such terms or not. Public discourses were affected as a result – and previously accepted frameworks challenged. The importance of building genuinely affordable housing was highlighted in the second case, part of a wider shift in public attitudes, recognising the urgency of the need for more council housing, subsequently highlighted by the tragedy of the Grenfell Tower fire disaster in 2017. There were shifts in public attitudes as a result of the first example too, part of wider mobilisations for environmental justice, despite the inherent limitations of local campaigning per se. Subsequent chapters return to explore ways in which popular education and participatory action research might contribute to the development of such wider mobilisations.

6

Making connections: linking issues and struggles across space and time

The previous chapter focused on the importance of taking account of differences, both differences in terms of people's interests and differences in terms of communities' organisational cultures and styles. This chapter moves on to focus on the commonalities, the links between people's immediate concerns in different contexts, pursuing the connections between jobs, health and the environment, for example, along with the links between housing and planning, health and wellbeing, and building links across space and time.

With increasing globalisation, local issues are more likely to have wider links as well. Obvious examples include a number of pressing environmental concerns, the toxic fumes that blow across borders for a start. The impact of austerity provides further illustrations of these interconnections, with the loss of local jobs as well as the loss of local services following the international financial crisis of 2007–08.

The first part of this chapter looks back to previous experiences of organising solidarity across international borders through participatory action research, campaigning to address people's health and environmental concerns. This is followed by reflections on experiences of popular education and research over time, linking communities' varying concerns in the context of industrial decline and planning for urban regeneration. The chapter concludes with more recent experiences, building mutual support systems to connect popular education and participatory action research initiatives in different contexts here in the UK.

Looking back to the Highlander Research and Education Center's approach to making connections

Chapter 2 introduced the Highlander Research and Education Center, in Tennessee, USA, with Myles Horton's conversations with Paulo Freire. As Paulo Freire summarised Highlander's approach, the contents of their learning programmes came from the participants and their issues, as they stood back to reflect on their experiences (Bell et al, 1990: 157). The educators at Highlander 'have been educators but have accepted *to be educated* too' in processes of dialogue, he explained (1990: 156), educators and participants each learning from these processes in turn. This was how the Highlander educators worked, from their first experiences of working with the labour movement from the 1930s through to the 1970s and beyond, starting from what labour movement activists perceived their problems to be. 'That was what they wanted.'

But the Highlander educators wanted to broaden their agendas too: '[W]hat we wanted in addition to that was to help them understand that they should work with a larger community. They should work with farmers, they should work with integration, they should be part of the world' (Bell et al, 1990: 164), building alliances for equalities and social justice. The methods included drama and role play, 'singing and dancing and laughing and telling stories' (1990: 168), a range of techniques to engage participants – making the links in the process of active learning. 'We'd go into why you had to involve everybody and why you shouldn't discriminate' (1990: 166) – key issues indeed in the context of the US South as the Civil Rights movements so amply demonstrated. So this was 'a holistic approach to education, not just a bunch of segments' (1990: 168–9), a rigorous approach but one that was also described as joyful. This was important, as Myles Horton subsequently reflected, emphasising the importance of positivity and hope, concluding with the warning that, without these, '[h]opeless people make good fascists' (1990: 228).

Highlander's history in the Civil Rights movement in the 1950s and 1960s, along with its support for anti-poverty and community action work in the 1970s, was further enriched with its environmental and economic development work in the 1980s and 1990s. This included support for community development and empowerment, on an increasingly international scale, identifying parallel issues and movements and developing shared learning accordingly. International exchanges between communities were organised as part of these learning processes, strengthening grassroots voices through participatory forms of education and research (Gaventa, 2002).

Highlander's approach to making links and building alliances has been demonstrated particularly clearly in relation to environmental issues at local, regional and international levels. Residential workshops had been researching occupational and environmental hazards in coal mining, for example, connecting leaders across different coal fields and forcing regional institutions to respond to their concerns. When Juliet Merrifield and John Gaventa, from Highlander, were invited in 1984 by the Society for Participatory Research in Asia (PRIA; also introduced in Chapter 2) Highlander's knowledge and experiences were shared with non-governmental organisations (NGOs) and workers in India. Because of these links Highlander and PRIA were able to respond quickly to the Bhopal disaster, an environmental catastrophe that took place later that year.

In December 1984, more than 40 tons of methyl isocyanate (MIC) gas leaked from a pesticide plant in Bhopal, India. Official Indian government figures estimated the death toll as about 1,700, but press reports gave a higher estimate of 2,500 deaths while local relief workers suggested that as many as 5,000 people died. In addition, the disaster was the subsequent cause of significant health problems and premature deaths among thousands more – up to 20,000 premature deaths, according to some estimates, over the following two decades. The company involved, Union Carbide, attempted to evade responsibility for this disaster, blaming the local subsidiary company and resisting demands for proper compensation for the victims and their families. At every point, it has been argued, the company has 'attempted to manipulate, obfuscate and withhold scientific data to the detriment of victims' (Broughton, 2005: 3), including obfuscation about MIC's health effects, thereby exacerbating victims' suffering, both at the time and in the longer term. To add insult to injury, the company finally moved on without cleaning the industrial site up effectively, leaving this as a continuing hazard for the local community.

This was a company with a poor record with safety equipment and procedures and especially so in India. Standards in India were far below the standards that were operative in the company's sister plant in West Virginia, USA for example (Broughton, 2005). Which is where Highlander's expertise comes into the story so significantly. Following the Bhopal tragedy Highlander worked with Bhopal activists to build international support and solidarity, linking them with people in the US who had also been affected by Union Carbide. Together with the support of PRIA and the Centre for Science and Environment in Delhi, Highlander facilitated the production of the report *No Place to Run: Local Realities and Global Issues of the Bhopal Disaster* (Agarwal et al, 1985), setting out the facts and the analysis of their implications both local and internationally.

As this report explained, the Union Carbide disaster 'shocked and numbed people across the world' (Agarwal et al, 1985: 1). Highlander responded by establishing linkages with concerned groups and activists, building on their existing relationships sharing information on aspects of the situation that were being obscured in India. PRIA had developed a collaborative relationship with the Center for Science and

Environment (CSE), further strengthening this collaboration through the actions that followed the Bhopal disaster.

Information was also sought from other organisations and groups across the world, exploring Union Carbide's record in their area along with information about local struggles in response. This enabled Indian activists to obtain a much fuller picture of Union Carbide's operations, from India to New Zealand, from Scotland to Japan, from Chile to the US. Together, Highlander, PRIA and CSE produced the joint report in question, bringing the facts and the analysis together, exposing Union Carbide's record, worldwide, with the aim of contributing 'towards building awareness among citizens and workers, mobilizing and energizing activists and promoting collective action worldwide to confront the issues so starkly posed by the Bhopal disaster' (Agarwal et al, 1985).

The Bhopal story provides a case study of solidarity, building connections across national boundaries, illustrating the scope for sharing participatory action research to address environmental issues in the community as well as in the workplace. Shared initiatives included Highlander's production of a videotape with communities in the southern United States which were also affected by similar processes, including Union Carbide's operations there too. This tape showed local people's reactions to the tragedy, with increasing awareness of 'the interconnectedness of workers and communities affected by multinationals' demonstrating how the chemical industry was operating with a double standard, both internationally and among 'minority and working class communities within the United States, exposed to environmental and occupational risks' (Agarwal et al, 1985: 35). There needed to be more popular education with workshops, seminars, exhibitions, songs and popular theatre, the report argued, to raise awareness across the world, building on the work that had already taken place.

Meanwhile, Highlander and PRIA had sponsored a delegation of health and worker activists from India, who had visited the US, sharing their story and visiting local communities. The Indian delegation learned more about the experiences of NGOs dealing with occupational and environmental health issues (Gaventa, 2002). PRIA's Center for Occupational and Environmental Health was established, as Rajesh Tandon of PRIA reflected some 15 years subsequently. And there was 'heightened awareness in the North of their common vulnerabilities with communities in other parts of the world' (Gaventa, 2002: 265) as a result of these exchanges. There were important gains in the process of these international collaborations then, as a result of these experiences of shared learning and participatory action research.

Still much remains to be achieved. The Indian government's response has been described as 'uncertain and tardy' (Agarwal et al, 1985: 3). Their initial reassurances were described by journalists at the time as sounding 'much like the pronouncements of Carbide officials' (Agarwal et al, 1985: 4). There was growing distrust and resentment as a result. In phrases with a contemporary ring, the government's 'Operation Faith' initiative was described by local activists as 'Operation fake'. Indian governments have been (and continue to be) concerned with attracting foreign investment, even if this has involved being somewhat relaxed about a number of environmental regulations, it has been suggested.

The report had raised vital questions about the use of chemicals that pose such hazards to workers, neighbours and consumers, however. Were there alternative development paths for the future, including paths that could lessen dependence on western technology and the multinational corporations so inextricably linked with this? The report reflected that: 'The reaction from around the world to the Bhopal tragedy gives hope that much can be done to build international pressure for change' (Agarwal et al, 1985: 33). Toxic products such as pesticides still continue to cause unnecessary deaths via hazards that affect both those who produce them – and those who use them, subsequently.

But the struggle continues, as the Bhopal Survivors Movement study has demonstrated (Scandrett, 2019). Since the disaster a remarkable social movement had been sustained, demanding basic rights from governments, tenaciously campaigning for justice from perpetrators and audaciously taking on multinational corporations and their logic of globalisation, it was argued (Scandrett, 2019). The participatory action research team that produced this study had encountered unbelievable strength, bravery and feistiness, they pointed out (2019), as well as witnessing the survivors' unimaginable pain. The movement they encountered was squabbling and struggling but vibrant and creative, the authors continued (2019). This was solidarity in action, involving activists from different castes, religions and classes, women as well as children, only too aware of the impact of the implications for future generations.

Community-based action research and local planning over time: building on previous links to develop holistic alternatives

The second set of examples includes illustrations from my own experiences of community-based research and community organisation in the context of urban regeneration in East London. These experiences have related to a range of concerns, from employment and training to housing, planning, and local amenities through to health, wellbeing and environmental issues – underpinned by equalities concerns and the importance of tackling racism. Like the story of the Holloway site in Chapter 5, these experiences illustrate some of the ways in which community mobilisations build on the legacies of the past, the links and the shared understandings that have been developed over time, along with the accompanying relationships of trust.

The historical context: building on links developed from the past

East London's Docklands was an area with a celebrated history of struggle. The 1888 Match Women's Strike had long ago demonstrated women's, including young women's, courage and determination, fighting for health and safety and fair treatment at work. Their strike had forced the employers, Bryant and May, to address the shocking effects of working with white phosphorus, leading to what was then described as 'phossy jaw' (Raw, 2009). This was a landmark in the history of the development of trade union organisation – even before that better-known strike in London's East End, the 'Great Dock Strike' of 1889, subsequently described as a milestone in the growth of the new unionism.

This militancy continued subsequently, up to and including more recent times, together with the area's histories of mobilising against racism, fascism and the Far Right. The Battle of Cable Street in 1936 has been symbolic of this tradition, as local activists mobilised in solidarity with Jewish activists to stop Oswald Mosley's fascists from marching through the area. Chapter 3 has already offered a more recent account of anti-racist campaigning in East London, with the story of the guided political education walk for Labour Party activists. This had involved a tour around Brick Lane, a battleground in terms of building challenges to racist and anti-Semitic violence, including the development of 'Rock against Racism' (RAR) in the 1970s (Rosenberg, 2011; Rosenberg and Browne, 2015). Activists had brought black and white bands to play together on the RAR stage at a series of gigs – to perform 'Music that breaks down people's fear of one another' (Saunders, 2018: 10). As one of the organisers has more recently reflected, 'RAR was a simple and very powerful idea, as valid today as it was 40 years ago: to mix music, culture and politics to fight racism amongst youth ... Resistance is in our history and our tradition' (Saunders, 2018: 11).

Without idealising the old East End (which has had its own share of racists as well as its own share of anti-racists), this could be described as an area with powerful traditions of militancy and social solidarity. These were the traditions that I came to learn about when I became involved as a community researcher in 1975, working for a coalition of local community and trade union organisations, the Joint Docklands Action Group (JDAG).

From 1975 to 1986 the JDAG team was provided with funding, initially by the five Docklands local authorities and the Greater London Council (subsequently abolished in 1986, during the Thatcher years). Our remit was to work with and for local communities to enable them to respond to the planning process, developing options for the area's redevelopment – with the aim of ensuring that redevelopment in the Docklands area would meet the needs of local people in a period of significant change.

By the 1970s jobs in well-organised industries, such as the docks, were disappearing, along with jobs in dock-related industries. Large tracts of land (5,500 acres) were being laid waste as a result, land that could be redeveloped in very different ways. Redevelopment could provide opportunities for the most profitable forms of private development such as city offices and housing for sale. Or alternatively redevelopment could be concerned with providing space for safeguarding and further developing quality jobs (especially skilled manual jobs) and genuinely affordable housing, along with the public services and community facilities that were so sorely needed in the surrounding area. These were the issues of pressing concern for local communities and trade union organisations – our starting points for shared processes of learning and participatory action research.

Our shared analysis drew on previous research, particularly research that had been undertaken as part of the government's Community Development Project (CDP). This programme had been launched in 1969, establishing small teams, supported by university-based research teams covering the 12 areas across the UK, tasked with exploring ways of addressing the problems of poverty and social deprivation. When CDP was launched, official explanations tended towards blaming the victims of poverty, caught up in pathological cycles of deprivation. Whole communities were being effectively characterised as inadequate or deviant (echoes of more recent examples of victim blaming, 'sink estates' supposedly populated by wastrels and benefit scroungers; Hanley, 2012; Jones, 2016).

By 1973, these types of explanation had been decisively rejected by many of the CDP projects (CDP/PEC, 1979), however. On the contrary, these projects argued, the concentrations of poverty and social deprivation that were being found in the CDP project areas represented the costs of industrial change (CDP, 1981). Industrial restructuring was the result of the continuing drive for profitability within capitalist societies, leading to the making – and then the breaking – of Britain's older industrial areas. Local communities were bearing the brunt of these underlying processes of change, processes with effects that successive governments had failed to mitigate (CDP, 1979). Without going into further detail here, the implications for Docklands can be summarised as follows: East London was being transformed by market mechanisms – although the market was actually being effectively subsidised through public investment in the infrastructure for these developments. Would the planning process facilitate the operations of these market mechanisms in the area? Or could the planning process intervene in order to safeguard community interests for the longer term (questions with continuing relevance, as the previous chapter has already illustrated with the story of the struggles for Housing for All)?

CDP has been criticised for being strong in terms of analysing the structural causes of people's problems, but weaker when it came to working with communities to develop strategies in response (Thomas, 1983) – with particular weaknesses in terms of working with women and ethnic minority communities. But this view has been contested in its turn (Banks et al, 2019). In East London we identified examples where the local CDP had been supporting minority communities to tackle their problems at work in very practical ways, making links as they built campaigns across workplace/community divides, as in the following case.

The case in question involved a furniture factory employing some 200 workers in East London (one of the area's traditional industries). Wages were below nationally agreed rates and working conditions were described as shocking, with major hazards to health and safety such as cutting machines without proper safety guards and workers exposed to choking fumes without proper safety masks (Morris, 1979). The relevant trade union, the Furniture Timber and Allied Trades Union (FTAT), had attempted to organise the factory in the 1960s, but without much success, in the face of management's intransigence – and threats – and the vulnerability of so many of the workers, women and men from ethnic minority communities (about 80% of the workforce were from a range of Asian backgrounds). The fact that many different languages, including different Asian languages, were being spoken in the factory further compounded these organisational problems.

By 1975 the local Newham-based CDP project had come together with community workers and lawyers, along with FTAT, to explore different approaches. This was a joint initiative, drawing on the CDP team's expertise in community organising and participatory action research. The first step was to identify contacts via community members from the surrounding area. Workers were then visited at home, in the evening, with an interpreter, to discuss their issues and concerns, their poor wages and conditions and their precarious employment situations. Through this community-based approach the relevant information could be safely researched, without jeopardising people's jobs. And contacts could be made, identifying those who were prepared to get further involved.

The next step was to call a meeting in a hall nearby. The speakers included activists from factories that were already organised elsewhere in East London – a Pakistani activist and a Tamil activist – as well as a well-known Indian socialist and the FTAT District Organiser, speakers who inspired confidence and trust, engendering enthusiasm for joining the union to take up people's issues collectively. This approach achieved some successes, both in terms of recruitment to the union and in terms of gaining improvements in pay and conditions as a result. When union members were subsequently re-visited at home, in the community, it emerged that most of the workforce had received wage rises. These increases compared favourably with the wages that were being paid in other factories in the area.

But it was becoming increasingly difficult to maintain trade union organisation within the furniture factory itself, with union members facing threats of dismissal and fears that management had recruited spies to attend workplace meetings. While there were gains then, these were also limited. Lessons had definitely been learned about ways of researching and organising through linking the workplace with the community. These were particularly valuable lessons that could be applied elsewhere, when mobilising extremely vulnerable workers, in precarious employment.

The following year, 1976, was a year in which there were important developments, responding to an upsurge in racial violence (the context for the development of RAR, as already outlined above). Militant Asian workers' organisations worked with the local labour movement, building alliances both inside and outside the local trades council. Reflecting on his experiences via CDP, Morris concluded that 'though defeats matter, the gains from these previous struggles can be built upon' (Morris, 1979: 110). These were connections to be developed for the future.

Planning for people not profit

This was the overall context within which we began working with local communities and trade union organisations at JDAG from 1975. There were four of us, covering three posts (with two job sharers covering one post between them). Two of the team were professionally qualified planners along with a community researcher and an administrator, working together as a collective. Our remit was to facilitate community and trade union responses to the planning proposals that were emerging from the Docklands Joint Committee (DJC) consisting of the five boroughs involved at that time. The DJC set out to produce papers, addressing the key topics involved, including topic plans for industrial development, transport, housing and community facilities. And we facilitated community responses to each in turn. Working together with local organisations and groups, JDAG researched each topic, identifying the issues and facilitating collective discussions as the basis for developing each set of responses, embodying local communities' aspirations for the future.

While the planning process itself was central to JDAG's work, the focus was also wider, in practice. JDAG's response to the DJC's plans for industrial development was based on a series of background studies, for instance, exploring the causes and the extent of industrial decline, industry by industry, from docks and dock-related industries, through engineering and print to furniture and clothing. These studies provided the basis for developing plans for stabilising and improving existing jobs and encouraging the creation of new jobs, supported by training initiatives to enable local people to benefit, as a result.

My memory is that we were working with local trade unionists who were only too well aware of the issues to be faced within their own industries already, but rather less aware of how the underlying causes of the area's industrial decline were impacting on other industries in the locality. In the process of completing these industry studies and discussing them, dockers and engineers shared understandings with printers and clothing workers, along with workers in the public sector (where public expenditure cuts were beginning to be felt from 1977, as the research on the cuts, and the need to reverse these, so clearly demonstrated; JDAG, 1977). These were learning processes for us all, sharing our different fields of knowledge, processes of popular education as well as participatory action research in practice – although that is not exactly how we would have described them at the time. The end result was a more holistic response to the planning process overall, based on a shared analysis of the market forces that were impacting on the area – and how to develop alternative strategies in response.

The final plan that emerged, the Docklands Strategic Plan, took account (or at least some account) of trade union and community responses to these topic papers. The Plan included the overall aim of using the availability of land and water to redress some of the problems that were facing the Docklands boroughs' residents, providing access to quality employment and training, housing, education, health and community facilities. So far so good. But this was in 1976.

By 1979 the whole approach to the redevelopment of Docklands had changed, with the election of the Thatcher Conservative government committed to transforming the planning process to free up the untrammelled operations of market forces. The land had already been made ready for development – via the investment of public funds. The benefits of this investment programme were then to be realised by private developers. The local authorities were side-lined with the establishment of a development corporation (the London Docklands Development Corporation, LDDC) along with the establishment of an Enterprise Zone in the Isle of Dogs – to remove planning restrictions that might discourage private developers.

JDAG continued to work with communities and trade union organisations in response. The struggle continued. Together JDAG produced an alternative plan for London's docks, for example, in response to the Port of London's proposals to close the upstream docks. This alternative plan pointed to the problems that this would cause, with some 5,000 jobs at risk in the docks themselves plus a further 15,000 to 25,000 jobs at risk in dock-related industries and services in the area (JDAG and Tower Hamlets Action Committee on Jobs, 1978). Rather than accepting the closure of the upstream docks, JDAG made the case for investment in new technologies, demonstrating ways in which the docks could be modernised to adjust to the requirements of the most rapidly expanding areas of trade. But this was not to be the outcome, as it turned out.

As the report on *Employment in Docklands* produced by Tower Hamlets, Southwark and West Ham Trades Councils in 1981 explained, Docklands had become the testing ground for national policies, policies that were market-driven, rather than focused on meeting social needs. In their evidence to the House of Lords Select Committee on Docklands (which formed the basis for *Employment in Docklands*), the trades councils built on the previous research reports that had already analysed the causes of the area's problems, now increasingly compounded by the cuts. They pointed to the particular problems for women and ethnic minority communities as a result of these processes of change, underlying the need for alternative approaches. There were three options for the future in their view:

- the market-led approach that was being promoted by the government, with continuing industrial decline, as developers found more profitable uses for the land, including the spread of offices, (providing few opportunities for local employment) along with the spread of private housing, especially on riverside sites;
- the boroughs' approach, attempting to encourage private investment but without a strategy to manage the spread of city fringe offices and warehousing (providing very few jobs); or
- an alternative economic strategy, developing long-term plans for investment and jobs, along with the local employment policies of the Greater London Council (GLC).

The contemporary parallels would seem striking, including the parallels with the development of alternative industrial strategies, involving communities and trade union organisations in the process of building these from the bottom up.

The GLC, in the early 1980s, was committed to just such approaches, bringing their industrial and training strategies together, alongside strategies for land use planning, taking account of the needs of women, black and minority ethnic communities and people with disabilities. Here too the planning process involved consultations, sector by sector and area by area, building on previous research, including previous participatory action research.

There were two GLC reports on plans for East London, for example, building on past research including JDAG's report on the Docks Connection (JDAG, 1979). As the East London File explained in 1983, the GLC was committed to

> an alternative *approach* to planning – not only to an alternative *outcome*. So the GLC puts key emphasis on starting from the bottom up – taking local people's own definitions of their needs seriously, considering the alternatives which are put forward by local organisations and individuals; and involving local people and organisations at every stage, in the implementation process. (GLC, 1983: 5)

The East London File Mark 2 updated this process, with GLC and borough officers working with trade union and community organisations in Newham, Tower Hamlets and Hackney (GLC, 1985a). (A similar report was compiled in West London, with a road show of consultations with local communities and trade union organisations across the area too; *The West London Report*, GLC, 1984.)

Unlike the government of the day's approach, the GLC had set out to prioritise meeting social needs, developing new ways of 'intervening to combat the market forces which are actively destroying East London's economic opportunities' (GLC, 1985a: 3). 'People before Profit', as local banners proclaimed, with a poster project, the Docklands Community Poster Project, to illustrate these alternative perspectives most visibly across the area. In addition to addressing employment and training issues, the GLC reflected local concerns with transport, health, housing, retailing and leisure facilities, taking account of the impact of government cuts in public spending. The London Industrial Strategy brought these different threads together, sector by sector, including sectors of particular concern to women, such as domestic work and childcare, homeworking and cleaning (GLC, 1985b).

This was the context for the development of The People's Plan for the Royal Docks in Newham, East London (Newham Docklands Forum/GLC, 1983), a locally-based initiative that emerged in response to the plan to build a short take-off and landing airport for city-to-city travel (STOLport) in the Royal Docks. Local people had come together to oppose this plan on the grounds that an airport would generate noise and nuisance – without generating many jobs to offset high unemployment levels in the area. The GLC agreed to support their campaign, funding the People's Plan Centre to develop alternative plans, popular planning from the bottom up.

The People's Plan for the Royal Docks (1983)

The People's Plan that was produced as a result began by acknowledging the support that had been provided by JDAG and by other local organisations, the Docklands Forum and the Docklands Community Poster Project. The staff at the People's Plan Centre had worked alongside local trade union and community organisations and groups in the area, building on previous knowledge and established networks of trust. The initial focus had been the need to respond to the proposals for the STOLport, proposals which were the subject of a public inquiry. But this proposed STOLport had provided the opportunity for local people to respond with wider proposals of their own, popular planning to meet local needs more holistically.

The timescale had been extremely tight, to put it mildly, with only four months to gather local views. Given these constraints the scale of the consultation process was impressive. The People's Plan included views from a wide range of organisations, individuals and groups, including inputs from meetings with an unemployed people's centre and with trade union representatives, women shop stewards, employers from local businesses, tenants, home helps, mothers and toddlers groups, women in a keep fit class, women in two different localities (including a meeting with black women) and meetings with older people. Evidence was also collected from a survey of existing firms, identifying jobs that might be retained and employment opportunities that might be enhanced.

Jobs were key. There were proposals for investing – and so safeguarding and increasing jobs – in the docks and dock-related industries, for example. But this was not only about jobs in transport and manufacturing. The plan was also concerned with the creation of jobs, including good quality part-time jobs, to meet social needs, such as jobs in childcare. There were proposals for co-operative developments. And there were proposals for training to enable local people to skill up for the future. As the People's Plan explained, their proposals 'are not simply an alternative to the airport in its use of land in the docks – they point to an alternative approach to creating jobs and strengthening the community' taking account of local needs (Newham Docklands Forum/GLC, 1983: 9).

While jobs were centrally important, so were a range of other issues: the need for improved public transport in a relatively isolated area, with more frequent buses, together with more homes with gardens and better security for flats in the area, as well as sheltered housing for the elderly and housing for people with disabilities. There were proposals for a new secondary school and for facilities for young people, with ideas for a 'Kids Kingdom' with theatre, music and dance, along with opportunities for sports (including water sports). There were suggestions for shopping (shopping having declined in the area in step with the area's industrial decline) and for leisure activities, including parks with trees and facilities for young children, along with an urban farm. This was a creatively presented plan, set out with pictures, diagrams and maps. The next step was to get the plan to become part of the local planning process, the plan concluded, working alongside the local authority and the GLC, organising to win.

In the event, the GLC was unable to buy the docks to implement alternative futures for the area. The STOLport did happen (London City Airport) along with some private housing. And the GLC itself was abolished by the Thatcher government in 1986. So this is in no way suggesting that these experiences were unproblematic. On the contrary.

There were competing pressures and inherent contradictions throughout (Brownhill, 1988). Sue Brownhill, a planner working with the Docklands Forum at the time, subsequently reflected on what she described as the 'hopefulness and naivety of establishing a mass campaign in four months' (Brownhill, 1988: 16). My own memory of that summer of 1983 is that the pressures were certainly intense. It was clearly challenging to reach out to engage those who were not already actively involved – although there were significant achievements in these respects.

More fundamentally Sue Brownhill questioned how far this had been a bottom-up process in any case. 'Was it a *people's* plan or a *GLC* plan? Did it empower people in Newham's Docklands or merely co-opt them into the GLC machinery and the political programme (of the GLC)?' (Brownhill, 1988: 15). She pointed to the fact that some people in the area had actually supported the STOLport proposal, believing that this was the best outcome that was realistically achievable at the time. She argued that not enough was done to engage everyone, especially women, and that not enough was done to take account of the full range of local interests and views, including the views of those who supported the STOLport proposal.

There were genuine dilemmas here. The timing was not of the GLC's choosing, of course. And there were indeed different interests within local communities and between local communities and the GLC – by definition – the GLC having a wider brief for London as a whole. Popular planning from the bottom up had to engage with wider interests and power structures and these needed to be analysed and understood from the outset, as the following chapter argues in further detail.

Meanwhile Sue Brownhill's subsequent reflections were far from being entirely negative. 'It [The People's Plan] was an alternative and a visionary one, and it did build confidence to some extent' (Brownhill, 1988: 20). Local ideas were included, and local people introduced different sections of the People's Plan at the public inquiry – a novel approach and a novel experience for those involved. Local people had commented that 'It's made people realise you can do something. The general person believes, I can't change things, it's all sewn up, there's no point in me getting involved'; 'It's putting those ideas in people's minds that there are other ways in which society can be organised'; '… this gives people a political perspective' (Brownhill,

1988: 19–20). Rather than suggesting that this was a Utopian venture then, this is simply to point to the People's Plan's achievements as well as to its inherent limitations, building on previous experiences and connections, as these have been developed over time. Here too there were legacies for the future. These processes of political education and trade union and community mobilisations have been credited with contributing towards the London Docklands Development Corporation's subsequent withdrawal, with their powers returned to the local authorities.

Before moving on to the questions of power and power analysis that are to be explored in the following chapter, there remains a more contemporary example to be included here, illustrating ways of linking popular political education initiatives together, building networks of solidarity and support.

The World Transformed

As Chapter 1 outlined, The World Transformed (TWT) started in 2016 as a festival of political discussion and cultural events, planned by a small but dedicated group of volunteers. The initiative was launched in the context of the resurgence of progressive politics, part of wider movements on the left, with the election of Jeremy Corbyn as leader of the Labour Party. Young people were engaging in politics for the first time and older people were re-engaging as the spaces for alternatives to neoliberal globalisation and the politics of austerity began to be opened up. As Chapter 1 also suggested, popular education was centrally important in this particular context, offering opportunities for building broad and well informed support for such alternative approaches from the bottom up.

The first TWT events were organised to take place alongside the Labour Party's annual conference – in Liverpool that year – a fringe with a difference. The following year's events, organised alongside the 2017 Labour Party conference in Brighton, were even more successful, attracting over 5,000 participants, popular political education on a massive scale. As they planned for TWT 2018 in Liverpool, the organisers reflected on how they could build on these successes, aiming to identify ways of facilitating popular political education on a year-round basis, reaching out more widely on a national basis.

TWT's 2018 events in Liverpool did indeed extend the process, providing over 250 hours of political discussion, debates, workshops, training, exhibitions, performance, music and sports, spread over three days. The festival was bigger and more diverse that ever with over 350 speakers, many of them international speakers, engaging with over 6,000 participants, supported by some 200 volunteers. This was definitely about making the links, internationally as well as more locally. As the programme explained, the aim was to provide a place

> where the international left can come together to share ideas and practices and forge links of solidarity. Together we are creating an open space for collective political education that strengthens our entire movement. Together, we are imagining the world we want to live in, and planning how to get there (The World Transformed, 2018: 2).

The range of topics and events was impressive: from sessions on the economy and a shared vision for a socialist government in the UK to the World Transformed Pub Quiz; from challenging the growth of the Far Right internationally to colonialism, neoliberalism and climate change; from reading groups on deconstructing neoliberalism to interactive arts workshop; from sessions on race, gender, and sexuality to sessions on education, health and housing through to the walking tour of Liverpool's 'History of Slavery'. There were well-known experts, writers and politicians from a wide variety of contexts. And TWT 2018 gave platforms to dozens of grassroots campaigns and organisations, including international campaigning organisations as well as more locally focused groups. Much of the content was recorded, enabling the proceedings to be made available as free resources for the broader movement.

The feedback was overwhelmingly positive. Journalists' reports referred to the festival's buzz, along with the intellectual space that it had provided for new discussions of radical ideas. More than half of those who completed a post-festival survey gave it the maximum score, with over three quarters rating it 4 or 5 out of a possible score of 5. As a volunteer reflected, "Working together with such positivity with other volunteers, being part of something that felt important, (was) inspiring and significant." "It was great to be given a safe space in which big political ideas could be discussed with a wide representation of voices," added a first time participant.

Most importantly, given the organisers' interests in developing TWT for the future, the 2018 festival included a stream on political education per se (with four sessions devoted to this, in total). This stream included an opening session on making the case for political education, a session on the history of popular education in the 20th century and a session on the need for a 'Popular Education

Forum: Let's Build a Network!' – a session that I attended as a participant. This session was run as a participatory workshop, so we broke into groups with flip chart sheets and sticky notes, a popular education approach which worked surprisingly well, given the number of participants that crowded into this session. There were over 60 people of all ages there, younger as well as older people from a diverse range of backgrounds and communities. Between us we produced a total of 193 sticky notes.

After the organisers' introductions, the first group task was to map our knowledge of existing popular political education provision across the country. Each group shared their knowledge of what was being provided, starting with their own experiences, writing these onto sticky notes to be stuck onto their flip chart sheet. This was followed by discussions within each group – sparking off the identification of further examples in the process. And then we walked around the room, noting the contents of other groups' flip chart sheets and bringing these back to share with our original group. The findings were certainly diverse, although there were some emerging patterns. I noted the following headings – listed in no particular order:

- Local reading groups/study groups, sometimes self-standing and sometimes attached to other organisations, such as a local Friends of the Earth group.
- Popular education sessions and events organised by labour and trade union linked organisations, including film showings, plays and other events at festivals.
- Political education in political parties, including the Green Party as well as the Labour Party (typically at constituency or ward level).
- Popular education projects, working with communities and/or specific groups such as young people, including projects working with young black and minority ethnic (BAME) people, providing the ideas and the skills needed for activism.
- Popular education linked to universities, including popular education events and Teach-Outs arising from the University and College Union (UCU) strike earlier that year, events that had brought staff, students and communities together to promote political discussion and debate rather than events organised as part of mainstream curricula and timetables.
- In addition there were also examples of universities providing safe spaces for small group and one-to-one discussions on challenging topics such as Israel, Palestine and anti-Semitism.
- And there were examples of popular education via digital media.

This is not an exhaustive list by any means, simply a set of examples, for illustration. I was surprised by the range and so, I think, were others, who had not fully appreciated just how much popular education was actually taking place already.

The next task was to identify the gaps, the areas with least or no provision, and the groups that were being left out. Perhaps unsurprisingly, big cities seemed the most likely to be relatively well-provided, along with university towns. Small towns and rural areas seemed to be the least well-provided. But the gaps were not only geographical. The use of arts and media as learning resources seemed somewhat patchy, for example. Once again we discussed these questions in small groups before sharing the responses, together, to build up the wider picture more comprehensively.

The scene was then set for the third and final task, to share ideas about how to move forward, how to develop the links, supporting each other to provide popular political education more holistically. There was broad agreement about the need for a network here, with links to the academic network that had already been set up, earlier in the year. The new network would need an effective website, enabling people to identify relevant initiatives elsewhere. This website could also provide links to learning resources, with links to speakers with expertise on particular topics, area by area. There was some interest in developing shared learning programmes in addition. But the majority seemed to favour a more flexible approach, taking account of the range of interests and the different priorities involved. While there were some differences of emphasis about the most effective next steps then, the shared enthusiasm for building such a network was inspiring.

Since then TWT have been taking these ideas forward. The ideas that came from the 2018 Liverpool workshop have provided the basis for developing the network, with plans to:

- provide skill-share and training events;
- develop resources to respond to current gaps in the materials available;
- pilot programmes in diverse areas to develop models of practice, reaching different groups more effectively;
- develop a speakers' network (with a database of academics, activists and other experts willing and able to speak at events across the country); and
- offer support through a digital hub, with web-based resources, including training materials for popular educators.

The mapping exercise has also provided the basis for more in-depth research to:

- identify examples of positive practices, including examples of training materials;
- identify a more systematic map of the gaps, both geographically and in terms of under-provided groups and communities;
- identify research needs, including the need for high quality monitoring and evaluation;
- identify resource gaps;
- identify training needs for training the trainers/educators; and, most importantly,
- build the network through this process of participatory action research.

Meanwhile, an electronic questionnaire circulated soon after TWT 2018 elicited 600 replies, indicating the range and depth of support for taking these initiatives forward. Of those who responded 76% were interested in organising political education in their areas, with 71% adding that they needed help in accessing political education resources such as expert speakers. A clear majority expressed interest in networking with others to develop political education more widely. At the time of writing this was an ongoing project – to develop TWT from an annual festival to a network to promote, improve and scale-up radical popular political education, building labour movement and community involvement, working for progressive social change. TWT's 2019 festival demonstrated how these initiatives were being taken forward for the future.

Conclusions

This chapter started from previous experiences of building links and making connections, both internationally and more locally, across space and time. There were examples of popular education and participatory action research linking workplaces with community-based mobilisations and struggles. There were instances where communities and workplace-based organisations had developed shared plans for their area's future. And there were cases where solidarity had been developed as a result, both within and across geographical boundaries, building on existing knowledge and previous experiences of activism.

As the final example from TWT illustrates, there is evidence of considerable interest in building connections for the future. This is particularly necessary when resources are so scarce; so many initiatives have been operating on a shoestring. There is evident enthusiasm for developing networks of support, as part of wider strategies for the promotion of knowledge and critical understanding for social change. This raises the question of how such support networks can increase popular educators' capacities to 'enable people to make sense of the causes of hardship and oppression', as the 19th-century proponents of 'Really Useful Knowledge' argued, 'with a view to challenging them' (Hughes, 1995: 99). And how can they enable popular educators to draw on past experiences as well as more recent experiences together, building support for alternative agendas in the contemporary context?

7

Power and power analysis

The previous chapter concluded with a focus on the development of support networks, linking popular educators together to pool ideas, identifying ways of sharing resources. This chapter moves on to focus on ways to identify potential allies, along with ways of identifying potential opponents. Who has the power and influence to make a difference, whether positively or negatively, depending on the issues and interests concerned? Who might be won over, depending on their own interests and views? And how can popular educators facilitate such analyses of power and influence in specific contexts?

The first part of this chapter summarises different approaches to the notions of power, authority and influence as these have been understood from varying perspectives, over time. This sets the framework for the discussion of power analysis tools, more specifically, with examples of how these have been applied in popular education contexts. Having focused on power analysis, taking account of the different and often competing interests and structural inequalities that communities need to address, the chapter concludes by focusing on power and power analysis within communities and groups themselves. This final aspect includes some discussion of the powers associated with leadership (whether formal or informal) as well as the negative powers that people can exert, whether consciously or unconsciously, undermining others, preventing their voices from being effectively heard. Subsequent chapters explore the issues for popular educators, more specifically, including the challenges involved in working with people's emotions (the focus of Chapter 9).

Power, legitimacy and influence

The Local Trust's report on *The Future for Communities: Perspectives on Power* described a powerful community as 'one where people feel they belong and where everyone can contribute' (The Local Trust, 2018: 32). People would be able to debate their differences in safe spaces where difficult conversations could take place. But people would also need to share understandings of how power works, the report continued, 'how to evaluate the information they are given and to find out how to navigate complex and often opaque power systems'

(2018: 49). And they would need to recognise that change also needed to come from beyond the community. Power holders 'in the public sector and business – need the will and the skills to work effectively with local communities' (2018: 47).

So what do we mean by power in the first place? Classic sociological writings on the subject, such as Weber's, focus on power as 'the ability to control others, events or resources – to make happen what one wants to happen in spite of obstacles, resistance or opposition' (Johnson, 1995: 9). Weber referred to this as 'the probability that an actor in a social relationship will be in a position to carry out his will despite resistance' (quoted in Lukes, 2005: 26). This type of power – over others, events or resources – can be all too real, highly visible and backed by physical force, whether wielded by an individual or by an individual or individuals acting on behalf of an organisation. The police can arrest demonstrators, for example, and the courts can impose custodial sentences on those who break the law. This type of power is not only about enforcing controls. The state can exercise power positively as well as negatively, of course, promoting particular behaviours as well as restricting others, compelling parents to send their children to school for example, or ensuring that people pay their taxes – with the threat of imprisonment for those who fail to comply. But this needs further unpacking.

As Weber and others have also pointed out, power is not just a matter of the ability to use compulsion. Power can be accepted as legitimate, the authority that a democratically elected government can command, for instance, or the authority that can be wielded by a charismatic leader, persuading people to accept their commands. People may accept the legitimacy of the state's demands that they pay their taxes for instance (even if they don't necessarily comply in practice, employing tax experts to minimise their contributions).

So how does this work in practice? People can and do challenge the powerful, just as they can and do challenge the underlying structures of power. The legitimation of power is an ongoing process, in other words, the processes involved in maintaining the consent of the governed, accepting the justifiability of the rules that manage them (Beetham, 1991). There are crucial issues here for popular educators to consider; how do people come to question the legitimacy of power structures that oppress them? And how do they come to develop collective strategies for change, based on their understandings of power in their own particular contexts?

But first, before coming on to focus on ways of addressing these questions, the nature of power needs to be questioned in other ways too. So far the discussion has centred on the powers that governments and charismatic leaders can wield over others, whether as a result of their control of the use of force or whether because the legitimacy of their authority has achieved and maintained widespread recognition – and compliance. But this leaves further questions about the underlying sources of their power, and the class influences that underpin their positions.

Marxist approaches to the state in capitalist society have focused on the relationships between power and social class, power as the capacity of one class to realise its interests over the interests of other classes. Economically based power is centrally important here, the power of the capitalist class, including the power of multinational corporations and financial institutions, just to mention the most evident manifestations of this type of power in action in contemporary Britain. There are versions of Marxism that treat the state in capitalist societies as the instrument of capital, describing the state in terms that Marx and Engels themselves used in the Communist Manifesto – as 'a committee for managing the common affairs of the whole bourgeoisie' (Marx and Engels, 1968: 37).

Without minimising the significance of capitalist interests, however, other writings, including Marx and Engel's own writings, recognise that there are other dimensions of power to be taken into consideration as well. Class power may be exercised in other ways, whether directly or indirectly, including ways with particular relevance for popular education. Chapter 3 has already outlined Gramsci, the Italian Marxist's thinking, focusing on his writings on the power of dominant ideas (Gramsci, 1968).

The less powerful can be persuaded to give their consent, recognising the legitimacy of existing power structures, whether these are economically based, as in employers' claims concerning the 'right of managers to manage', for example, or whether these are more politically or more ideologically based. The question is not only whether rulers are seen to have legitimate authority – or not. Processes of legitimation also represent the ways in which dominant ideas are produced and reproduced, re-enforcing the 'common sense' views that are so widely accepted in capitalist societies.

Some Marxists have emphasised the structural bases of class power, leaving little space for human agency in contrast (Althusser and Balibar, 1968; Poulantzas, 1973), let alone space for considering the significance of ideological struggles. But Gramsci and others have emphasised precisely this. The legitimation of power is a continuing process. Consent is conditional. The less powerful can challenge previously accepted norms and values, such as the neoliberal emphasis on individualism and the dominance of the profit motive, just as the less powerful can campaign for alternatives, rooted in very different types of 'common sense'. There is, in summary, a continuing battle of ideas to be waged.

Different dimensions of power

The writings of Steven Lukes (2005) bring these issues together in ways that have particular relevance for popular education and participatory action research. Lukes starts from the limitations of what he describes as the one-dimensional view of power. This is the concept of power in terms of the ability of someone (or some people or groups) to get another/others to do something that they would not otherwise do. From this perspective, power can be measured by examining the outcomes of particular conflicts of interest, focusing on observable behaviours and their results. Which persons or groups of people actually win out? How far do elite preferences actually prevail (assuming that their preferences reflect their underlying interests anyway)? Or to what extent can the interests of the powerful be challenged? This type of approach can be effective as a way of analysing the strengths and limitations of different interest groups as reflected in the outcomes of specific conflicts of interest – conflicts over the (re)development of particular sites, for example, or campaigns to prevent asbestos plants from causing environmental pollution.

But one-dimensional approaches fail to capture crucial aspects of power, in Lukes' view, presenting misleadingly straightforward accounts of politics and power and the ways in which these can be measured and understood. So Lukes moves on to reflect on the contributions of two-dimensional approaches to power, drawing on the writings of Bachrach and Baratz (1970). In their view, power has two faces – or two dimensions in Luke's terminology. The first is the open face that can be measured by studying the outcomes of particular decision making processes, whereas the second face or dimension of power is less evident. This second dimension consists of the power to decide which issues are up for discussion – and which issues are not. Which issues are simply not on the agenda? Public consultation exercises can illustrate precisely this type of power in practice. The public may be invited to respond to particular questions, such as which option should be chosen for the route of a new road, for example. But what the public may not be invited to challenge may be the consultation paper's underlying assumption about the case for the new road in the first place. Is the proposed road really desirable anyway, or might there be more environmentally friendly solutions to the transport problems in the area in question? Researchers need to explore this type of 'non-decision making', as well as focusing on decision making if they are going to uncover this less visible dimension of power, in Lukes' view.

This leads into the discussion of Lukes' third dimension of power: the mobilisation of bias in ways that may not even be recognised at the conscious level, the ways in which particular forms of the prevailing 'common sense' may become internalised in people's own heads. Paulo Freire identified with Gramsci's thinking here on the ways in which oppressors' thinking could be internalised within the heads of the oppressed themselves, as Chapter 2 has already explained (Freire, 1972). Oppressive social relationships could be seen as inevitable, even justifiable in fact. These were the taken-for-granted assumptions that needed to be challenged through processes of popular education, promoting constructive dialogues, built on relationships of trust. So many examples have emerged already, from the Civil Rights Movement and Women's Liberation groups onwards and beyond.

In the second edition of his book on power Lukes added reflections on a number of thinkers who had been pursuing these questions further – and in varying ways. These included Foucault whose work has particular relevance here. Foucault explored the connections between power and knowledge (Foucault, 1980). These connections remain central for popular educators and participatory action researchers, concerned as they have been with enabling people and communities to unpack the underlying causes of their concerns, armed with the knowledge and skills that they need, in order to develop alternative strategies for social change.

In addition, Lukes pointed to the significance of Foucault's writings on the microphysics of power, the ways in which power 'reaches into the very grain of individuals, touches their bodies, and inserts itself into their very actions and attitudes, their discourses, their learning processes, their everyday lives' (Foucault, 1980: 39, quoted in Lukes, 2005: 89). Just to give an example for illustration, Foucault points to the ways in which women and girls can internalise particular body images. These can lead them to engage in dieting regimes with potentially damaging effects, blaming themselves if they fail to achieve unrealistic targets for their weight rather than questioning such body images in the first place.

Such an all-encompassing conception of power identifies relations of domination and subordination as being involved whenever and wherever social relations exist. These relations permeate our lives, whether we are aware of them – or not. Foucault's is a finely tuned approach, it has been argued, identifying the micro practices that normalise and so reproduce social inequalities, including inequalities within families and communities as well as inequalities between those governing and the governed.

One take on Foucault's work suggests that if power is everywhere all around us and within us – and if we are all involved in reproducing unequal relationships of power – then how might these inequalities be effectively challenged? Foucault himself can be quoted as suggesting that power's ubiquity implies precisely this, with 'no liberation from power, either within a given context or across contexts' (Foucault, 1980: 142, quoted in Lukes, 2005: 91). But Foucault has also argued that where there is power there is resistance. Rather than taking a deterministic approach, this conclusion leaves scope for human agency, starting from Foucault's finely tuned analysis of power, with the knowledge and skills to develop collective strategies for social change.

There is not the space to explore competing concepts of power, authority and influence in further detail here. In summary, the points to emphasise are simply these. Knowledge is power, including knowledge about power. This needs to be understood as being three-dimensional if unequal power relationships are to be effectively challenged. Popular education needs to include an emphasis on the importance of understanding and addressing the problems associated with unequal relationships of power wherever these occur, within communities as well as beyond them. The following section explores some of the tools that have been developed in order to apply these understandings of power in popular education contexts.

Tools for analysing power and influence in particular contexts

Popular educators have developed a range of tools to apply these differing dimensions and varying aspects of power. John Gaventa's power cube (Gaventa, 2006) offers a particularly useful approach to start from, drawing on Steven Lukes' thinking about the different dimensions of power and influence. Building on Lukes' writings, Gaventa's power cube has been developed and applied in international development contexts as well as in more local contexts here in the UK. This brings the different aspects of power together, adding an additional dimension, to take account of the increasing significance of globalisation since Lukes' *Power: A Radical View* was first published in the 1970s. The power cube has been applied in a wide range of contexts, including international development contexts, to explore forms, levels and spaces of power (Gaventa, forthcoming).

The power cube (illustrated in Figure 7.1) sets out these different dimensions in the form of a Rubik's cube, representing the different levels, spaces and forms of power which have been characterised as follows.

The levels of power are situated at:

- the global level
- the national level and/or
- the local levels.

The spaces of power are:

- closed spaces (where decisions are taken behind closed doors, away from public scrutiny);
- invited spaces (such as public consultation spaces where people may be invited to participate); and
- claimed or created spaces (where communities have gained access, opening previously closed spaces up for public engagement).

The different forms of power are:

- visible forms (as with government structures, for example);
- hidden forms (as with the issues that never emerge on public agendas, because they are being resolved behind closed doors); or
- invisible forms (the attitudes that are internalised, and the self-limitations that ensue as a result).

Together these different sections of the power cube illustrate Lukes' three dimensions of power, its visible forms and its less visible manifestations. These less visible forms include the spaces where citizens are invited to consider – but to confine their considerations to – predetermined agendas. And they include such invisible forms of power as where people or entire communities internalise oppressive relationships, accepting these as the norm, the 'common sense' that is beyond challenge. These different dimensions of power can be identified at different levels, as the power cube also illustrates, from the very local though to national and international levels, aspects with particular relevance in the context of neoliberal globalisation.

If we want to change power relationships, to make them more inclusive, Gaventa has explained, 'we must understand more about

Figure 7.1: The power cube

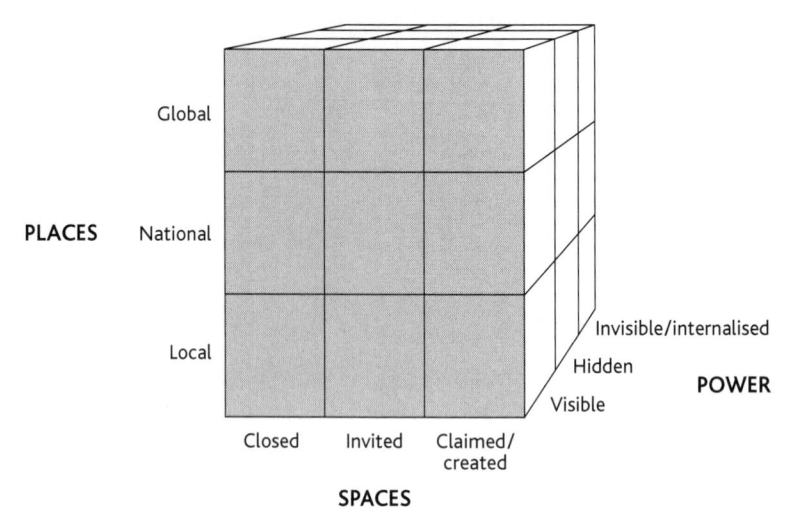

```
              Global

PLACES        National
                                              Invisible/internalised
              Local                         Hidden
                                                        POWER
                                         Visible
              Closed   Invited   Claimed/
                                 created
                         SPACES
```

Source: © Institute of Development Studies

where and how to engage' in differing contexts (Gaventa, 2006: 23), enabling citizens to recover a sense of their capacity to act. The power cube provides a tool for 'actors seeking to change the world to reflect on where and how they do so, and how they work across boundaries with others who are also working for change' (2006: 31), finding the spaces for change within the wider structural constraints. This sets the scene, facilitating the development of effective strategies, taking account of the differences that need to be addressed, along with the levels as well as the spaces and forms of power to be understood.

Power mapping

Power mapping provides an additional tool – or set of tools – for popular educators, useful as a way of facilitating collective discussions. How to identify those with the power and influence to support – or to obstruct – progressive social change? And how to develop the most effective strategies as a result?

At its simplest, this exercise starts by providing small groups of participants with a blank sheet of flip chart paper. Each group is then invited to draw a power map, illustrating the different interests involved in the particular issue in question. So, for example, one such concern was how to respond to a major scheme for urban redevelopment in an inner London site. This proposed development was impacting on the participants' neighbourhood, raising fears that local people were at risk of being squeezed out by rising property prices, processes of 'gentrification' that were proceeding apace elsewhere in the city at the time (processes that were and still are global, as well as national and more local in this global city of capital).

Each group devised a different map. One map looked like a spider's web, for example, with the development site in question in the middle, linked by a variety of lines, going to and from the centre as well as linking up with each other, illustrating the lines of connections between the various communities affected, across two different local authority boundaries, with their respective local politicians and officials. Another map included central government departments at the outer edges of their diagram, adding a further dimension to their picture. And a third included the property developers in question, taking account of the wider financial interests that were impacting on the decision-making processes involved, along with the underpinning structural constraints, taking account of central government's pro-marketisation policy framework.

The groups then shared their power maps, each explaining the reasons for their choices to the other groups. Each map illustrated relevant aspects of the situation, as they readily agreed. It was the subsequent discussion that enlarged everyone's take on the powers and interests to be addressed, providing the basis for a more strategic approach.

A more recent example of power mapping relates to the discussion of the redevelopment of the Holloway prison site, in Islington, north London, an issue that has already emerged in Chapter 5. As this previous chapter has already outlined, the proposed closure of Holloway prison had been announced in November 2015. There were concerns about how to mark the prison's history in positive ways, celebrating the achievements of the suffragettes and others, while highlighting the importance of providing support services for women, addressing the problems that had led to their incarceration in the first place. And there were particular concerns about the type of redevelopment that would be taking place subsequently on this major site. Would developers have the opportunity to build highly profitable, luxury homes on the site? Or would this be an opportunity to build more genuinely affordable social housing along with much needed facilities to meet community needs, including women's needs?

This example was used to illustrate power mapping as part of a course on 'Tackling the Current Housing Crisis', organised early in 2018. The exercise started from the need to share clear understandings about the different interests involved – the potentially competing interests as well as the potential allies. So the first element was to identify these, as the following list illustrates.

Potential opponents of prioritising social housing and community facilities might be expected to include:

- Landowners, property developers and their financial backers
- Private landlords (including more commercially minded housing associations)
- Residents more concerned with maintaining the value of their properties/safeguarding their views, rather than with meeting housing needs
- Local authority interests (at different levels of governance)?
- (some) Political parties?
- Central government?
- Much of the media.

Potential supporters/allies of prioritising social housing and community facilities might include the following:

- Tenants and residents and their networks both locally and more widely
- Other housing activists and experts
- Trade unionists (especially trade unionists directly involved in housing provision)
- Local authority interests
- Local MPs (the local MPs were both known to be sympathetic)
- Other levels of governance (such as the Greater London Authority, GLA)?
- (some) Political parties?
- Some of the media (such as sympathetic local papers)
- Faith groups
- Voluntary organisations (such as advice centres).

Once the different interests involved in the area had been identified, these were mapped onto a diagram, illustrating the key decision makers and the competing interests that needed to be taken into account. This provided the basis for further discussion. Who had the power to decide which types of housing should be built on particular sites, for instance? And who might be prepared to campaign for progressive housing priorities to meet social needs rather than to maximise private profits? While there was a groundswell of support for prioritising the provision of genuinely affordable housing, a position that was shared by the local

Power and power analysis

authority, as well as by many local organisations and groups, there were competing interests to be considered. These included the Ministry of Justice – with its interest in obtaining the best possible price for the land – along with the private developers, who could be expected to share this interest in maximising the profits from developing the site.

The 'power map' in Figure 7.2 summarises the situation – and the challenges to be faced, as these were seen at the time.

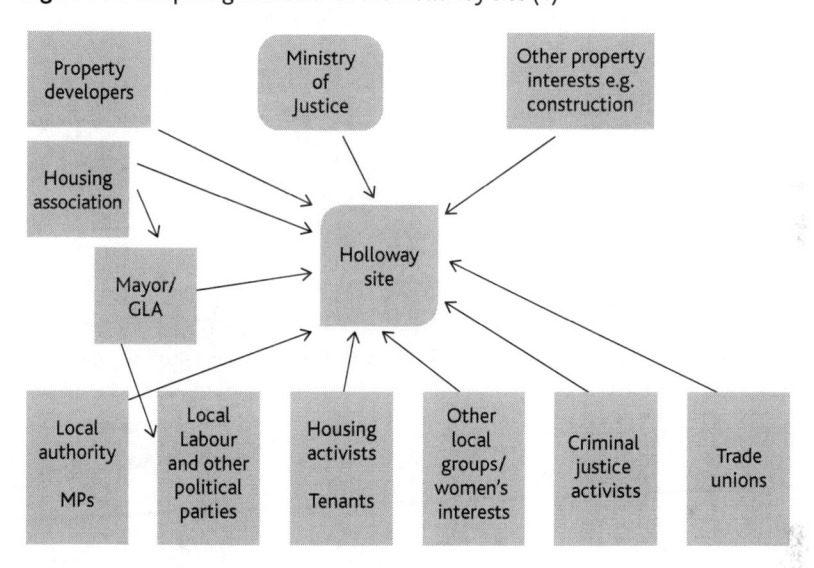

Figure 7.2: Competing interests for the Holloway site (1)

[Diagram showing the Holloway site at the centre with arrows from: Property developers, Ministry of Justice, Other property interests e.g. construction, Housing association, Mayor/GLA, Local authority MPs, Local Labour and other political parties, Housing activists Tenants, Other local groups/women's interests, Criminal justice activists, Trade unions]

Competing interests for the Holloway site

Property development/market interests

The diagram was absolutely not comprehensive. This only began to map out the competing interests involved. But you can begin to get the picture. Those concerned with social housing and community facilities may be 'the many, not the few', to coin a contemporary political slogan. But they have been facing very powerful interests, concerned with developing the Holloway site in the most profitable way possible.

The arrows illustrate some of the different groups' interests in the Holloway site. But what about the links *between* the different interests, on either side? If these were to be included the diagram might look more like Figure 7.3.

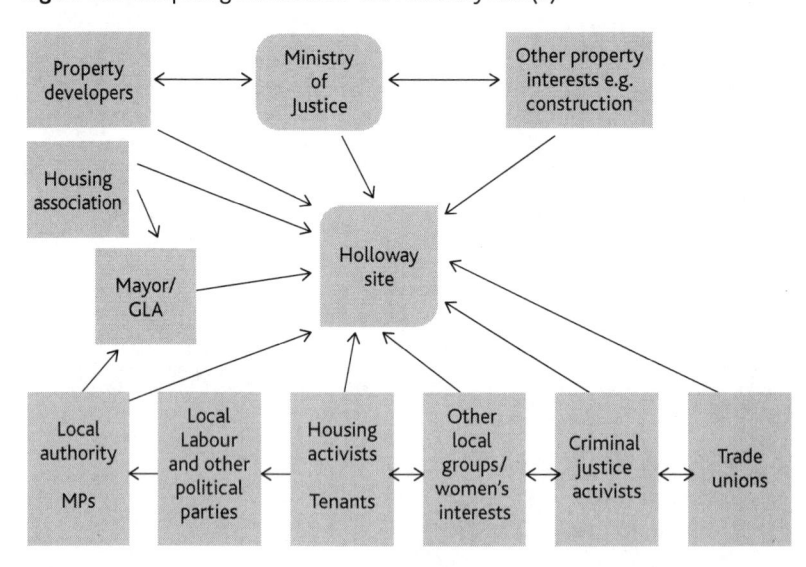

Figure 7.3: Competing interests for the Holloway site (2)

[Diagram showing relationships between: Property developers, Ministry of Justice, Other property interests e.g. construction, Housing association, Mayor/GLA, Holloway site, Local authority MPs, Local Labour and other political parties, Housing activists Tenants, Other local groups/women's interests, Criminal justice activists, Trade unions]

Or would it? There were potential differences on either side as well as potential points of common interests, running between and across each side of the overall divide. Could some of those with different property development interests be persuaded/pressured to take more account of community interests? This continues to be a work in progress.

The Ella Baker School of Transformative Community Organising's power mapping tool

Meanwhile the following example illustrates another approach to power mapping. This has added a further element in ways that have been very productive, in terms of stimulating the group discussions that followed. This tool has also proved to be very productive in terms of developing effective campaigning, as it emerged subsequently.

In 2018 a group of popular educators took part in a residential workshop to share skills and experiences – with a view to identifying opportunities for future collaborations. The session, led by the Ella Baker School of Transformative Community Organising, provided the power mapping tool under discussion here.

Each group was given a flip chart sheet. The first task was to draw a simple diagram, a cross consisting of a vertical line going *down* the middle of the sheet, intersecting with a horizontal line going *across* the middle of the sheet. The horizontal axis was to represent the extent to which individuals or groups would be sympathetic to the issue/

campaign in question. The vertical axis was to indicate how powerful (or influential) these individuals and groups were. The grids on the flip chart sheets looked like those in Figure 7.4.

Figure 7.4: Power and sympathy mapping grid

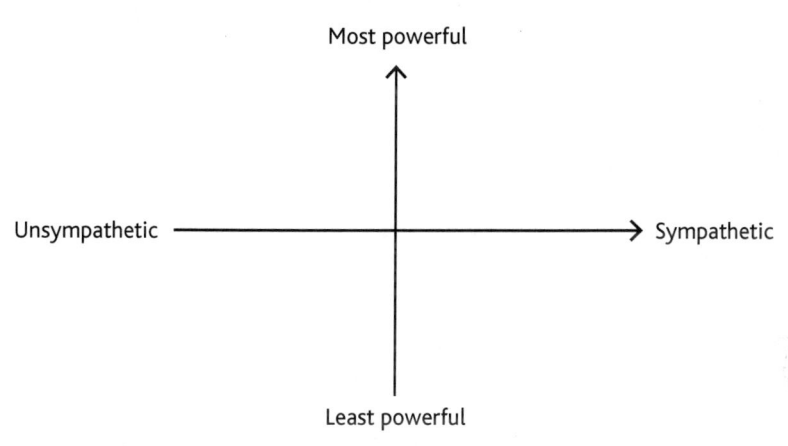

Most powerful

Unsympathetic ⟶ Sympathetic

Least powerful

Source: Based on the Ella Baker power mapping tool

The groups then set to work, plotting examples from their own experiences in order to test the power analysis tool out in practice. This seemed straightforward enough at first sight. But the process actually generated plenty of discussion and debate, demonstrating the tool's value as a way of bringing underlying power dynamics to the surface, strengthening strategic planning processes in specific contexts. The use of sticky notes made it easy to move pieces around, as the discussion developed.

On the day in question, we focused on sharing our own analyses, drawing on our previous experiences in the group. It was only subsequently that I had the occasion to ask the presenter if he would like to share an example from his own experience, explaining how the tool had been used to develop a successful strategy in the past. He explained a particular use of the tool in Hackney.

Challenging the Far Right in Hackney, East London

In the run-up to the Greater London Authority mayoral elections for 2004, Hackney Trades Council had a tip-off. The Far Right British National Party (BNP) was planning to place an advertisement in the local paper, the *Hackney Gazette*. These elections were seen as offering particular opportunities for minority parties like the BNP to gain ground, because the mayoral voting system combined elections for locally-based candidates with elections for London-wide positions, on the basis of proportional representation. So minority parties that failed to win a single seat in any local constituency might still muster enough votes across the city to take a seat via the London-wide list (which they actually did manage to achieve, some four years later in 2008).

As the Hackney Unite's *Introduction to Community Organising* explained subsequently, it had been 'hard to describe the level of fear and anger this created' (Hackney Unites, undated: 25). Hackney has been an ethnically very diverse area, 'and one that has suffered terribly from racist gangs in the past, from Oswald Mosley's blackshirts in the 1930s and 1950s, to the skinhead gangs of the National Front in the 1970s' (Hackney Unites, undated). This was a threat that needed to be challenged. But how to stop the BNP from advertising their socially divisive propaganda across this very diverse area? Hackney Trades Council had just five days to plan their response.

Activists set about undertaking a power analysis. Who were the key players? How to analyse the different interests involved? Who might be supportive, understanding and sharing the Trades Council's concerns? And which of these potential supporters would have the most power and influence? Who might be won over? How could all this be achieved, within these particular time constraints?

The groups that might have been expected to support the Trades Council included the printers working on the *Hackney Gazette*. The print industry has had a history of trade union organisation and activism, having organised boycotts in such situations in the past. This could have been a very effective tactic. But it wasn't seen as realistic to organise a boycott by printers on the *Hackney Gazette* within this timeframe. Nor would it have been realistic given that this would have had to be a wildcat strike, trade union legislation being far more restrictive than it had been when such actions had been successfully organised in previous times.

A parallel suggestion was to invite the journalists to strike. But this wasn't seen as realistic within the same constraints either. Nor was it seen as realistic to approach the advertisers to persuade them to refuse to advertise alongside the BNP. Advertisers do have very significant power in general, being essential to the media's financial viability. But here again, it was seen as unrealistic to organise such a boycott within the relevant time frame.

Then came a suggestion that has been described as a stroke of genius. The potential supporters who were identified as having significant power to intervene included the newsagents who used to sell the paper in their shops, across the borough. These newsagents were predominantly from black and minority ethnic communities themselves. So, as Hackney United explained, 'they would not need convincing of why we wanted to keep a toxic gang of racists from recruiting in our borough' (Hackney Unites, undated: 26). As the *Hackney Gazette* didn't represent a major source of their income either, they could actually afford to act by refusing to sell it.

So the Trades Council decided to produce a leaflet, setting out the arguments in support of taking such action on one side of the leaflet, with a pro-forma cancellation form on the other side. As this leaflet pointed out to the *Hackney Gazette*, 'if you do print the advert for the racist organisation, then please cancel my order for your paper' (Hackney Unites, undated: 25). Then Trades Council members and other activists went around to their local newsagents with this leaflet, having a conversation with the newsagent in question, explaining the issues and seeking their support. As a result 100 local newsagents filled out the pro-forma to cancel their order and faxed this to the *Hackney Gazette*, explaining their reasons for doing so. And this strategy worked. The advertisement was dropped.

To summarise this particular example, then, the use of power analysis was seen as having been an extremely useful tool, facilitating popular education and participatory action research, assisting Hackney Trades Council in developing their strategy in response to this particular threat. This was a very focused campaign as a result. Activists targeted potential supporters very effectively, engaging with them on the basis of their common interest in challenging the Far Right.

Power, authority and influence *within* communities and groups

Power mapping can enable communities to develop more strategic ways of addressing their issues, understanding the power dynamics involved and thereby maximising support for their causes. But what about the dynamics of power, authority and influence *within* communities and groups as well? Power can be understood as being everywhere, whenever and wherever social relations exist, according to Foucault, as the previous references to his writings on power have already suggested (Foucault, 1980). Particular individuals and groups can – and too often do (?) – dominate, whether directly, or more subtly, to the effective marginalisation of other individuals and groups, potentially silencing less dominant voices. So how do organisations and groups come to identify and challenge such processes of effective exclusion, developing more inclusive ways of working together transparently?

As Chapter 5 has already mentioned, community groups, labour movement organisations and social movements tend to have different ways of organising themselves, whether formally or less formally, vertically or more horizontally. These are differences that popular educators need to consider if they are to work effectively across diverse organisational structures and styles. So how do power differentials manifest themselves *within as well as between* such varying patterns?

Vertically structured organisations such as trade union organisations and political parties tend to have relatively transparent decision-making processes. There tend to be formal elections for leadership positions, for example, and clear hierarchies between committees, with differentiated powers for each, spelt out at national, regional and local levels. One-dimensional approaches to power would seem to have relevance here.

But two-dimensional approaches would seem to have relevance too: the power to decide which issues should be up for discussion, which motions are to be taken at conferences for instance and which, conversely, are to be ruled out of order. The members, as represented by their delegates, may have the ultimate power to decide. But this is not to discount the potential impact of less formal influences, less immediately visible forms of power.

Similar arguments can be made in relation to the potential relevance of three-dimensional approaches to power analysis. Whose voices have had the greatest influence and whose voices have had significantly less? And how far have such power differentials been internalised – viewed as the norm, the generally accepted 'common sense'? Women have had to struggle to challenge 'common sense' views about women's places in the trade union movement, for example, counterposing such views with the principle that 'a woman's place is in her union'. Women, LGBTQIA+ groups, black and minority ethnic communities and people with disabilities continue to have to struggle to realise their rights in practice, despite formal commitments to equalities across a wide variety of organisations and structures.

Horizontally organised groups and social movements have their own issues to address too when it comes to questions of power, accountability and inclusivity. Without formal hierarchies, power is to be shared among participants. There are no formal leaders – in principle – leadership being a collective responsibility. Everyone takes part in the decision-making processes, exploring the issues until consensus can be reached. So far so inclusive? This could be argued in the context of one-dimensional understandings of power. But how far does this hold in relation to two-dimensional understandings, let alone three-dimensional understandings of power?

Second wave feminists[1] have been among those who have developed a more critical approach, exploring the power imbalances that could lurk beneath apparently consensual organisational forms. They identified this in terms of what was described as the 'tyranny of structurelessness' – the hidden ways in which particular voices could actually dominate, even in supposedly non-hierarchical groups. And being less transparent, these power relationships were all the more difficult to challenge. Groups could simply fail to recognise that there were discrepancies between their principles and their practices, as three-dimensional understandings of power might predict, failing to question the extent to which the 'common sense' norms that they had internalised were being reflected, in reality. They could be in denial about the ways in which their agendas were actually being set and their decisions were being taken, in fact, whatever their formal commitments to power sharing, with everyone involved on an equal basis for all. Such unacknowledged power imbalances represent continuing challenges within communities and social movements, just as they represent challenges within partnerships between communities, social movements and formal organisations, including community–university partnerships, as Chapter 8 considers in further detail.

There is not the space here to explore these issues further. The point is simply to raise awareness of such power imbalances in order to minimise the risks of reproducing them in popular education contexts. How to ensure that participants feel safe and sufficiently confident to express their views and to voice their concerns – without being disrespectful to others? How to ensure that different voices can be heard, and that minority opinions can be expressed – and challenged – without any such challenges becoming personalised? And most importantly, how to avoid situations in which the more confident and the more articulate participants dominate group discussions while the less dominant, the less confident and the less articulate become effectively silenced?

Popular educators have a variety of tools to address such challenges, supported by plenty of materials, providing information, advice and guidance. Small group discussions can be less intimidating for those who struggle to express their views in plenary sessions for example, just as the rotation of roles can encourage the shy to step up to take their turn. There are so many ways in which popular educators can promote inclusive approaches to learning within groups. And this includes sharing responsibility for inclusivity with the learners themselves, starting from shared understandings of how everyone plans to work together in collaborative and mutually respectful ways.

Power analysis has relevance here, enabling participants to identify the different dimensions of power within the group, whether formal and overt or hidden and obscured. These dimensions need to be made explicit if the group is to take collective responsibility for addressing them. Ground rules can be agreed from the start, for instance, on the basis of group discussions about how to work together inclusively, agreeing rules such as:

- treating each other respectfully
- no racist, sexist or other discriminatory forms of language
- not dominating discussions
- waiting to take turns to speak
- not interrupting or speaking across others
- not personalising disagreements, and most importantly,
- listening to each other, giving others our full attention and respect.

Different groups come up with their own variations on these types of theme, whether these are ground rules in popular education groups or codes of conduct in other settings, such as political party meetings, for example. The point is absolutely not to suggest that ground rules or codes of conduct solve the problems associated with power imbalances and relationships of domination. In my experience they don't. Rather the point is to go through the process of agreeing them together, establishing shared commitments to abide by such norms. This can then facilitate the development of shared responsibility for challenging unacceptable behaviours effectively, working towards more inclusive ways of learning for social change.

So far the discussion has focused on the implications of power analysis for popular educators, highlighting the importance of recognising the less visible dimensions of domination within communities and groups. It can be just as important to recognise the hidden as well as the more overt power imbalances to be found in the context of partnerships between organisations and groups, including partnerships established between communities and universities, in the pursuit of participatory action research. The following chapter explores these aspects more fully, taking account of the power differentials to be addressed. If knowledge is power, as Foucault pointed out, then universities are likely to be more powerful, by definition, even if not always in practice.

Conclusion

This chapter has focused on the analysis of power, taking account of power's different dimensions. Popular educators can enable communities to identify the powerful interests that they need to challenge, just as they can enable communities to identify the interests that can be enlisted to support them, including the interests that could be won over to their cause. Most importantly in addition, popular educators can enable communities to identify the less visible dimensions of power, the ways in which issues do – or do not – emerge on public agendas, the taken-for-granted assumptions that they may need to challenge. And this includes the taken-for-granted assumptions, the 'common sense' views that they have internalised, the oppressors within their own heads that may be just as, if not even more, difficult to challenge.

Most importantly, popular educators can also enable individuals and communities to appreciate the powers that they themselves possess. Power is so unevenly spread, increasingly unevenly, in fact, in too many contexts. But even the relatively powerless may have some power, some room for manoeuvre. Where there is power there is resistance, according to Foucault, after all. This may be very limited – the power to say no when faced with discrimination and oppression, for example. But even such limited powers can be enhanced and extended through collective organisation, facilitating the development of more effective strategies for social change.

Conversely, there are more negative possibilities too, however. Even the relatively powerless may have power over others, whether such powers are evident – or not. Relationships of domination and submission are to be found within families and communities, just as they are to be found within the rest of society at large. Lukes' approach to understanding the different dimensions of power applies across these divides, the hidden dimensions of power, including the insidious ways in which oppressive power relationships can be internalised within people's heads, within communities and groups as well as between them. If knowledge *is* indeed power, then this includes knowledge *about* power in its various guises, within us as well as between us, and the structures of power that need to be challenged. Chapter 9 explores some of these themes in further detail, taking account of the emotional dimensions that popular educators need to address.

Note

[1] 'Second wave feminism' refers to the feminism that was developed from the 1970s, as distinct from the first wave feminism of the suffragettes.

8

Community–university partnerships

If knowledge is power, as the previous chapter has suggested, then universities and colleges should have particularly important contributions to make. Universities should be embedded within their communities rather than simply focusing on serving elites, in Paulo Freire's (1996a) view, supporting the development of popular education and participatory action research as central to their remits for knowledge creation and knowledge dissemination more generally. As joint UNESCO Chairs in Community-Based Research and Social Responsibility in Higher Education, Budd Hall and Rajesh Tandon have been building on the ideas of Paulo Freire and Orlando Fals Borda and others in more recent times, as previous chapters have illustrated, advocating the co-construction of knowledge and respectful partnerships between communities, universities and governments. Much is being done to develop strategies for taking these types of partnership forward for the future. The Knowledge for Change (K4C) consortium represents precisely such an outcome from the joint UNESCO Chairs in Community-Based Research and Social Responsibility in Higher Education, providing training for community-based researchers within and outside academia.

The possibilities for developing such partnerships could be expected to expand, if the expansion of universities were to be the key determinant. In UK alone, the number of universities has grown from 46 to over 140 over the past three decades or so, part of wider international trends (Collini, 2017). But universities' expansion is only one aspect of recent developments. Before reflecting on the lessons, as well as the achievements, of community–university collaborations, past and present, this chapter summarises some of the issues to be faced in the contemporary context. Like communities in so many contexts, universities and colleges have been facing major challenges. Processes of marketisation have been impacting on their capacities to engage, impacts that have been compounded by the effects of austerity, as Chapter 3 has already suggested. These processes pose fundamental questions as to what universities should actually be for, along with fundamental questions about the very nature of knowledge, whose knowledge and whose truth – to be explored in whose interests?

What are universities for? And why does it matter?

Marketisation is far from being a new phenomenon, as E.P. Thompson's reflections on 'Warwick University Ltd' demonstrated, some 50 years ago (Thompson, 1970). But marketisation has been proceeding on a different scale in more recent years. Stefan Collini's book *What are Universities for?* (Collini, 2012) addresses these issues head on, exploring the pressures on universities in the current context, making the case for higher education as a public good. This is a very difficult case to present, in a populist age, he points out, an age in which neoliberal assumptions have been so predominant. Universities are so often discussed in terms of their contributions to economic growth, with scientific research to the fore, in terms of the potential impact on the creation of wealth.

The only forms of justification that politicians in populist democracies think that the wider public (their electorates) will accept are as follows, he suggests: 'first manpower planning, the training of future employees in a particular economy; and second, certain narrowly defined benefits of "research", especially the medical, technological, and economic benefits' (Collini, 2012: 91). Justifications in terms of the cultivation of civic values have had far less purchase in the UK, in his view, although these aspects have been considered more relevant elsewhere, as in France and the United States, for example. In the UK, in contrast, universities have had to face charges of elitism if they are seen to be defending wider educational purposes. The benefits of open-ended enquiry may seem even less relevant in a populist climate, which Collini describes as being characterised by widespread bitterness, resentment and sneering towards academics in their supposedly ivory towers.

For individuals, the benefits are presented in similarly reductionist terms, he continues, as personal forms of investment, to be recouped by consequently higher earnings, subsequently. The market in higher education is supposed to operate accordingly, encouraging students to invest in the most potentially lucrative programmes of study. So the money is supposed to follow the student, encouraging universities to tailor their offerings according to this logic, operating in increasingly marketised – and increasingly managerialised – fashions. Meanwhile, governments 'empower' students 'by loading high levels of debt onto them', Collini suggests (in a subsequent publication – Collini, 2017: 105), illustrating some of the fundamental contradictions inherent in this type of approach. Individuals can indeed benefit, of course, although the benefits would seem to be disproportionately distributed to those attending the most prestigious institutions (universities that are still disproportionately attended by those who have been educated at 'public' – private – schools). Meanwhile there have been increasing doubts as to whether degrees from some of the less prestigious institutions, leading to less effectively marketable qualifications, are actually outweighing the initial costs, in terms of the subsequent burdens of student debt.

While Collini's books specifically focus on the situation in the UK, under previous as well as more recent governments, the challenges can be identified more widely too. In his view 'the managerialism of universities has not, for the most part, gone as far in continental Europe as it has in Britain' (Collini, 2017: 212). But

> any gathering of European university rectors reveals their deep concern about what they see as going on here, concern not just because it was a system which, though differentiated from their own in various ways, they nonetheless largely admired, but also because they see that Britain is the guinea pig in an experiment in extending free market dogmas into higher education, an experiment that cross-cutting market-orientated parties in their own countries may wish to emulate. (Collini, 2017: 212)

Martha Nussbaum (2010) develops parallel arguments in relation to the situation in the United States and beyond, including reflections from India. Despite the diversity, there are common threads, in her view, amounting to no less than a worldwide crisis in education – 'a crisis that is likely to be, in the long run, far more damaging to the future of democratic self-government' (Nussbaum, 2010: 1–2), more damaging even than the economic crisis that began in 2008. While science and technology teaching have centrally important roles, in her view, this should not be to the detriment of learning for democracy and active citizenship, 'the ability to think critically; the ability to transcend local loyalties and to approach world problems as a "citizen of the world"; and finally the ability to imagine sympathetically the predicament of another person' (2010: 7). Nussbaum's thinking has particular relevance in relation to the growth of the Far Right, and the contributions that universities could be making to popular education for social justice and democracy, both in Britain and beyond. Henri Giroux has come to similar conclusions, pointing to the implications of what he described as 'the slow death of the university as a centre of critique, vital source of civic education and crucial public good' (Giroux, 2011: 151). What is at stake, he has continued, extends to the very possibility of enlightened literacy, politics and democracy itself' (2011: 153). This needed to be resisted in his view.

Internal contradictions and stories of resistance

For Marxists it would be unsurprising if such processes were to have inherent contradictions. This is the logic of a dialectical analysis, identifying the scope for alternative approaches, embedded within the prevailing 'common sense' of marketisation. Universities can engage with external partners in very different ways in this context. At one end of the spectrum, corporate interests can encourage universities to produce knowledge to fuel Far Right agendas, providing resources that are spent for such purposes – but below the public radar (Monbiot, 2018: 1). But governments can also provide resources to encourage universities to engage with communities in very different ways. And universities can work in partnership with communities to challenge public policy agendas, where needed, opening spaces for the development of alternative approaches, as the previous chapter has already suggested in relation to the discussion of the different dimensions and spaces of power.

The pressure on academics to provide evidence of the impact of their research provides one such example of the potential contradictions at play. From 2014, the Research Excellence Framework (REF, which had been introduced in place of the previous Research Assessment Exercise) included the requirement that universities should demonstrate that their research was of 'demonstrable benefit to the wider economy and society' (quoted in Collini, 2012: 169). This could be interpreted in more than one way. 'The wider economy' comes first, before 'society' more generally, posing particular challenges for the humanities, Collini reflected. How to make the case that books on Anglo-Saxon history or 19th century poetry could be directly contributing to economic growth?

But this requirement to demonstrate impact could also be met in less economistic ways, including via research that is of benefit in terms of 'informing public policy' and 'improving public services' (Collini, 2012). This could be defined in a variety of ways in its turn, whatever the original intentions of the policy makers in question. This could be about researching new ways of improving cost-efficiency perhaps or promoting resilience to enable communities to cope with the reduction of much needed public services. But universities might conversely focus on achieving 'impacts' via community partnerships, co-producing research for social justice agendas, collaborating with community partners, including voluntary organisations, even if such partnerships contained their own potential tensions, especially if they involved large power differentials (Martikke et al, 2019).

The pressures on students to focus on higher education as an investment could have similarly contradictory possibilities. If future employability is to be promoted as the key objective, then students need to be concerned with developing their curriculum vitaes (CVs). Internships in prestigious organisations, such as prestigious financial institutions, have evident value here (whether paid or unpaid). But experiences of community engagement can have relevance too, as the popularity of student unions' initiatives to facilitate volunteering have been demonstrating in recent years.

But before moving on to explore examples of such forms of engagement in practice, other forms of engagement also need to be taken into account. There have been more direct forms of resistance too, as the collection of essays on *The Assault on Universities: A Manifesto for Resistance* has illustrated (Bailey and Freedman, 2011). Faced with the prospect of higher fees in 2010, students engaged in occupations in 46 universities, occupations that were accompanied by wider questioning processes. These included a conference on 're-imagining the university' at one university and a 'camp for education', at another. As a student activist reflected, 'the occupations serve as a fast track apprenticeship for action' (Kumar, 2011: 139). Without idealising their achievements, these protests can be seen to have contributed to wider processes of questioning, raising possibilities for new approaches to community–university partnerships.

Staff and students mobilise

Goldsmiths, University of London offers an illustration of these processes of mobilisation in action. This is far from being the only case. But it is the one with which I am most familiar, which is why the story is included in summary here.

Following on from the challenges of 2010, the university lecturers' strike over pensions, in the early part of 2018, sparked off a range of discussions about the nature of universities in contemporary Britain (Benn, 2018). Who runs them and how could they become more genuinely democratic institutions, generating knowledge for the many not the few? Reflecting on these mobilisations Melissa Benn quoted the example of Goldsmiths, where a group of academics had produced a 'Gold Paper', setting out transformative alternatives for students and staff and for the wider community (*The Gold Paper*, 2018).

The first version of *The Gold Paper* had actually been produced some time before the 2018 strike. This had been in response to the government's 2015 Green Paper, which had proposed further marketisation in the higher education sector. As *The Gold Paper* (2018: 7) explained, this was about 'altering the nature of the university and its relationship with its students, transforming it into an economic relation based on the provision, purchase and consumption of services or goods'. In contrast *The Gold Paper* set out its own alternative vision, aiming to build a more democratically accountable university for the future, valuing academic freedom and autonomy, committed to the collaborative pursuit of understanding and knowledge – with the active participation of the local community, as well as with the wider higher education community. 'Goldsmiths should take a proactive approach to involving the surrounding community', the report recommended, with 'a culture of co-research' which 'should be encouraged wherever possible' (*The Gold Paper*, 2018: 27), demonstrating commitment to community–university partnerships as a central feature. *The Gold Paper* has been followed up in a number of ways subsequently, as I have been able to explore for myself as a (retired but still interested) member of staff.

The background to these developments around *The Gold Paper* can be traced back to even earlier initiatives at Goldsmiths, including the 'People's Tribunal'. This had been organised as a popular education event, marking the fifth anniversary of the vote in Parliament that had resulted in the trebling of student fees, in 2010, a decision that had sparked off demonstrations, leading to a number of student arrests, at the time. The ways in which student mobilisations had been (mis)handled had raised concerns about civil liberties and the right to protest, issues of continuing concern in the contemporary context.

The 'People's Tribunal' had offered a safe space for students to explore their feelings about what had been going wrong in the university system, using drama and other creative ways of sharing their concerns. The approach had been specifically Freirean overall, starting from people's issues and reflecting on these through processes of dialogue. There had been contributions from invited experts and from staff, drawing on their own areas of expertise and skills. And there had been contributions from the students themselves. Sessions had included the use of drama to explore particular issues such as finance and the impact of austerity policies, for example. And sessions had included testimonies from students, reflecting on their experiences of stress-related mental health issues, issues that were discussed in ways that took account of the underlying social factors, the political as well as the personal dimensions. Counselling and individual therapies had their place but this had been about focusing on the systematic factors as well.

These discussions had included an important contribution from a lecturer with particular expertise concerning the social and more personal issues to be addressed. Tragically this particular lecturer took his own life, only too vividly illustrating the lethal effects of stress within universities, in the contemporary context, the ways in which 'free market dogma gives primacy to the competitive; increasing our workloads, shortening our leisure time and placing immense strain on personal and familial relations', in the words of a subsequent commentator.[1]

There had also been discussions about governance and democracy, raising underlying questions about the role of the university in the contemporary context – who was actually running universities and for whose interests? And how to understand university finances? These types of concern – about governance and marketisation and about mental health more specifically – have represented continuing themes for students and staff. There have also been ongoing concerns about housing and the high cost of rents in student accommodation, together with concerns about the disposal of student accommodation units, selling these off to private providers. Here too there have been collaborations with those concerned with housing issues in the wider community, including the Renters Union. Together these themes have been providing the background for subsequent collaborations to take *The Gold Paper* initiative forward.

The 2018 Universities and College Union (UCU) strike proved a catalyst in a number of ways. What could have been a relatively specific dispute about the protection of academic staff's interests (in relation to their pensions) turned into a much wider affair, building on these previous staff and student initiatives in the College. The strike stimulated further discussions around these broader concerns about higher education, marketisation and the need for the democratisation of knowledge for social justice agendas. As one of the organisers reflected, the strike had brought people together in totally amazing ways. She hadn't known anything like this, previously.

Picketing had been a novel experience for many of those involved. The approach had been to engage staff and students in discussion if they expressed anxieties about supporting the strike, rather than behaving in more confrontational ways to try to prevent them from crossing the picket lines. A more aggressive approach might have been counterproductive – and far less likely to promote the kind of discussions that had actually taken place between staff and students. This approach had proved very successful. People had communicated in ways that had never happened before.

It had been really important that there had been such strong support from the students. This had taken a very visible form with a student-run tea stall at the entrance, demonstrating their solidarity in very practical ways. When other students came up to the picket lines, expressing very understandable anxieties about missing their lectures (especially when they were being charged such high fees to attend them in the first place), they were invited to discuss their concerns with their fellow students who would explore the issues with them, recognising these concerns while clarifying the reasons why there were students supporting the strike. This support was carried on with incredible energy and creativity from the students throughout the strike. It was a learning experience for everyone involved, participants explained.

During the 2018 strike the governance theme took on particular prominence. At Goldsmiths, as at a number of universities, there were common interests in collaborating to identify the financial issues that were underpinning the pension issue which was at the heart of the dispute. Those with accountancy expertise supported research accordingly, sharing the findings from their forensic investigations across a network of universities. Expertise was shared on other issues too, including how to respond to casualisation and to threats of redundancies. And there was action research around governance issues more locally, as well, including research at Goldsmiths to explore whether there were property development interests involved within the governing body, potentially involving conflicts of interest over developments such as the disposal of student accommodation.

Overall, in summary, there had been an effective balance between the provision of support and expertise from the top down, including support from the union and from other universities, and the generation of energy and support, including students' energy and enthusiasm, coming from the bottom up.

Meanwhile popular education events were organised throughout the strike. There were 'teach-outs' in the forecourt, in front of the main building, with contributions from academics and from well-known authors and journalists, along with well-known politicians. These sessions explored a range of topical issues, facilitating discussions with staff and with students along with others from the local community and beyond. There were creative events as well, drawing on specific areas of expertise within the university – a design workshop on 'designing dissent' for instance, and visual cultures events that included a tour round the area's lamp posts, on which advertising slogans for higher education were mounted, illustrating theoretical arguments from a Marxist perspective (Marx's 'Theses on Feuerbach') and their continuing relevance in the contemporary context. There were reading groups, including reading groups in local pubs. There were art and drama-based happenings on the picket lines, happenings that actively involved some of the visiting speakers as well. It became a 'photo opportunity' in some ways, as trade unionists and activists from different contexts came to express their solidarity. And there were workshops in the Students Union in the afternoons. "It was very beautiful", an academic staff member reflected subsequently, "very Goldsmiths", another staff member added, sharing knowledge and skills together collectively, and in such creative ways.

These events were Freirean in another sense too, acting as catalysts for collective action on the basis of people's shared reflections. At the time of writing, one of the most significant outcomes has been the successful campaign for Justice for the Cleaners. Like so many universities, Goldsmiths had outsourced its cleaning services. As the Goldsmiths' UCU website has explained, this has meant that colleagues 'have been treated like a second tier workforce: entitled to only statutory minimum in relation to holiday and sick pay (with many reported that they do not even receive this) suffering heavy workloads and lack of job security'.[2] The cleaning staff had been particularly vulnerable, the website continued, being predominantly from a migrant and/or black and minority ethnic background.

Shortly after the UCU strike, the company that had been contracted to provide cleaning services at Goldsmiths proposed changes to their staff's conditions, including changes in their shift patterns. These changes presented major problems for the staff concerned, including reductions in pay and/or the loss of their jobs. Many of the cleaners had more than one job (the pay being so low that it took more than one job to earn enough to make ends meet). But the new hours clashed with many of the cleaners' other jobs. There were also concerns for safety since the new hours involved more night travel – along with increasing workloads for those that still had jobs under the new work patterns.

The response to these challenges demonstrated the strength of the solidarity that had been developed, building on the experiences of staff and students, organising together over the UCU strike. The different trade unions collaborated to organise a joint campaign. This included calling a meeting at which the cleaners testified before going to lobby the College's governing body, the Council, which was also meeting that day. This had been very risky for the cleaners involved, given their inherent vulnerability as migrant workers. But the effect had been very powerful, raising the issues in such immediate ways with the decision makers concerned. The end result has been that the College has agreed, in principle, to bring the cleaning services back in-house. Cleaners' representatives have attended staff/student meetings subsequently, keeping these issues on the agenda for the future.

To summarise the impact of the 2018 strike overall, this had been a very creative period, building on previous mobilisations to take *The Gold Paper* initiative forward. But it was not only at Goldsmiths that there had been such hubs of popular education and campaigning activities. This was far from being the only example, as it has already been suggested. A number of universities had already organised successful campaigns to take their cleaning services back in-house for example, campaigns with potential lessons for the Goldsmiths campaign. Other universities had organised alternative happenings too. This emerged in the context of the popular education workshop at The World Transformed in Liverpool, in September 2018, as Chapter 6 outlined. The strike mobilised staff and students alike, coming together to defend and improve conditions, setting a counterexample to the challenges of marketisation, working for the democratisation of higher education and the transformation of learning – for students, for staff – all staff – and for the wider community.

Public policy initiatives

Meanwhile there have been public policy initiatives as well as contestations with relevance for the development of community–university research partnerships. And there have been contestations within such public policy initiatives, as the story of the government's Community Development Projects (CDPs) has already demonstrated, illustrating ways in which public policy agendas could be widened to address the structural causes as well as the more immediate symptoms of communities' problems (CDP, 1977; CDP CDPPEC, 1979). Previous chapters have identified similar issues and tensions within more recent government programmes, as the stories of Active Learning for Active Citizenship (ALAC) and the Take Part initiatives have demonstrated (Mayo and Annette, 2010; Mayo et al, 2013). Public policy initiatives can open up new spaces for popular education and participatory action research, whatever the challenges in the policy context more generally.

The Connected Communities programme is a case in point. The UK Arts and Humanities Research Council launched this cross-research council initiative with the aim of achieving 'new insights into community and new ways of researching community that puts arts and humanities at the heart of research and connect academic and community expertise'.[3] This was an ambitious programme with a wide range of projects involving community partners, working collaboratively with universities 'to build new knowledge, address longstanding silences and exclusions, and pluralise the forms of knowledge used to inform common-sense understandings of the world' (Facer and McKay, 2019: xii). The themes covered a wide range of arts and humanities concerns including creative and digital aspects, along with participatory arts, civil society and social innovation, diversity and dissent, health and wellbeing, culture and heritage, the environment and sustainability, and methods and theory – plenty of scope for addressing community issues via community–university partnerships in other words.

As part of this programme one of the participating research councils, the UK's Economic and Social Research Council, funded a five-year project (2013–17), entitled 'Imagine – Connecting communities through research'. This was to be a collaborative project involving research partnerships between 'people from communities of place, interest and identity largely based outside universities, and academics largely based within universities' (Banks et al, 2019a: xiii) – community–university partnerships backed with public funds, despite the wider context, with austerity policies continuing to impact on communities and universities alike. Against this background, as the programme's website explained, 'researchers from a range of disciplines worked with community partners to explore the changing nature of communities', taking account of their historical, cultural, democratic and social contexts over time. 'Research was done collaboratively *with* communities rather than *to* them', the website continued, 'allowing academic researchers to experiment with different forms of community building that ignite imagination about the future and help to build resilience'.[4] This was going to demonstrate impact, in other words, illustrating new ways of combining academic rigour with social relevance, taking up the REF's pressures to collaborate – in socially progressive ways.

The Imagine project's initiatives connected communities with experiences from the past, as well as identifying ways forward for the future. Projects included community–university partnerships in former CDP areas (in the North East and the West Midlands), linking local histories and past experiences with future aspirations for their neighbourhoods and beyond (Banks et al, 2019b). In addition, the universities that have been actively involved in the 'Imagine' programme have included international connections, opening possibilities for further collaborations subsequently.

Like the Imagine team's initiatives elsewhere, the North East team identified their approach as being based on community development principles, summarised as starting from people's own experiences, enabling communities to identify their own needs, developing collective strategies to challenge unequal power relationships, promoting social justice and inclusion to improve the qualities of their own lives and those of their communities and the wider societies of which they were part. Their view of co-produced research drew on similar traditions explicitly, focusing on 'participatory and action-orientated research, inspired by radical social movements concerned to democratise knowledge production' (Banks et al, 2019b: 23), citing Fals Borda, Freire and others, including reflections on the lessons from the CDPs. These CDP experiences formed the background for 'Imagine North East', focusing on Benwell, Newcastle and North Shields between 1973 and 1978, just as 'Imagine Hillfields' in the Hillfields area of Coventry was developed against the background of the CDP in that area too.

Imagine North East worked with 12 community-based organisations (four from North Shields and seven from Benwell, together with the Discovery Museum in Newcastle, an example of museums' engagements in popular education and participatory action research). The projects involved workers and volunteers in each organisation, 'engaging with residents and service users to explore aspects of the past, present and future of their neighbourhoods' as Banks and her colleagues explained (Banks et al, 2019b: 28). Together they used a range of creative methods, such as graffiti art, as well as oral histories and archival research, to explore their neighbourhoods' pasts as the basis for developing their hopes for the future.

The projects' evaluations provided evidence of learning and 'the development of new knowledge, understandings, skills and community capacity' it has been argued (Banks et al, 2019b: 30). The creative work consolidated existing skills and developed new ones, from interviewing and archiving skills through to script writing and film making. These skills were enhanced through group work, including intergenerational group work, in a number of cases, with a 'sharing of ideas and a crossing of cultures', as in the case of a project partnering young people with graffiti artists in North Shields, for example (Banks et al, 2019b:

31). Young people were able to express their hopes for their areas' futures in these innovative ways.

One of the most significant themes to emerge related to these neighbourhoods' pasts and local people's concerns with the importance of challenging their areas' stigmatisation. Both Benwell and North Shields had been selected as CDP areas in the late 1960s, because they had been categorised as being 'deprived'. The CDPs had challenged the view that these areas' problems were due to the deficiencies of their residents, demonstrating that these areas' problems stemmed from de-industrialisation and the failures of public policies, in response, as previous chapters have already pointed out. But decades later, what has been described as 'territorial stigmatisation' (Wacquant, 2007) was continuing to blight people's lives. As a member of a local history group in North Shields commented, reflecting on the portrayal of such negative stereotypes in a BBC television programme called 'Living with Poverty: The Queen of North Shields in 2013', 'everyone's out of work, no one wants to work, everybody lives on the borderline ... it was awful the way it was portrayed' (Banks et al, 2019b: 33). Small wonder then that challenging stigma emerged as a major concern for residents who wanted to change the reputations of the areas in which they lived.

One response was provided by a local history group, producing a timeline in Meadowell, North Shields, presenting the community's strength and resilience, despite the challenges that had been faced, over the years. Meanwhile in Benwell, Newcastle, a Heritage and Culture Partnership produced an intergenerational cross-community felt project, with an estimated 350 people producing representations of significant and valuable aspects of the area's stories – in felt. The results were displayed as an exhibition in Newcastle's main library, thereby reaching wider audiences before being permanently displayed in a local community facility. These felt pictures were described as helping to 'put the area on the map as a place of interest for reasons of culture and heritage rather than for its history of poverty, disadvantage and social unrest' (Banks et al, 2019b: 36). 'We had expected some of the felt pictures to show negative images', the group's report continued, given the large areas of former industrial land that remained empty patches of mud and the failed promises of large scale regeneration. But 'this did not happen. Instead there was a clear emphasis on the positive' although there was also 'a distinct sense of loss embodied in several of the pictures representing valued places and organisations that had disappeared or declined' (Banks et al, 2019b: 36).

The area's objective realities have remained challenging to say the least. Cultural strategies were never likely to reverse so many decades of industrial decline, accompanied, as they have been, by the limitations of successive public policy responses. But cultural strategies have particular relevance in the context of the growth of Far Right populism, replacing alienation and hopelessness with more positive feelings of pride in past achievements and solidarity in the pursuit of alternative futures.

While participatory action research had contributions to make in these regards, the Imagine North East team was realistic about co-inquiry's inherent challenges, bringing academics together with voluntary and paid workers from community organisations and a museum. There had been resistance to the idea of quarterly co-inquiry meetings from some members of community organisations, for example. They had other pressures on their lives and felt resistant to spending time getting to know each other and undertaking group exercises as part of the initial planning phase. Learning did take place and connections were made nevertheless, including connections beyond the local to the international, beyond the here and now (through exploring history and through imagining the future) and beyond talking and writing (through visual and audio materials and exhibitions). But this all took time. As the team concluded, one of the main messages was that 'it takes time to build a community–university partnership' (Banks et al, 2019b: 43). 'When working with diverse groups and organisations with different priorities and understandings, it takes time and commitment to create together a shared learning space that facilitates co-existence, cross-fertilisation and eventually collective action' (Banks et al, 2019b: 44).

There were similarities as well as differences in the experiences and challenges facing 'Imagine Hillfields'. Like Imagine North East, this had also been a CDP area with a history of deprivation, despite a series of regeneration initiatives, over past decades. Like Imagine North East, Imagine Hillfields faced similar challenges as a result of territorial stigmatisation, described as a place that 'made most middle class people in Coventry shudder' (Kyneswood, 2019: 159). Residents spoke of the problems of putting a Hillfields address on a job application form because of the stigma attached to living there (Kyneswood, 2019: 161), a situation that had worsened in recent years with increasing community fragmentation as a result of the effects of austerity cuts. The community–university partnership developed via Imagine Hillfields focused on addressing this stigmatisation, working in partnership with the Herbert Museum and WATCH, an organisation whose remit included ownership of the local radio station Hillz FM. Using a community development approach, the researcher set out to co-produce research, integrating stories of Hillfields' lives more positively via existing and new local radio shows (building on the researcher's previous experience in community radio).

As in Imagine North East, volunteers had their own priorities, however. And local residents had their own priorities in their turn. When introduced to new people, the researcher would be asked about his motivation. '"Why are you doing this?", "Who is it for?" were the two most familiar questions, the answers to which needed to be "for the people of Hillfields" if I was to get any of their time', he reflected (Kyneswood, 2019: 164). Building relationships of trust took time here too.

In the event, a photography project was developed instead, focusing on more positive aspects of the area. From this initiative a very different image emerged, depicting contemporary Hillfields as 'a diverse place of hard work and enterprise' (Kyneswood, 2019: 165). When the photographs were exhibited at the Herbert Museum they were described as presenting 'a powerful counter to the stigmatisation of Hillfields' (Kyneswood, 2019). This led to the development of a visual history of the area, working with a local history group, illustrating – and challenging – the processes of stigmatisation and their effects over time.

The next step was to plan an exhibition of these photographic narratives. But this entailed its own inherent tensions. There was concern that such an exhibition would only be taken seriously by opinion formers in Coventry if this were to take place in a prestigious venue, with inputs from professional photographers as well. This excited the team, in the researcher's view, but 'excluded and challenged the community group in several ways' (Kyneswood, 2019: 170). So further photography was commissioned, but on a different basis this time, enabling the community group to be more directly involved, partially resolving the feelings of marginality that had been experienced, during the previous commissioning phase.

The exhibition itself was very successful with over 2,000 people attending over the 18 days that the exhibition was open to the public. While there were positive responses though, some visitors were described as expressing 'discomfort at how their perception of the area had been challenged' (Kyneswood, 2019: 175). For some, there were feelings of disappointment, with 'appreciations of the past but not of Hillfields today' (Kyneswood, 2019). 'It's terrible now, a real dive' (Kyneswood, 2019), as one visitor regretted, reflecting the diversity of views within local communities in the area and beyond.

Reflecting on co-producing knowledge more generally, the researcher pointed to the limitations of a formally structured approach to community–university partnership working. What had actually emerged had been more experimental – a more iterative process, building relationships of trust and shared understandings over time. It had been important to take account of the different interests and priorities involved and the different paces of life within communities, as well as taking account of the differences between communities and academic researchers. People needed to be involved on their own terms.

These were conclusions that were re-iterated by other Imagine authors, recognising the different pressures on voluntary and community organisations and university-based researchers, along with the limitations of community–university partnerships in the current policy context more generally. Much of the co-production in Imagine had taken place with small groups for a very short period of time, it was also pointed out, but 'is that transforming the landscape of community research? I'm not sure it is', another researcher questioned (Bell et al, 2019: 106). The co-production of research 'which brings experiential knowledge of people outside universities to the surface, enables them to create new knowledge that can lead to positive change in their communities', Ward and his colleagues concluded (Ward et al, 2019: 204), but this did not mean that the co-production of research was unproblematic. On the contrary, the limitations and criticisms of co-production had been only too evident. 'This had been a learning process for all those involved' (Ward et al, 2019: 208). There had been no such thing as 'perfect co-production' (Ward et al, 2019). But that should not discourage others from engaging in the effort, the researchers concluded.

Conclusions

Community–university partnerships have a long and varied history. Power imbalances have inhibited the co-production of knowledge, and so have the competing pressures on universities and voluntary and community-based organisations alike, including pressures to convince funders that more is being produced with less, in the context of austerity. Such pressures potentially challenge the very basis of academic approaches to research – starting from the 'findings' to be obtained rather than from the questions to be explored. But there have been more positive approaches to the production and dissemination of knowledge as well, earlier approaches with continuing relevance for more recent times. Learning and the production of knowledge has been advocated in less instrumental ways, as the Russell Report argued in 1973, referring back to the views of the Ministry of Reconstruction after the First World War, emphasising that

> The value of adult education is not solely to be measured by increases in earning power or productive capacity or by any other materialistic yardstick, but by the quality of life it inspires in the individual and generates for the community at large contributing to providing '*the fullest opportunities for personal development and for the realisation of a higher standard of citizenship*'. (The Russell Report, 1973: 4, quoting Ministry of Reconstruction, 1919: 153; emphasis in original)

From the CDPs through Taking Part and on to Connected Communities, public policies have supported learning and knowledge production, working *with* as well as *for* communities. Whatever the official motivations for such initiatives may have been, those involved have identified spaces for co-producing knowledge for social justice and equalities, despite the countervailing pressures that characterised the contemporary policy context in recent years. Meanwhile popular education and participatory action research continue to be pursued by academics and activists alike, demonstrating their recognition of the increasing need for alternative approaches to knowledge and knowledge creation in the contemporary context. This still leaves more fundamental questions about the nature of knowledge, whose knowledge and what forms of knowledge, experiential or otherwise, questions to be revisited in the final chapters.

Notes
[1] https://thepanoptic.co.uk/2017/08/06/repoliticising-depression-late-mark-fishers-vital-lesson/
[2] http://goldsmithsucu.org/justice-for-cleaners/
[3] https://connected-communities.org/index.php/about/
[4] http://www.imaginecommunity.org.uk/about/

9

Taking emotions into account

However important as an ingredient in developing strategies for social change, evidence-based research needs to be complemented by popular education approaches that take account of people's emotions. The roots of people's concerns need to be understood and addressed, as previous chapters have already suggested. Popular educators and participatory action researchers have experiences to share in these regards, engaging with people's emotions, including emotions of anxiety, envy, fear and hatred of the 'other', as the basis for developing more hopeful strategies for the future.

This chapter starts by summarising ways of understanding the connections between people's emotions and their social contexts. This sets the framework for considering examples of community-based learning strategies to engage with people's feelings and the issues about which they feel passionate. These examples include 'Hope Not Hate' workshops, along with 'Kick It Out' and 'Show Racism the Red Card' initiatives to challenge racism and other forms of discrimination in football, here in the UK. While these specific types of initiative have major contributions to make, the principles that underpin them have wider implications for popular educators too, re-enforcing the importance of engaging with people's passions as well as engaging with their immediate concerns. Whether working through sports or the arts, this is about managing to 'connect the prose in us with the passion' as the novelist E.M. Forster expressed this (Forster, 1989: 187) – building relationships of trust as the basis for engaging in transformative dialogues for social change.

Working with emotions

There is an embarrassment of riches when it comes to writings on working with emotions in contemporary contexts. The work of Arlie Hochschild has already been cited in Chapter 1, for example (Hochschild, 2016), exploring feelings of anger and mourning on the American Right. Sara Ahmed's study of the cultural politics of emotions adds insights into the emotions of hate (of 'the other') and fear (including the fear of loss) as well as insights into the reverse, emotions of love (for one's family and country, love for the white racial family) (Ahmed, 2015). There is so much of relevance for popular educators. So first a disclaimer: there is no way that this chapter could provide a systematic account of the theoretical underpinnings that would be required for a comprehensive understanding about and working with emotions. This would be far beyond the scope of this particular book. The aim of this chapter is far more modest here – to identify a number of concepts with particular relevance for popular educators, exploring ways of taking account of feelings more effectively in the contemporary context, addressing the challenges posed by Far Right populism.

Although I come from a background in social policy and community development, drawing on Marxist, socialist-feminist and anti-racist perspectives, I have also come to appreciate the contributions of a psycho-social approach, recognising the value of exploring the interconnections between the personal and the political in these ways. Through researching the challenges and dilemmas of development work, in collaboration with Paul Hoggett and Chris Miller, I came to appreciate the ways in which people explained their motivations and values. As I reflected at the time (Hoggett et al, 2009: 5), 'with little if any prompting, they (the participants) began by outlining their own formative experiences, exploring the influences of family and community as well as the subsequent influences of the workplace and political and community engagement'. Paul Hoggett's psycho-social insights enabled us to develop a more comprehensive and critical understanding of the dilemmas facing frontline public service workers, holding onto public service values in the teeth of the countervailing pressures of marketisation and increasing managerialism. His writings have particular relevance for popular education and participatory action research, and especially so in the current context, a decade later.

Taking account of 'structures of feeling'

Raymond Williams had previously coined the term 'structures of feeling' to capture the ways in which different form of thinking can emerge, before being articulated in fully worked out forms. He defined this as being 'as firm and definite as the term "structure" suggests, yet it operates in the most delicate and least tangible parts of our activity' (Williams, 1973: 64). This is about emergent approaches and tones of argument, before these become more formally defined and classified. Far from seeing cultures as fixed or predetermined, as in dogmatic versions of Marxist analysis, Williams was more concerned with focusing on the ways in which cultures are dynamic, in continuing processes of change. The term could be applied to ideas that were still barely formed (Williams, 1977), including ideas that were potentially subversive of the prevailing cultural hegemony, Williams' own particular interest as a theorist drawing on Marxist approaches to the study of culture and society.

But the notion of 'structures of feeling' could be applied more widely too. Hoggett uses the term to explore communities' partially articulated emotions and emergent ideas, expressing the collective mood music that predominates in particular contexts over space and time (Hoggett, 2016). Rather than either focusing on the individual or focusing on society, this type of approach focuses on the creative ways in which people interact with the wider society as social beings, two-way processes that shape us in our social contexts.

These collective feelings can be positive or negative – or some combination of both, just as individuals' feelings can combine positivity and negativity, love and hate, hope and fear. People speak of depressed communities, for instance, contrasting depressed communities with places with more positive feelings of community spirit. And writers refer to the 'zeitgeist', the spirit of a particular age.

People can also be courageous and heroic, just as they can be cowed in fear before imagined enemies. And they can be swayed by emotions to act against their own best interest, turkeys voting for Christmas – although Hoggett is absolutely not suggesting that emotions are inherently in opposition to rationality. On the contrary, in fact, as it will be suggested in more detail subsequently.

In the contemporary context, meanwhile, Hoggett focuses on the significance of what he describes as generalised 'affects', such as free floating feelings of anxiety. These free floating 'affects' have no apparent focus or target, flitting from one thing to another. But populists can give them a focus, turning these free floating 'affects' into more specific emotions, particularly the emotions of fear, envy and even hatred of the 'other'. This is particularly toxic in the contemporary context, given the extent of such generalised anxieties, and the precariousness of so many people's lives, especially, although by no means only, affecting young people lacking housing or job security. There is plenty for them to worry about in 21st-century Britain.

Such feelings of anxiety and related feelings of envy and fear can be experienced by people in a range of other social contexts too, though. Reflecting on the image of Edvard Munch's 'The Scream' – an image displayed as part of an exhibition at the British Museum entitled 'Love and Angst' – Jones has described Munch's masterpiece as 'the face of our political age' (Jones, 2019: 8). The image was reproduced in

Peter Brookes' cartoon depicting Donald Trump's inauguration as US president, for instance, with every person in the crowd metamorphosed into 'the wraith-like figure from "The Scream"'. And it has been reproduced as an emoji representing fear and shock, 'a handy emoji if you're traumatised by Brexit … or climate change, or plastic in the oceans', Jones continued. 'We have hit a time of maximum anxiety that all of us feel incredibly strongly' (Jones, 2019: 8). Hugo Chapman, the keeper of prints and drawings at the British Museum, commented in similar vein, as he reflected on the eve of the vote in the House of Commons on Theresa May's Brexit deal on 15 January 2019.

This brings the discussion to the concept of 'ressentiment'. Ressentiment refers to more than the term 'resentment', including, as it does, more generalised feelings of anxiety and envy, along with feelings of weakness and powerlessness, when people believe that others are being treated more favourably, being given the respect that they feel that they deserve – but fail to receive (Clarke et al, 2006). Such feelings have been described as being emotions of opposition to unequal and unjust situations.

Inequalities and injustices can give rise to feelings of anger in positive ways, inspiring people to take action to work for equalities and social justice. But they can also give rise to more negative emotional responses. Where injustice occurs we may rightly feel the emotion of resentment towards the group that is responsible for it. But if our capacity to express this resentment is blocked (because, for example, no group or party exists which might act on our behalf in pursuit of redress) then the anger turns in on itself leading to the more generalised affect of ressentiment – a mixture of bitterness, complaint, envy and shame. Richard Sennett and Jonathan Cobb (1993) have described such feelings in terms of the hidden injuries of class. People can feel shame for their situations, accepting stigmatising stereotypes of themselves as feckless no-hopers, 'welfare scrounging chavs' (Jones, 2011; Tyler, 2013; McKenzie, 2015; Shildrick, 2018), blaming themselves for their own oppressions – internalising the oppressor inside their own heads, as Freire described such processes. The term 'social suffering' has been applied to such situations, stigmatised contexts in which the emotional 'habitus' reflects more generalised feelings of helplessness and hopelessness, shame and despair.

In supposedly meritocratic societies the gap between formal and substantive equalities may prove particularly problematic. If everyone is supposed to have an equal opportunity to succeed then failure can be perceived as being one's own fault – which is precisely how poverty and deprivation are so often publicly portrayed. This can have a profoundly demoralising effect on individuals and communities alike, as the previous chapter outlined, impacting on communities over generations in stigmatised areas such as the former Community Development Project (CDP) areas. This was precisely why it was so important for people in these areas to have the opportunity to reclaim their histories in more positive ways, the recovery of the past as an essential resource of resistance, as Stuart Hall has put this more generally (Hoggett, 2000: 93).

The CDP areas had been designated as suffering from material forms of social deprivation (although the original policy papers had included references to them in terms of so-called 'cultures of poverty' – implying that these communities were deficient in non-material ways as well). But negative feelings of 'ressentiment' can be experienced in other areas and contexts too, feelings of powerlessness, resentment and envy that can emerge in identity politics more generally. Hoggett (2000) refers to Nancy Fraser's (2008) distinctions between struggles for material equalities and struggles for social recognition and acceptance (along with political struggles for the right to participate, to make your voice effectively heard). These types of feelings of powerlessness and resentment can of course be identified in materially deprived neighbourhoods, as illustrated by young people's responses when feeling disrespected/'dissed'. But such feelings can be identified far more widely too. Maslow's hierarchy of human needs has parallels here; the view that it is only when people's most pressing biological/material needs have been met that they can address their less material but no less vital needs, including the need for esteem and respect (Maslow, 1943, 1954). The educational implications of Maslow's writings have been significant (if contested) in subsequent debates, pointing as they do to the importance of addressing these needs, as well their material needs for food and shelter. Learners need to feel safe and most importantly, they need to feel respected before they can learn effectively.

Demertzis has added more specific reflections on the links between feelings of social and cultural losses and the rise of Far Right populist movements through the example of Greece (Demertzis, 2006). He suggests that a range of emotions can be involved, including nostalgia as well as angst, helplessness, hatred, vindictiveness, melancholy, anger, fear, indignation, envy, spite and resentment. Such emotions could be identified among lower middle class groups in Greece, he argued, feelings of nostalgia and cultural loss as well as feelings of anxiety about the state of the economy and material insecurities (and this was written before the financial crisis of 2008). There would seem to be resonances here with so many of the concerns that have been emerging from studies of the Far Right in the UK and the US subsequently, as Chapter 1 suggested. Brexit slogans such as 'Take Back Control' have appealed to wide sections of the population in Britain too, chiming with feelings of nostalgia for a mythical golden age, an age when Britain – like the US – was seen to have been great, when shared cultures were valued and communities were believed to have been strong. 'It don't feel like our country any more' has been a view that has by no means been confined to those feeling economically left behind.

Politicians from the Far Right do not create such feelings out of thin air, Hoggett (2016) explains. But such generalised feelings can be manipulated. Moral panics can be whipped up by the media – fear can sell copies – and politicians can play on such fears for their own ends, professing to be standing up for the 'little man' and/or the 'silent majority'. Such outcomes are especially evident in times of stress, Hoggett suggests. When free floating anxieties are focused this can lead to feelings of fear along with feelings of envy and hatred, emotions that can too readily become projected onto the 'other'. So the 'other' becomes a convenient focus for what would otherwise remain a free floating 'affect'. Problems with the lack of secure housing and jobs can be explained in terms of there being too many migrants, for example, just as more generalised anxieties can be explained in terms of fantasies about there being too many Muslims, stereotyped as potential paedophiles and rapists, if not actually terrorists, the very people who may be believed to be receiving more favourable treatment from public authorities.

Hoggett (2016) points to research that suggests that people who have been better informed may be noticeably less affected by populist politicians' rhetoric. But this is not to pose rationality against emotions. On the contrary. He explicitly rejects such binary oppositions, as it has already been suggested. Reasoned responses need to have engagement with people's passions too, supporting them to move from shame to pride – from grief to the type of anger that mobilises them to take action against injustice. Common interests need to be addressed together, he concludes, while differences need to be recognised and understood through processes of deliberation and dialogue based on mutual respect (Hoggett, 2016).

Finally Hoggett recognises the challenges that such approaches involve. Working with people's emotions requires understanding and resilience on the part of the workers and educators concerned, understanding their own emotions if they are to cope with the feelings of others (Hoggett et al, 2009). There are implications here for the universities and colleges that provide education and training for those engaged in this type of work. And there are implications for workers (whether paid staff or unpaid volunteers/activists), who need to appreciate the importance of developing their own networks, offering solidarity as well as providing more practical forms of mutual support. The Popular Education Network (PEN) and the networks being developed via The World Transformed provide examples of just such possibilities, as outlined in Chapter 8.

Engaging with emotions via the arts and sports

As recent usages of Munch's 'The Scream' have illustrated, the visual arts can tap into popular moods, reflecting back the anxieties and fears of an era. So can the performing arts, as previous chapters have documented too. There is a rich literature exploring the contributions that the arts can make, including community arts and cultural engagements that can – and do – contribute to community development, popular political education and active citizenship (Clover and Sanford, 2013; Rooke, 2013; Tiller, 2013; English and Irving, 2015). Boal's use of drama provides a case in point, building on Freirean approaches to learning for social transformation. Street theatre based on such principles can offer people creative opportunities to reflect on their issues, exploring alternative scenarios, testing out new roles and new ways of challenging oppressive situations – in the safety of the drama (Boal, 1979).

Whether more or less directly, the arts can also be provocative. They can stimulate people to question previously accepted ways of seeing their worlds – without necessarily presenting recipes for taking action, as a result. Films and plays do not need to be directly didactic in order to engage with people's emotions for instance, providing challenges with contemporary relevance without telling their audiences what to think and/or do next. There are so many examples for reference. The play based on the book about 'The Jungle' (Agier et al, 2018) did not need to tell audiences how to respond to the plight of migrants and refugees encamped around the French port of Calais, for example. The dramatisation of their struggles – and their resilience – told their stories in ways which could engage audiences' emotions so powerfully. This was far more effective than simply providing the facts about migrants' situations, I felt; a form of popular education that enabled migrants to speak for themselves with dignity, rather than being portrayed as passive victims to be pitied, let alone being portrayed as the threatening 'other' to be feared.

'Sweat', a play about effects of de-industrialisation on a community in Reading, Pennsylvania, USA, provides another example of just such emotional impacts. Based on oral testimonies, the play shows the destructive effects of job losses on the characters involved, the demoralisation and shame attached to long-term unemployment and the subtle ways in which racism can manifest itself, as some characters come to blame the 'other' in times of trouble, the black neighbour who is believed to be getting more favourable treatment. As the programme notes for the London performances explained, back in the US the project integrated live performances with film and projections, 'reframing the evidence of people's lives across mediums including dance, spoken word, montage, music, mural and immersion, and by reflecting the community back to itself', creating space and opportunity for re-imaging the community's future (Buckner, 2018). Seeing the play in London, audiences could engage with the emotions that were being portrayed, drawing their own conclusions about its potential relevance for themselves and their communities.

Drama can also be used as an approach to participatory research, enabling people to share their experiences, including their feelings about these experiences, with wider audiences. For example, through 'Me? I just put British!', a play that migrant women performed in 2019, audiences were enabled to feel the cruelty of these experiences for themselves, particularly the cruelty that was being meted out to those excluded from recourse to public funds. This was popular education for the audience as well as popular education for the migrant women who shared their experiences to put the play together in the first place.

Research was part of the process too. The play's performance was followed with forum theatre interventions. Members of the audience were invited to participate themselves, replaying scenes to test out alternative ways of coping with these women's challenges. Being more assertive might have seemed a good idea, for instance, but when this approach was tried out it became increasingly clear that this wasn't going to be much help after all; it was the policies themselves that needed to be changed. Meanwhile the researchers were recording the audience's reactions, inviting people to summarise their responses, providing further evidence through these innovative approaches to research.

The arts have major contributions to make in terms of engaging with people's emotions then. But so do sports. So many people are passionate about sports, especially, but by no means only, young people, whether as participants or spectators, or both. Football provides an obvious example, illustrating ways in which racism and other discriminatory attitudes can be challenged through popular education initiatives engaging players, managers and supporters, alike. Before moving on to explore the role of popular education in football, however, the following section illustrates more direct approaches to popular education to enable communities to challenge racist, xenophobic, anti-Semitic and Islamophobic attitudes and behaviours more effectively, focusing on the example of the Hope Not Hate campaign.

Hope Not Hate's approach

Hope Not Hate was founded in 2004 to provide positive antidotes to the politics of hate. The initial impetus came from the challenges posed by the electoral successes of the Far Right British National Party (BNP), which won votes in a number of local council elections. In response the campaign focused on working with communities, engaging with local people, realising that the BNP was tapping into a wider mood of alienation and hardship. So the campaign appreciated that it was important to tap into these issues of concern to voters, thereby contributing to the BNP's subsequent electoral decline, as a result.

Since then Hope Not Hate has put added emphasis on community politics and educational activities, setting out to build peaceful and positive forms of resistance to the BNP's successor, the English Defence League's (EDL) attempts to divide communities. Every year some 700 ambassadors go into schools, providing classes and exercises to prepare young people with the empathy, information and confidence they need to take a stand against prejudice. The campaign has also been providing popular education workshops for adults too including four-day residential workshops, 'Hope Camps', bringing people together to develop shared understandings and skills. These events set out to explore the bases for racist, xenophobic, anti-Semitic and Islamophobic attitudes and behaviours; and to examine ways in which participants could develop the skills to respond positively – and effectively – building community solidarity, replacing feelings of hate with feelings of hope. Some 40 participants attended the first event in 2016, with 80 participants at the second event in 2017.

The participants had applied for a Hope Camp place, responding to the invitation that had been circulated via Hope Not Hate's mailing list. They had been selected on the basis of ensuring that the group would be diverse in terms of race, ethnicity, gender and age, bringing people's different experiences together in a context in which people would feel safe and open to new ideas. Around half the participants had already been very actively involved in relevant ways, including those who had been active in their communities and people who had been active within black and minority ethnic groups and faith-based organisations. Others were new to activism in the UK, including asylum seekers, for example, bringing their own perspectives and experiences to share.

The sessions were co-facilitated in participative ways, with cabaret-style seating around tables in groups, rather than having participants lined up in rows, to be addressed from a top table of experts. Following an overview of the national scene, the table-based groups were organised, region by region, to discuss the situation in the participants' own particular regions. This set the context for the discussions that followed, discussions that were organised in similarly participative ways, including the use of games as a fun way of exploring the issues together.

Topics included:

- Organising for equality
- Power and privilege
- Power analysis
- Strategy and tactics
- Leadership
- Developing transformative conversations and
- Building networks.

The Hope Camps' aims were to explore these underlying issues and concepts, building on people's previous experiences and recognising the importance of their feelings, as the basis for developing a positive antidote to the Far Right. The focus was on enabling participants to have the confidence and skills to reach out to those who disagreed with them, engaging people in potentially transformative conversations rather than simply confronting them on the streets – or even simply telling people that they were wrong. Presenting people with the facts could actually be counterproductive, it was pointed out, re-enforcing people's feelings that they were being disrespected and patronised by the liberal elite.

The story of the Battle of Cable Street in 1936 has sometimes been misunderstood in this context, a Hope Not Hate educator and activist explained to me. This had been widely presented as an epic victory over Oswald Mosley's fascists – by physically preventing them from marching through London's East End. The reality was actually more complex though, in Hope Not Hate's view. The fascists had indeed been challenged on the streets. But popular support for them had already been undermined by community-based conversations developed through community-based struggles, supporting people facing evictions, for example, building shared understandings and trust as the basis for demonstrating solidarity in action.

Challenging Far Right demonstrations is only part of the strategy that is needed in the present context – and not necessarily the most effective way of winning people over, in Hope Not Hate's view. On the contrary, in fact, bystanders who witness – or hear about – violent confrontations between the Far Right and their opponents on the streets may be turned off, becoming even more fearful as a result. Rather, Hope Not Hate has been concerned with enabling activists to address the underlying causes of such fears, including fears about migration – as part of strategies to reach out to the people who disagreed with them, building community solidarity for the longer term. The success of this approach was to be judged by whether communities were more united in practice, rather than more frightened and divided, as a result.

So how has this approach been applied in particular contexts? The first example comes from Hope Not Hate's initiatives in Hackney, East London, where the Far Right planned to terrorise the Charedi Jewish community in 2015, threatening to march through the area on a monthly basis. Hope Not Hate worked with others to plan their response. As part of this response a leaflet was prepared, in English on one side and in Hebrew on the other, as a mark of respect for the Charedi community, illustrating the importance of encouraging Charedi and non-Charedi communities to stand together in solidarity. As a result of the united approach that was developed together, in a variety of ways, the Far Right came to appreciate that Hackney communities were not going to be intimated by such marches – and no more marches followed.

There was a similar story to tell about Hope Not Hate responses to Far Right threats to Jewish communities in Golders Green, North West London. Rather than planning a battle on the streets, Hope Not Hate organised community-based expressions of solidarity with Jewish communities in the area, working together alongside Jewish organisations. A petition was organised, seeking to have the threatened march relocated. Meanwhile, posters of support were displayed in people's windows, and gold and green ribbons decorated the area – not just the clock tower at the centre of the area but also on lamp posts and street furniture for about a square mile around.

The public narrative was changed, as a result. From being portrayed as 'the isolated Jewish community in Golders Green' the Jewish community was being portrayed within the context of 'the diverse community of Golders Green, standing together', building on positive feelings of solidarity. The Far Right got the message and issued no further threats to march through Golders Green. *The Jewish Chronicle* subsequently included an eight-page supplement in commemoration, including articles from the local Orthodox Christian community, a black community church and the local mosque, illustrating the solidarity that had been developed as a result.

The third example comes from Birmingham, with Tommy Robinson (aka Stephen Yaxley-Lennon) threatening to march, to intimidate Muslim communities in the city. The day before the scheduled event, Hope Not Hate organised a meeting in the Central Mosque, with councillors, several MPs, representatives from trade unions and other organisations and local activists. Table by table in groups, they shared ideas and developed strategies as to how to organise their response most effectively. In the end the march was relocated and the Far Right marched around virtually empty car parks outside the city centre, the following day – in pouring rain. Far from intimidating Muslim communities in Birmingham, the Far Right had been met with increasing community solidarity. From a narrative of fear and intimidation, there had been developed a narrative of solidarity and mutual support.

Overall, Hope Not Hate's approach has demonstrated successes then, listening to people's concerns, addressing their fears, and organising to build solidarity and hope within as well as between communities. The training camps have been part of this strategy, enabling activists to have the confidence and the skills to work with communities in these ways, promoting transformative conversations and building systems of mutual support. Hope Not Hate has identified former trainees playing leading roles subsequently, further demonstrating the effectiveness of their approach for the longer term. This approach has also been applied internationally, as well as in the UK, with a two-day training event in Prague in 2017, for example, focusing on tackling the Far Right across Eastern and Central Europe.

Challenging racism and discrimination in football

Sports can engage with people's emotions in very powerful ways too – whether positively or more negatively – providing correspondingly powerful opportunities for popular education, providing the basis for developing processes of critical reflection and dialogue. Freirean principles have been applied in such ways in Edinburgh, for example, working with football fans to develop critical literacy skills. Using media reports that participants brought in as the focus for discussion, the project succeeded in unpacking the underlying commodification of cultural, social and labour relations and the ascendancy of global finance capital in determining football success (Player, 2013). There would seem to be significant implications for tackling racism in sports in general, and football more specifically.

Racism and discrimination have been only too evident, both on the pitch and off it, attitudes and behaviours that have been challenged in a variety of ways over past decades. The 'Kick It Out' and 'Show Racism the Red Card' campaigns have been organising a range of interventions with players, trainers and managers alike, working with fans along with those involved in the sport professionally, going into schools and formal education settings, as well as developing training materials for popular education initiatives in different contexts. The importance of these approaches has been highlighted only too clearly with the emergence of Far Right Tommy Robinson's so-called 'Democratic Football Lads Alliance' in 2017, targeting young football supporters with a view to mobilising them for the Far Right.

Kick It Out had already been formed back in 1993 as 'Let's Kick Racism Out of Football'. This had been a time when racial violence, harassment and abuse had been described as being rife in the game (Kick It Out, 2017) – but the authorities had been described as being in denial (2017: 1). So the campaign set out 'to raise awareness about inequalities and exclusion and set an evolving agenda for action to enable the authorities, leagues, clubs, players, match officials and fans to tackle these issues' (2017: 1). Reflecting on the progress that had been made since then, the report on football's Equality (E), Inclusion (I) and Cohesion (C) (EIC) initiatives pointed to the achievements, while recognising the many challenges ahead and the remaining deficiencies and shortcomings to be addressed (2017: 1). Football is an important part of many people's lives, the report continued. Much had been done to make playing, watching, officiating and being active in the sport safer and more enjoyable.

The range of activities included the development of regulatory codes to address abusive and discriminatory activities, a series of initiatives to promote inclusivity and equalities within professional football, along with equalities and anti-discrimination training and education for all those concerned. Educational resources had included an Equality and Awareness online distance learning course developed with Solent University, Southampton, with other resources developed for particular issues/groups. There had been targeted campaigns and education programmes to tackle prejudice and hate, including the release of a film as part of Chelsea's campaign to tackle anti-Semitism, for example, a resource that other clubs were being encouraged to use. Equality ambassadors had been raising awareness among young people in schools and junior clubs. And the clubs' community programmes offered important ways to promote equalities and community cohesion more widely.

The report concluded that there had been considerable progress on the field at the top end of the professional game but more needed to be done. More recent instances of abusive behaviours served as reminders that these have been continuing challenges. There had been worrying reports of violence, reflecting 'a rise in reported and under reported hate crimes in wider society' (Kick It Out, 2017: 5). More remained to be done too in terms of the management and administrative culture of the game. Strong leadership was needed along with more effective coordination, linking activities to tackle discrimination within the football industry with activities to tackle racism and abusive behaviours on pitches and terraces.

These initiatives have been based on critical understandings of the underlying connections between racism and discrimination in their differing manifestations, whether among the fans or among the players themselves. Maslow (1943, 1954) and Fraser (2008) had both pointed to such connections in their different ways, demonstrating the links between people's material needs and their need for recognition, respect and esteem, needs that apply within the community as well as within the workplace. Tackling inequalities and discrimination within the professional football industry itself was as essential as tackling abusive attitudes and violent behaviours among the fans.

The evaluation of 'Show Racism the Red Card's 'Routes' project pointed to similar conclusions (Rodgerson, 2018). This particular initiative set out to provide specialist anti-racism educational interventions through schools and formal educational settings in Tyne and Wear, targeting young people aged between 13 and 18 years who had been identified as being at risk of being drawn into the politics of the Far Right. This was an area that had been identified as targeted by Far Right extremists. There had been demonstrations against refugees and against Islam, for example, in the context of a national rise in hate crime, hate speech, graffiti and physical violence.

The project was based on the recognition that racism is multifaceted and so needs to be tackled with flexibility, taking account of 'young people's sense of identity, sense of place in their communities and in the wider political and economic context' (Rodgerson, 2018: 5). Their concerns had to be addressed in 'a safe, non-judgemental space, in order to foster young people's self-expression and critical thinking skills' (2018: 5). And rather than telling young people what to think, the approach encouraged 'the exploration of where our ideas come from', via 'the development of critical thinking skills', enabling young people to experience 'a reduction in conflict and confrontation with themselves, their education provider and wider society, thus increasing their resilience to racist and far-right rhetoric' (2018: 5). Their needs for safety and respect had to be met, in other words, taking account of their own senses of identity, before the wider issues could be effectively addressed. This approach seemed to be working. Qualitative feedback from the young people and education providers involved provided some evidence that the project was 'being valued, needed and that objectives are being met' (2018: 5).

Whether consciously or less consciously these initiatives reflect Freirean approaches to popular education, in response to the challenges of racism and the growth of threats from the Far Right, approaches that emerge more explicitly from the following discussion with a longstanding activist, drawing on his educational experiences in the trade union and labour movement.

As a shop steward, this anti-racist activist had first become involved in educational work as a part-time tutor with the Workers' Educational Association (WEA). His personal experiences reinforced his appreciation of the importance of starting from learners' own concerns, respecting their existing knowledge as the basis for taking the learning process forward. This was particularly important when working with people who had had negative experiences of education at school – barriers to learning that had to be overcome. The approach needed to be participative and collective, he explained, engaging participants in active learning together as a group, rather than being talked at by big experts from the front. This was the basis for his anti-racist work as well.

Having worked as a tutor in different contexts, he had the opportunity to attend an advanced international education programme for experienced trade union activists. This brought him fresh insights, further re-enforcing his previous understandings, he explained. In summary, he had become more aware that this type of educational approach was not just about starting from where people were at, although this was indeed the basis on which you needed to work. But it was also about finding ways to engage people in processes of dialogue in order to move them on – from A to B. It was about having a plan as to where you were going forward as an educator, in other words. He summarised the basis for such a plan by quoting from Tony Benn, the radical politician who had been committed to working for a fundamental and irreversible shift in favour of working people. The goal was social transformation, in other words, working for equalities and social justice.

Although he hadn't initially been familiar with Paulo Freire's ideas, he had come to know them and so to recognise their relevance. There would seem to be parallels here with Paulo Freire's reflections on the influence of Gramsci's ideas on his own thinking, as Chapter 2 has already outlined, quoting him as explaining that 'I discovered that I had been greatly influenced by Gramsci long before I read him'. 'It is fantastic to discover that we have been influenced by someone's thought,' Paulo Freire had continued, 'without even being introduced to their intellectual production' (de Figueiredo-Cowen and Gastaldo, 1995: 63–4).

Freire's was the approach that he had developed more consciously in his anti-racist, anti-discriminatory work, since then, this activist explained, including his involvement in tackling racism and discrimination in football. He had been a football supporter himself as a young person in the seventies, but had stopped going to games in the early 1980s, because of the horrible level of racist abuse on the terraces. This was not an issue that could be tackled on an individual basis, he appreciated.

A more collective approach was needed, a view that had come to be recognised more widely too. Following the uprisings of the 1980s there had been increasing recognition of the importance of tackling racism, including the importance of challenging racism collectively within the trade union movement in general and trade union education more specifically. This was precisely where he became actively involved, himself.

These challenges were all linked, in his view, as he went on to explain. Racism was not only an issue on the terraces and pitches. Black players were also trade unionists, members of the Professional Footballers' Association (PFA). They needed to be supported to challenge racism and discrimination within the football industry as well as among the fans. The provision of anti-racist, anti-discriminatory training was being hampered by the lack of black trade union tutors, however, along with the lack of structures to support them; they were a tiny minority within the trade union and labour movement. They needed to be organised to have the power and the recognition to be able to challenge racism within the movement as well as within the wider society. So, far from being separate struggles, the struggles for the right to self-organise, for black sections and for black workers' conferences within the Labour Party and the trade union movement, were all inextricably linked, along with the struggle for a national black tutors' group and the struggle for anti-racist initiatives in football. 'We never saw these issues as separate.' There needed to be more black tutors, with the space to develop their own thinking, producing relevant training materials for trade union education, just as there needed to be more black football managers and trainers, if racism and discrimination were to be seriously addressed, in their varying manifestations. The aim was to build unity, within the trade union movement as well as beyond.

So these messages needed to be taken out to communities, including communities of football supporters, as well as to those working in football professionally. The trade union movement has massive human resources, he pointed out, with some 6 million members, many of whom would be football supporters, or have football supporters among their families and friends. These human resources could and should be mobilised to challenge racism and discrimination, wherever these occur, whether within the workplace or within communities including communities of football supporters across the country.

In summary, black activists needed to be taking leading roles in anti-racist campaigns. They did not need to be told what to do by white groups who thought that they had all the answers. But white groups did need to be actively involved as well, working alongside black groups, understanding and respecting where people were coming from as the basis for moving forwards, from A to B. This was the basis for challenging racism, anti-Semitism, Islamophobia and xenophobia, along with all forms of discrimination and oppression. It was not just about challenging the Far Right on the streets, although that was certainly necessary too. Rather it was about engaging with people, building a movement for change. And this involved being clear about 'what it is we stand for', putting out strong messages about what 'we are *for*, not just what we are *against*', through trade union and anti-racist education, working for the sort of society that we want to create, the fundamental and irreversible shift that Tony Benn had outlined as the basis for a transformative future. He concluded that he felt optimistic despite all the problems that he had just outlined, enthused by the current wave of engagement in politics, especially among young people. The struggle continues.

Conclusion

The reflections from this trade union educator and activist bring these discussions together, illustrating the interconnections between the different spheres of struggle. Far from being separate, let alone in competition with each other, these different sites of struggle have the potential to be mutually re-enforcing, linking trade union struggles in the workplace with complementary struggles around the issues that most concern people in communities. People's material concerns need to be addressed, but so do their anxieties and fears, along with people's feelings of humiliation and shame when they are treated without respect.

In addition, campaigns to challenge discrimination and racism in football illustrate the positive potential for engaging people, including young people, through their passions. Like the arts, sports can appeal to people's feelings, providing opportunities to stimulate new ways of thinking and new ways of behaving. Emotions can contribute to such processes rather than being in competition with them, as Hoggett's writings have already explained, demonstrating the relevance of psycho-social understandings more generally.

Finally, these reflections relate back to previous chapters' discussions on popular education, drawing on the writings of Paulo Freire and others, more generally. Popular education can be distinguished from populism in a number of ways, starting from its theoretical roots – based on critical understandings of the structural causes of people's experiences of exploitation and oppression, whether in terms of their class or their race, gender, sexuality, disability or faith, or some combination of these. Most importantly, popular education needs to start from where people are at, taking account of their emotions, their hopes and fears as well as their more immediate issues and concerns; but this is not where popular education ends. On the contrary. Rather, through processes of dialogue based on relationships of trust, popular educators aim to move people from A to B, to promote critical thinking as the basis for developing more transformative relationships of social solidarity. And this involves knowing where you are going, a lesson that I began to understand as a child myself, through the sport of dinghy sailing. Learning to sail a dinghy involves precisely this, in fact, identifying the mark that you aim to reach and then working out how to get there, tacking to and fro to take account of the wind if need be, but keeping your eye firmly on your objective if you are to avoid drifting way off course.

10

Looking backwards, looking forwards

Much has been written about the Far Right, fake news and post-truth since I began thinking about this book. This would seem to be a fast-moving situation. As one of those writing about the Far Right reflects, 'Things change so quickly' (Hawley, 2019: 1), and statements about such rapidly changing social movements 'can transition from being perfectly accurate to woefully outdated with shocking speed' (2019: 1). There is not space here to review these writings in detail, let alone to try to keep up with the shifting ground of Far Right movements in the UK and elsewhere. Rather, the point to emphasise is simply this: Far Right mobilisations continue to present serious challenges. And so do the underlying causes of the growth of Far Right populism, the political, social and cultural causes as well as the material causes, rooted in increasing insecurities, injustices and widening social inequalities.

Sadly I have not come across any convincing evidence to persuade me to the contrary. Rather the reverse. Since I began writing this book there have been disturbing increases in the incidence of racist, anti-Semitic, Islamophobic and homophobic hate crimes, both in the UK and elsewhere. And there have been horrific manifestations of White Supremacist violence – from Charlottesville, USA to Christchurch, New Zealand – illustrating the most extreme expressions of the politics of hate. Far from diminishing, these challenges seem to have been growing in recent years.

But so has the flip side of this particular coin, the growth of popular mobilisations for progressive alternatives for the future. So what might be the implications for popular education in populist times? And how might popular educators contribute to the development of these mobilisations for progressive alternatives, burgeoning movements for social transformation?

The first part of this chapter summarises the reasons why a structural approach to understanding the underlying causes of people's frustrations continues to have relevance, drawing on the insights to be offered by a Marxist analytical framework, along with the insights to be provided by feminist and psycho-social approaches. This leads into the discussion of the continuing relevance of popular education and participatory action research building on the approaches that have been developed by Paulo Freire and others, in their differing contexts.

These can provide the basis for developing strategies for the future, supporting wider movements for social equalities and justice. Finally the chapter concludes by summarising some of the remaining tensions and challenges for popular educators in the contemporary context.

The continuing relevance of Marxism

Around 2017 there were a number of conferences marking the 200th anniversary of the birth of Karl Marx. Were these simply academic exercises? Or were Marxist approaches still relevant to current struggles, whether in Britain and/or elsewhere? And if so, how might Marxist analyses have continuing relevance and in what ways?

In a contribution to the popular education journal *CONCEPT*, I argue that Marxism is more relevant than ever, and particularly so for popular education and development in the contemporary context (Mayo, 2019). Marxist analyses could contribute to the development of critical understandings about the growth of Far Right populism in different contexts, on a global scale. And these forms of critical thinking could contribute to the development of community-based responses, promoting strategies of hope not hate, working with movements for social justice and social solidarity. Marxism provides no simplistic, off-the-peg solutions to contemporary questions and dilemmas. Absolutely not. But it does provide the conceptual tools with which to develop alternative ways forward from the bottom up.

The first point to stress then is that this is absolutely not about trying to find apposite quotations from Marx and Engels' *Selected Works* (1968) and then applying/misapplying them to the contemporary context. Rather this is about the relevance of Marxist understandings, with a particular focus on the centrally important (if contested) concepts of class, and class consciousness. Class structures vary across time and space (Miliband, 1977). But the overall tendency has been towards polarisation, in Marx's view, splitting societies into the 'two great classes directly facing each other' (1977: 36), the '1% versus the 99%', or the 'Many rather than the Few', in more recent terminology. Although much criticised in the past for being too simplistic, this view would seem more relevant than ever, with the growth of precarious employment and zero hours contracts across a wide spectrum of occupations, including professional occupations (Standing, 2011). Neoliberal postmodernists may question the continuing relevance of class, but this doesn't magic class differences away, as Freire has also argued, pointing to class struggle as one of, if not the only, mover of history (Freire, 1996b).

This is not necessarily how people perceive their class situation though. On the contrary, the common sense perception of class is that of a ladder of occupational hierarchies, with opportunities for more or less social mobility between its rungs. Nor do people necessarily perceive class in terms of class conflict, although there so often are conflicts, including conflicts within as well as between social classes. Previous chapters have already outlined longstanding divisions between the 'respectable' as contrasted with the 'undeserving' poor, for example, conflicts that have been fanned by media attacks on so-called scroungers and benefit fraudsters, in recent times. There have been conflicts between newcomers and longer established communities, as previous chapters have also outlined, just as there have been conflicts within and between communities based on factors such as gender, sexuality, ethnicity, disability, age and faith. And there have, of course, been conflicts between capital and labour, with capital typically (although not always) supported by the forces of the capitalist state, as in the case of the 1984–85 Miners Strike in Britain, for example.

Addressing the causes of conflicts within and between different sections of labour has to be central to the development of strategies to challenge the Far Right politicians that seek to exploit them for their own ends. Marxists recognise the importance of understanding and addressing such divisions, just as they recognise the importance of understanding and addressing oppression in relation to gender, sexuality, ethnicity, disability, age and faith, alongside recognising the underlying significance of exploitation in relation to social class. As Mae Shaw and I explained in our introduction to *Class, Inequality and Community Development* (Shaw and Mayo, 2016) class cannot be experienced in practice outside these other forms of oppression, it cannot be 'lived outside of "race", "gender" or "sexuality" and the same is true of other categories', in the words of Dhaliwal and Yuval-Davis (2014: 35).

How then do people develop solidarity, taking account of such forms of oppression too? The Communist Manifesto argued that the working class was becoming concentrated in larger industrial units, engaging in workplace struggles which could lead to increasing class consciousness. But this wouldn't happen automatically. And it hasn't, a point of particular relevance in more recent times given the increasing fragmentation that characterises so many employment patterns today, with the growth of 'self-employment' and zero hours contracts. Political organisation has been needed and continues to be needed too – along with political, psycho-social and cultural analyses, as the previous chapter argued.

Community education and development workers have known this only too well. People can and do learn from their involvement in social movements (Foley, 1999). But they can draw reactionary conclusions rather than progressive conclusions from their experiences, becoming more exclusive, blaming the 'other' – reflecting and amplifying communities' darker sides (Kenny et al, 2015). The challenges involved in addressing such forms of alienation would seem greater than ever in the current context, with the growth of the gig economy in the world of work, along with the social fragmentation and the lack of security that so often accompanies rapid change.

From a Marxist perspective it is no wonder that so many people feel so angry and frustrated and so alienated from established political parties that attempt to manage capitalist crises with the politics of austerity. But these feelings are not to be explained simply in populist terms, focusing on corrupt politicians (although there may indeed be corrupt politicians as well as incompetent ones) or the arrogance of the elite (although that may indeed be an issue too). Rather, explanations need to go back to the operations of global capital, increasing financialisation, and the effects of the crisis of 2008 on those least able to pay. Without going into detail here the point is simply to emphasise the economic factors that have led to the politics of austerity, along with the case for developing alternative strategies.

This is absolutely not to suggest that politics can be explained simply in terms of the economy either. Nor is it to suggest that people's cultures and ideas can be read off in this way – an approach that has been described as 'vulgar Marxism'. Marx was absolutely not an economic determinist himself, arguing that people make their own history – if not in circumstances of their own choosing. Politicians could have made other choices then, despite the constraints, as others have also pointed out (Farnsworth and Irving, 2015). As it was, neither the politics of austerity nor even the politics of 'austerity light' were likely to address the underlying problems, nor were they going to address the immediate problems that people were facing as wages were falling in real terms while public services and benefits were being slashed, as has been the case in recent years in the UK, for example. Nor were populist politicians addressing the root causes of the wider feelings of alienation, anxiety and loss, the existential angst that has been explored in the previous chapter. Popular educators need to feel able to explore these issues effectively, engaging with communities through processes of dialogue based on relationships of mutual trust.

How then to build support for alternative strategies, building solidarity rather than increasing social fragmentation in the process?

Far Right populists set the people/the nation against the elites that are supposedly favouring outsiders while ignoring, if not actually despising, the very people that they are supposed to serve. Marxists, in contrast, start from a class analysis, exploring the conflicting interests and powers involved in any particular context, as Chapter 7 has already explained, including the relative strengths of progressive movements. Which exploited and oppressed groups have potentially common interests, despite their differences – questions that have also been explored in previous chapters? And where might they be able to gather support? How far might it be possible to win government support to meet people's needs, despite the limitations of the capitalist state – as happened to a significant extent with the development of the Welfare State in the UK, in the post Second World War period? And how might local struggles come together to achieve relevant reforms – while recognising the structural limits – making history despite not being in circumstances of progressive movements' own choosing? How to build solidarity across differences, working for effective reforms in the here and now while being only too aware of the need for longer-term strategies for social transformation? This brings the discussion to the continuing relevance of Paulo Freire and others, popular educators and participatory action researchers who have been developing strategies to work towards precisely such goals.

Drawing on the work of Paulo Freire and others, popular educators know just how important it is to engage in processes of dialogue on the basis of mutual trust, rather than attempting to harangue people and communities for being reactionary, racist, sexist, homophobic, xenophobic or whatever. Telling people that they are wrong is simply counterproductive, as the comments that have been quoted in previous chapters so clearly illustrate. There were so many expressions of resentment, feelings of frustrations and rage at being dismissed by liberal and financial elites, 'The rich cunts in the City ... calling us racists' (Winlow et al, 2017: 95). Myth-busting exercises have similar risks of being counterproductive, if people don't trust the source, potentially dismissing the information in question as fake news. The bases for people's feelings need to be addressed, as the previous chapter has also considered.

The continuing relevance of Paulo Freire

Like Marx, Paulo Freire has been taken out of context, filleted for quotations that can be (mis)applied, reduced to a set of educational tools. Crowther and Martin have described such approaches as bastardisation, the 'sanitisation and domestication of Freire's pedagogy' (Crowther and Martin, 2018: 12). But this pedagogy was still as relevant as ever, if not more so in their view, in the contemporary context. In a special issue of *CONCEPT*, focusing on 'Pedagogy of the Oppressed', the editors brought a range of popular educators and participatory action researchers together to share their thoughts on how and why Paulo Freire's work had influenced them, and, most importantly, why *Pedagogy of the Oppressed* still mattered in neoliberal times. This was absolutely not about presenting uncritical paeans of praise to the great Brazilian. On the contrary, contributors included reflections on the inadequacies of his writings that had disturbed them from the first, including the inadequacies of Freire's earlier writings in relation to gender (Tett, 2018). Rather the point was to share more rounded perspectives on the book's continuing relevance, its continuing uses as well its continuing abuses.

It had been 50 years since *Pedagogy of the Oppressed* was first published in 1968 (although it had only been published in an English translation subsequently). The editors' introduction went on to explain their reasons for bringing out this special issue, pointing to the book's profound relevance in times of fragmentation, in the face of neoliberal globalisation and the growth of the Far Right (Aitken and Shaw, 2018). Like Crowther and Martin's (2018) contribution in the same issue, they emphasised the importance of understanding Freire's theoretical underpinnings, approaching his work holistically, rather than treating this as a toolbox of methodologies to be applied pragmatically, for whatever particular agenda; whether to domesticate or to promote critical understanding, 'conscientisation' to use Freire's own terminology. Freire's writings had been misunderstood and misapplied in various contexts over time, they argued, as previous chapters have similarly pointed out. But *Pedagogy of the Oppressed* had also been internationally recognised for its transformative potential. As a result of this revolutionary potential it had been banned in South Africa, for example, categorised as a dangerous book during the Apartheid years (von Kotze, 2018), drawing, as it did, on what Crowther and Martin have described as Freire's 'eclectic and idiosyncratic brand of Marxism, Christianity and humanism' (Crowther and Martin, 2018: 8).

Education was essentially political for Freire, deciding whose side you were on, as Chapter 2 has already outlined. Exploitation had to be understood in terms of class politics, while taking account of other forms of oppressive relationships too. The causes needed to be understood and challenged at their roots. And this required popular education and participatory action research to produce 'really useful knowledge', as subsequent writers including Fals Borda, Hall and Tandon have also emphasised, knowledge to enable people to identify their collective interests, pursuing shared aspirations for a better future (Crowther and Martin, 2018; Ledwith, 2018). Chapter 2 has already considered their contributions in further detail, building on their critical reflections on the writings of Freire, among others.

In addition to class and class struggle, Freire demonstrated his understanding of the importance of Marxist understandings of ideology and culture. This included the importance of challenging the 'common sense' of 'hegemonic' ideas, to use the Gramscian term. As Popple's article in this collection points out, Freire also saw that political struggles include ideological struggles for moral and intellectual leadership within civil society (Popple, 2018). This needed to be about enabling people to question the status quo, challenging the 'common sense' internalisation of victim blaming, rather than people blaming themselves for their own exploitation and oppression. Freire's work on education for liberation draws on these insights, starting from people's everyday experiences, but building on these experiences through processes of dialogue based on relationships of trust. Through such processes people could begin to overcome the culture of silence, gaining the confidence and skills to work collectively for social transformation. As the trade union activist reflected in the previous chapter, this is not just about starting from where people are at, however important this most certainly is; it is also about moving forwards from A to B, based on shared understandings of the goals for social transformation. Freire shared similar reflections in *Pedagogy of Hope* (1996b), pointing out that starting from learners' existing knowledge was only the beginning, setting off down the road. 'I have never said, as it has sometimes been suggested or said that I have said, that we ought to flutter spellbound around the knowledge of the educands [the learners] like moths around a lamp bulb' (Freire, 1996b).

Rather, as other articles in this special issue of *CONCEPT* also emphasise, *Pedagogy of the Oppressed*'s approach is rooted in the importance of dialogue. But this is not simply about the value of dialogue per se. Crowther and Martin quote Allman's view that the Freirean approach involves 'a transformed type of communication and is therefore not a technique that can be used in isolation from an acceptance of and commitment to … the totality of Freire's philosophy' (Allman, 1987, quoted in Crowther and Martin, 2018: 13). This is fundamentally different from neoliberal approaches to learning or indeed from populist approaches, taking people's everyday consciousness as given, in the case of the latter, or viewing people as rational individuals responsible for investing in learning for their own individual advancement, preparing 'citizens for participation in the new welfare order' in the case of the former (Crowther and Martin, 2018: 9).

Chapter 8 focused on the impact of neoliberalism on universities and colleges, compounded by the impact of austerity policies in recent years. Although neoliberal approaches to learning have been predominant, however, universities could still play a potentially valuable role, 'becoming more accessible and working alongside communities', as Lucio-Villegas (2018) concludes, reflecting on his experiences associated with the establishment and functioning of the Paulo Freire Chair at the University of Seville, Spain. Crowther and Martin conclude on a similarly positive note. Freire's work asserts that fatalism and passivity can be challenged, enabling people and communities to lever themselves out of immersion in the culture of silence. They point to the fact that one of Freire's last books, published in 1996, a year before his death, was called *Pedagogy of Hope*.

Remaining tensions and challenges?

The pedagogy of hope might be the place to conclude, an upbeat outlook for popular educators and participatory action researchers in populist times. This might seem too simplistic, however, given the preceding discussion. Marxism provides a framework for critical analysis rather than a set of ready-made answers to the questions of the day, just as surely as does the legacy of Paulo Freire. Rather than providing a ready-made toolkit, his writings provide a framework for others to develop popular education and participatory research in their own specific contexts. Taken together with the insights to be gained from feminist analyses and psycho-social understandings, these approaches offer guidance, ways of promoting shared understandings and collective learning rather than offering prescriptions for the way forward, in the context of the effects of neoliberalism, the politics of austerity and the growth of the Far Right in the UK and beyond.

Rather than offering blueprints for the future then, this concluding section points to three continuing tensions and dilemmas for popular educators and participatory action researchers. Far from being entirely new, each of these dilemmas has its antecedents. But each has particular relevance in the contemporary context.

First, as Liam Kane (2005) reflected (as discussed in Chapter 2), the very definition of popular education has inherent tensions and challenges. Who exactly are the 'ordinary people' who are to be the focus of popular education to enable them to take their interests forward in the first place? And do they have real interests in common in any case? Who is to define these interests, and how to take account of differences within as well as between communities and social movements, including differences rooted in social class, gender, sexuality, ethnicity, religion (dis)ability and age? These are fundamentally problematic questions underpinning the very concept of popular education – and most especially so in the context of Far Right populism.

Second, there would seem to be continuing tensions inherent in the objective of starting from where people are at, validating the legitimacy of people's concerns while aiming to move people on. The very notion of conscientisation embodies this potential tension. Whose perspective needs to provide the focus for moving on? Who can legitimately claim to know best – and on what basis? Gramsci's concept of the organic intellectual has relevance here, the leaders and organisers, including the popular educators, who can act as strategic players, 'helping people make connections between their position and the need for change' (Popple, 2018: 86) – including change in the hegemonic as well as the material spheres.

So far, so good? Or is it? How far might this provide guidance that could be applied in particular situations in the current context? Whose knowledge really counts in any case and on what basis? The importance of valuing people's existing knowledge has been a continuing theme in previous chapters. This includes indigenous people's knowledge in the global south just as it includes people's existing knowledge about their situations in communities in the global north. As Chapter 6 demonstrated, workers may have a great deal of knowledge about their own particular industries, for example, even if this knowledge isn't necessarily linked to wider understandings about the effects of industrial restructuring more generally. But where are the boundaries between respecting people's existing knowledge on the one hand and colluding with more populist approaches on the other, accepting 'common sense' explanations without challenge, when people blame the 'other' rather than unpacking the underlying structural causes of their problems?

Here too popular educators need to use their judgement, recognising the inherent dilemmas that may be involved. When to challenge people's existing explanations and beliefs? And when and how to confront their prejudices? Too soon, before establishing the basis for such dialogues – based on relationships of trust – and you can actually make the situation worse, re-enforcing people's resentments about being told what to think by representatives of the liberal elite. Too late and you may be effectively reinforcing damaging stereotypes and divisive relationships within communities as well as between them.

As Hoggett and others have pointed out, the very nature of a dilemma is that there are no right answers to be had. Whichever way you decide, you can be left wondering whether an alternative approach might have been more justifiable and/or more effective (Hoggett et al, 2009), as Chapter 9 pointed out. There are implications here for popular educators themselves, and for the types of support that they might need to sustain them, as it will be suggested subsequently.

The third set of tensions relates to the realm of emotions, the feelings that have been underpinning people's reactions to neoliberal globalisation and the effects of austerity in recent years. The previous chapter has already outlined some of the ways in which individuals and communities can respond – and do respond – to their circumstances, both positively and more negatively – and not necessarily rationally. Turkeys can indeed vote for Christmas – although this can, of course, be counterproductive for them, as previous chapters have also suggested. But how to work with people's emotions productively? How to achieve complementary rather than competing relationships between the spheres of rationality and the spheres of emotions, mobilising people's passions for social justice agendas, as the previous chapter has also proposed, maintaining the energies and enthusiasms of activists as they engage with the contemporary challenges that they collectively face?

This brings the discussion to the emotional needs of popular educators and participative action researchers themselves. Working with emotions is potentially challenging whatever the context, let alone working with emotions in the context of Far Right populism, surrounded by feelings of anxiety, powerlessness, resentment, shame, fear and hatred of the 'other', a context in which expressions of homophobia, racism, anti-Semitism, Islamophobia and xenophobia have been becoming increasingly normalised. Coping with such emotions requires resilience, with the ability to contain your own feelings as well as the ability to contain the feelings of others (Hoggett et al, 2009). It involves the ability to cope with uncertainty and ambiguity along with the capacity to act, even in situations when there is no obviously right course of action to be pursued. And this requires the ability to be reflexive, applying Freirean principles to oneself as well as to the learning of others. These requirements pose continuing challenges, with no immediate prospect of becoming redundant in the contemporary context.

There are implications here for those concerned with the education and training of popular educators and participatory action researchers. Universities and colleges need to ensure that they provide their staff and students with safe spaces for ongoing cycles of reflection and action within their programmes of learning. Employers also need to recognise the importance of providing support as part of continuing professional development for their staff. And activists need to develop their own support strategies, finding ways of looking after themselves and managing the stresses that they experience effectively. They need to do this as individuals. And they need to do this as members of mutual support networks, sharing experiences and reflecting on these together as the basis for building wider movements for social transformation.

Dreams and utopias have too often been portrayed as useless, if not actually impeding progressive social change. But dreams and utopias were essential, in Paulo Freire's view: vital components of any educational practice with the power to unmask what he has described as the dominant lies (Freire, 1996b) – and to share alternative scenarios for the future. Hope was an ontological need, he argued. But even this was not enough. It was *critical* hope that was needed for the fierce struggle to build a better world. Which is why popular education and participatory action research are more relevant than ever, supporting movements for justice, solidarity and social transformation.

References

Agarwal, A., Merrifield, J. and Tandon, R. (1985) 'No Place to Run': Local Realities and Global Issues of the Bhopal Disaster, Highlander Center and Society for Participatory Research in Asia.

Agier, M., Bouagga, Y., Trépanier, M. and Fernback, D. (2018) The Jungle: Calais's Camps and Migrants, Cambridge: Polity Press.

Ahmed, S. (2015) The Cultural Politics of Emotions, 2nd edition, London: Routledge.

Aitken, A. and Shaw, M. (2018) 'Editorial', CONCEPT, 9 (3): 3–7.

ALAC (2006) Active Learning for Active Citizenship, London: Department for Communities and Local Government.

Alfred, D. (1987) 'Albert Mansbridge' in P. Jarvis (ed), Twentieth Century Thinkers in Adult Education, London: Routledge, 17–37.

Althusser, L. and Balibar, E. (1968) Lire le Capital, Paris: Maspero.

Andrews, G., Kean, H. and Thompson, J. (1999) Ruskin College: Contesting Knowledge, Dissenting Politics, London: Lawrence and Wishart.

Austin, R. (1999) 'Popular history and popular education', Latin American Perspectives, 26 (4): 39–68.

Bachrach, P. and Baratz, M. (1970) Power and Poverty: Theory and Practice, Oxford: OUP.

Bailey, M. and Freedman, D. (eds) (2011) The Assault on Universities: A Manifesto for Resistance, London: Pluto.

Banks, S., Hart, A. and Ward, P. (2019a) 'Preface and acknowledgements' in S. Banks, A. Hart and P. Ward (eds), Co-producing Research: A Community Development Approach, Bristol: Policy Press, xiii.

Banks, S., Armstrong, A., Bonner, A., Hall, Y., Harman, P., Johnston, L., Levi, C., Smith, K. and Taylor, R. (2019b) 'Between research and community development: Negotiating a contested space for collaboration and creativity' in S. Banks, A. Hart, K. Pahl and P. Ward (eds), Co-Producing Research, Bristol: Policy Press, 21–48.

Barca, S. and Leonardi, E. (2016) 'Working-class communities and ecology: reframing environmental justice around the Ilva steel plant in Taranto (Apulia, Italy)' in M. Shaw and M. Mayo (eds), Class, Inequality and Community Development, Bristol: Policy Press, 59–75.

Bauman, Z. (2001) Community, Cambridge: Polity Press.

Bedford, J., Gorbing, S. and Hampson, S. (2010) 'The five Cs: Confident, challenging, co-operative, constructive and critical women' in M. Mayo and J. Annette (eds), Taking Part?, Leicester: NIACE, 186–210.

Beetham, D. (1991) *The Legitimation of Power*, London: Macmillan.

Bell, B., Gaventa, J. and Peters, J. (eds) (1990) *We Make the Road by Walking: Conversations on Education and Social Change: Myles Horton and Paulo Freire*, Philadelphia: Temple University Press.

Bell, D., Pool, S., Streets, K. and Walton, N. (2019) 'How does arts practice inform a community development approach to the co-production of research?' in S. Banks, A. Hart and P. Ward (eds), *Co-producing Research: A Community Development Approach*, Bristol: Policy Press, 95–114.

Benn, M. (2018) *Life Lessons*, London: Verso.

Boal, A. (1979) *Theatre of the Oppressed*, London: Pluto.

Boal, A. (1995) *The Rainbow of Desire*, London: Routledge.

Boal, A. (1998) *Legislative Theatre*, London: Routledge.

Boffo, M., Saad-Filho, A. and Fine, B. (2019) 'Neoliberal capitalism: The authoritarian turn', in L. Panitch and G. Albo (eds), *A World Turned Upside Down?, Socialist Register 2019*, London: Merlin, 247–70.

Borg, C. and Mayo, P. (2006) *Learning and Social Difference*, London: Paradigm

Boughton, B. (2005) '"The Workers' University": Australia's Marx Schools' in J. Crowther, V. Galloway and I. Martin (eds) (2005), *Popular Education: Engaging the Academy*, Leicester: NIACE, 100–109.

Bowie, D. (2017) *Radical Solutions to the Housing Supply Crisis*, Bristol: Policy Press.

Brookfield, S. (1987a) 'Eduard Lindeman' in P. Jarvis (ed), *Twentieth Century Thinkers in Adult Education*, London: Routledge, 119–43.

Brookfield, S. (1987b) *Developing Critical Thinkers: Challenging Adults to Explore Alternative Ways of Thinking and Action*, Milton Keynes: Open University Press.

Brookfield, S. and Holst, J. (2011) *Radicalizing Learning: Adult Education for a Just World*, San Francisco: Jossey-Bass.

Broughton, E. (2005) 'The Bhopal disaster and its aftermath: a review', *Environmental Health*, 4 (6), available at: www.ncbi.nlm.nih.gov/pmc/articles/PMC1142333/

Brownhill, S. (1988) 'The People's Plan for the Royal Docks: Some Contradictions in Popular Planning', *Planning Practice and Research*, 4: 15–21.

Buckner, J. (2018) *Programme Notes to Sweat*, London: Donmar Warehouse Theatre.

Butterwick, S. (2012) 'The politics of listening: the power of theatre to create dialogic spaces' in L. Manicom and S. Walters (eds), *Feminist Popular Education in Transnational Debates*, Basingstoke: Palgrave Macmillan, 59–73.

References

CDP (1977) *Gilding the Ghetto: The State and the Poverty Experiments*, London: CDP Inter-Project Editorial team.

CDP (1981) *The Costs of Industrial Change*, 3rd reprint, CDP.

CDP/PEC (1979) *The State and the Local Economy*, Newcastle: CDP/PEC in association with PDC.

Chan, L.H. (1996) 'Talking pain: Educational work with factory women in Malaysia' in S. Walters and L. Minicom (eds), *Gender in Popular Education*, London: Zed, 202–28.

Clarke, S., Hoggett, P. and Thompson, S. (eds) (2006) *Emotion, Politics and Society*, Basingstoke: Palgrave Macmillan.

Clover, D. (2012) 'Feminist artists and popular education' in L. Manicom and S. Walters (eds), *Feminist Popular Education in Transnational Debates*, Basingstoke: Palgrave Macmillan, 193–208.

Clover, D. and Sanford, K. (eds) (2013) *Lifelong Learning, the Arts and Community Cultural Engagement in the Contemporary University*, Manchester: Manchester University Press.

Clover, D. and Stalker, J. (2007) 'Introduction' in D. Clover and J. Stalker (eds), *The Arts and Social Justice*, Leicester: NIACE, 1–18.

Cohen, M. (1992) 'Revolutionary education revived: The Communist challenge to the Labour Colleges, 1925–1944' in B. Simon (ed), *The Search for Enlightenment*, Leicester: NIACE, 137–52.

Collini, S. (2012) *What are Universities for?*, London: Penguin.

Collini, S. (2017) *Speaking of Universities*, London: Verso.

Copsey, N. and Worley, M. (eds) (2018) *'Tomorrow Belongs to Us': The British Far Right Since 1967*, London: Routledge.

Corfield, A. (1969) *Epoch in Workers' Education: A History of the Workers' Educational Trade Union Committee*, London: WEA.

Cornwall, A. (2008) 'Unpacking "participation": models, meanings and practices', *Community Development Journal*, 43 (3): 269–83.

Cornwall, A. and Coelho, V. (2007) 'Spaces for change? The politics of participation in new democratic arenas' in A. Cornwall and V. Coelho (ed), *Spaces for Change?*, London: Zed, 1–29.

Craik, W. (1964) *The Central Labour College*, London: Lawrence and Wishart.

Crick, B. (2002) *Democracy: A Very Short Introduction*, Oxford: Oxford University Press

Cross-Durant, A. (1987) 'John Dewey and lifelong learning' in P. Jarvis (ed), *Twentieth Century Thinkers in Adult Education*, London: Routledge, 79–97.

Crossley, N. (2002) *Making Sense of Social Movements*, Buckingham: Open University Press.

Crowther, J. and Martin, I (2018) 'Why Freire still matters', *CONCEPT*, 9 (3): 8–14.

Crowther, J., Martin, I. and Shaw, M. (eds) (1999) *Popular Education and Social Movements in Scotland Today*, Leicester: NIACE.

Crowther, J., Galloway, V. and Martin, I. (2005a) 'Introduction: Radicalising intellectual work' in J. Crowther, V. Galloway and I. Martin (eds), *Popular Education: Engaging the Academy*, Leicester: NIACE, 1–7.

Crowther, J., Galloway, V. and Martin, I. (eds) (2005b) *Popular Education: Engaging the Academy*, Leicester: NIACE.

D'Ancona, M. (2017) *Post-Truth: The New War on Truth and How to Fight Back*, London: Ebury.

Dalton, A. (1979) *Asbestos Killer Dust: A Worker/Community Guide: How to Fight the Hazards of Asbestos and its Substitutes*, BSSRS publications.

David, M. (2016) *Reclaiming Feminism: Challenging Everyday Misogyny*, Bristol: Policy Press.

Davis, E. (2017) *Post-Truth; Why We Have Reached Peak Bullshit and What We Can Do About It*, London: Little Brown.

de Figueiredo-Cowen, M. and Gastaldo, D. (eds) (1995) *Paulo Freire at the Institute*, London: Institute of Education.

Della Porta, D. and Diani, M. (1999) *Social Movements*, Oxford: Blackwell.

Della Porta, D. and Tarrow, S. (eds) (2005) *Transnational Protest and Global Activism*, New York and Oxford: Rowman & Littlefield.

Demertzis, N. (2006) 'Emotion and populism' in S. Clarke, P. Hoggett and S. Thompson (eds) (2006) *Emotion, Politics and Society*, Basingstoke: Palgrave Macmillan, 103–22.

Denny, B. (undated) 'Present and correct', Dissertation, Ruskin College, Oxford.

Dhaliwal, S. and Yuval-Davis, N. (eds) (2014) *Women against Fundamentalism*, London: Lawrence and Wishart.

Dorling, D. (2010) *Injustice*, Bristol: Policy Press.

Dorling, D. (2018) *Peak Inequality*, Bristol: Policy Press.

Elsey, B. (1987) 'R.H. Tawney – "Patron saint of adult education"' in P. Jarvis (ed), *Twentieth Century Thinkers in Adult Education*, London: Routledge, 62–76.

Engels, F. (2009) *The Condition of the Working Class in England*, Oxford: Oxford World Classics.

English, L. and Irving, C. (2015) *Feminism in Community: Adult Education for Transformation*, Rotterdam: Sense.

English, L. and Mayo, P. (2012) *Learning with Adults*, Rotterdam: Sense.

References

Etmanski, C. (2007) 'Voyeurism, consciousness-raising, empowerment; Opportunities and challenges of using legislative theatre to "practise democracy"' in D. Clover and J. Stalker (eds), *The Arts and Social Justice*, Leicester: NIACE, 105–24.

Facer, K. and McKay, G. (2019) 'Series editors' foreword' in S. Banks, A. Hart and P. Ward (eds), *Co-producing Research: A Community Development Approach*, Bristol: Policy Press, xii.

Fals Borda, O. (1985) *Knowledge and People's Power*, New Delhi: Indian Social Institute.

Fanon, F. (2001) *The Wretched of the Earth*, Penguin Classic.

Farnsworth, K. and Irving, Z. (eds) (2015) *Social Policy in Times of Austerity: Global Economic Crisis and the New Politics of Welfare*, Bristol: Policy Press.

Fekete, L. (2009) *A Suitable Enemy: Racism, Migration and Islamophobia in Europe*, London: Pluto.

Fekete, L. (2018) *Europe's Fault Lines: The Rise of the Far Right*, London: Verso.

Fieldhouse, R. and Associates (1998) *A History of Modern British Adult Education*, Leicester: NIACE.

Fisher, J. (2005) *Bread on the Waters*, London: Lawrence and Wishart.

Foley, G. (1999) *Learning in Social Action*, Leicester: NIACE.

Forster, E.M. (1989) *Howards End*, Harmondsworth: Penguin.

Foucault, M. (1980) *Power/Knowledge: Selected Interviews and Other Writings, 1972–77*, Brighton: Harvester.

Foweraker, J. (1995) *Theorizing Social Movements*, London: Pluto.

Fraser, N. (2008) *Adding Insult to Injury*, London: Verso.

Freire, P. (1972) *Pedagogy of the Oppressed*, Harmondsworth: Penguin.

Freire, P. (1996a) *Letters to Cristina: Reflections on My Life and Work*, London: Routledge.

Freire, P. (1996b) *Pedagogy of Hope*, London: Bloomsbury.

Fryer, R. (2010) *Promises of Freedom: Citizenship, Belonging and Lifelong Learning*, Leicester: NIACE.

Gaventa, J. (2002) 'Crossing the great divide: building links and learning between NGOs and community-based organisations in the North and South' in D. Lewis (ed), *The Earthscan Reader on NGO Management*, London: Earthscan, 256–70.

Gaventa, J. (2006) 'Finding the spaces for change: A power analysis', *Institute of Development Studies Bulletin*, 37: 6.

Gaventa, J. (forthcoming) 'Applying Power Analysis: Using the 'Powercube' to explore forms, levels and spaces' in R. McGee and J. Pettit (eds), *Power Analysis*, London: Routledge.

Giroux, H. (1997) *Pedagogy and the Politics of Hope*, Oxford: Westview Press.

Giroux, H. (2010) *Politics After Hope*, London: Paradigm.

Giroux, H. (2011) 'Beyond the swindle of the corporate university' in M. Bailey and D. Freedman (eds), *The Assault on Universities: A Manifesto for Resistance*, London: Pluto, 145–56.

GLC (Greater London Council) (1983) *The East London File*, London: Greater London Council.

GLC (1984) *The West London Report*, London: Greater London Council.

GLC (1985a) *The East London File II*, London: Greater London Council.

GLC (1985b) *The London Industrial Strategy*, London: Greater London Council.

Gott, R. (2008) 'Orlando Fals Borda', obituary in *The Guardian*, 26 August.

Gramsci, A. (1968) *The Modern Prince and Other Writings*, New York: International Publishers.

Grayson, J. (2010) 'Borders, glass floors and anti-racist popular adult education' in M. Mayo and J. Annette (eds), *Taking Part?*, Leicester: NIACE, 156–68.

Hackney Unites (undated) *An Introduction to Community Organizing*, London: Hackney Unites [accessed at: https://drive.google.com/file/d/1wwUqws89SVwWca96tJ7v_OCKqJ1RrUdf/view].

Hall, B. and Tandon, R. (2017) 'From action research to knowledge democracy: Cartagena 1977–2017', Conference presentation to the World Conference on Action Research, organized by the Action Research Network of the Americas, June 2017.

Hall, B., Clover, D., Crowther, J. and Scandrett, E. (eds) (2012a) *Learning and Education for a Better World: The Role of Social Movements*, Rotterdam: Sense.

Hall, B., Clover, D., Crowther, J. and Scandrett, E. (2012b) 'Introduction' in B. Hall, D. Clover, J. Crowther and E. Scandrett (eds), *Learning and Education for a Better World: The Role of Social Movements, in Britain*, Rotterdam: Sense, ix–xvi.

Hall, S. (1991) 'Old and new identities, old and new ethnicities' in A. King (ed), *Culture, Globalization and the World System*, Basingstoke: Macmillan, 41–68.

Hanley, L. (2012) *Estates: An Intimate History*, London: Granta Books.

Hartley, T. (2010) 'Proving a point; effective social, political and citizenship education in South Yorkshire' in M. Mayo and J. Annette (eds), *Taking Part?*, Leicester: NIACE, 141–55.

References

Harvey, D. (1990) *The Condition of Modernity*, Oxford: Blackwell.

Hawley, G. (2019) *The Alt-Right*, Oxford: Oxford University Press.

Hochschild, A. (2016) *Strangers in Their Own Land: Anger and Mourning on the American Right*, New York: New Press.

Hoggett, P. (2000) *Emotional Life and the Politics of Welfare*, Basingstoke: Macmillan.

Hoggett, P. (2016) *Politics, Identity and Emotion*, London: Routledge.

Hoggett, P., Mayo, M. and Miller, C. (2009) *The Dilemmas of Development Work*, Bristol: Policy Press.

Holford, J. (1994) *Union Education*, Nottingham: Department of Adult Education, University of Nottingham.

Holst, J. (2002) *Social Movements, Civil Society, and Radical Adult Education*, London: Bergin and Garvey.

hooks, b. (2015 edition) *Ain't I a Woman*, London: Routledge.

Hughes, K. (1995) 'Really useful knowledge: Adult education and the Ruskin Learning Project' in M. Mayo and J. Thompson (eds), *Adult Learning, Critical Intelligence and Social Change*, Leicester: NIACE, 97–110.

Jarvis, P. (ed) (1987) *Twentieth Century Thinkers in Adult Education*, London: Routledge.

JDAG (Joint Docklands Action Group) (1977) *Rebuilding Docklands: Cuts and the Need for Public Investment*, London: JDAG.

JDAG and Tower Hamlets Action Committee on Jobs (1978) *London's Docks: An Alternative Strategy*, London: JDAG.

JDAG (1979) *The Docks Connection*, London: JDAG.

Johnson, A. (1995) *The Blackwell Dictionary of Sociology*, Oxford: Blackwell.

Jones, J. (1992) 'Foreword' in B. Simon (ed), *The Search for Enlightenment*, Leicester: NIACE, 7–8.

Jones, J. (2019) 'Primal scream: the face of our political age', *The Guardian*, 15 January, 8–9.

Jones, O. (2012) *Chavs: The Demonization of the Working Class*, London: Verso.

Kane, L. (2001) *Popular Education and Social Change in Latin America*, London: LAB.

Kane, L. (2005) 'Ideology matters' in J. Crowther, V. Galloway and I. Martin (eds), *Popular Education: Engaging the Academy*, Leicester: NIACE, 32–42.

Kane, L. (2012) 'Forty years of popular education in Latin America', in B. Hall, D. Clover, J. Crowther and E. Scandrett (eds), *Learning and Education for a Better World: The Role of Social Movements, in Britain*, Rotterdam: Sense, 69–83.

Kenny, S., Taylor, M., Onyx, J. and Mayo, M. (2015) *Challenging the Third Sector*, Bristol: Policy Press.

Kick It Out (2017) *Football in Pursuit of Equality (E), Inclusion (I) and Cohesion (C)*, Kick It Out.

Knowles, M. (1970) *The Modern Practice of Adult Education*, Cambridge: Cambridge Book Company.

Kotze, A. von (2005) 'People's education and the academy: An experience from South Africa' in J. Crowther, V. Galloway and I. Martin (eds), *Popular Education: Engaging the Academy*, Leicester: NIACE, 11–21.

Kotze, A. von (2018) 'Celebrating Freire: A message of solidarity from South Africa', *CONCEPT*, 9 (3): 96–7.

Kotze, A. von, Walters, S. and Luckett, T. (2016) 'Navigating our way: A compass for popular educators', *Studies in the Education of Adults*, 48 (1): 96–114.

Kumar, A. (2011) 'Achievements and limitations of the UK student movement' in M. Bailey and D. Freedman (eds), *The Assault on Universities: A Manifesto for Resistance*, London: Pluto, 132–42.

Kyneswood, B. (2019) 'Co-production as a new way of seeing: Using photographic exhibitions to challenge dominant stigmatising discourses' in S. Banks, A. Hart and P. Ward (eds), *Co-producing Research: A Community Development Approach*, Bristol: Policy Press, 155–80.

Laclau, E. (2005) 'Populism: What's in a name?' in F. Panizza (ed), *Populism and the Mirror of Democracy*, London: Verso, 32–49.

Lazaridis, G., Campani, G. and Benviste, A. (eds) (2016) *The Rise of the Far Right in Europe,* Basingstoke: Palgrave Macmillan.

Ledwith, M. (2018) 'Reclaiming the radical: Paulo Freire in neoliberal times', *CONCEPT*, 9 (3): 15–25.

Ledwith, S. (2019) 'Cruel cut to Ruskin's role and reputation', *The Guardian*, 7 March, 7.

Lenin, V. (2014) *The State and Revolution*, CreateSpace Independent Publishing Platform.

LEWRG (London Edinburgh Weekend Return Group) (1979) *In and Against the State*, London: Pluto.

Lissard, K. (2012) 'Venus in Lesotho' in L. Manicom and S. Walters (eds), *Feminist Popular Education in Transnational Debates*, Basingstoke: Palgrave Macmillan, 93–109.

Lucio-Villegas, E. (2018) 'Freire at the university', *CONCEPT*, 9 (3): 90–93.

Lukes, S. (2005) *Power: A Radical View*, 2nd edition, Basingstoke: Palgrave Macmillan.

References

Malik, K. (2018) 'No reds under beds, but the young are awake to the flaws of capitalism', *The Guardian*, 21 January.

Martikke, S., Church, A. and Hart, A. (2019) 'A radical take on co-production? Community partner leadership in research' in S. Banks, A. Hart and P. Ward (eds), *Co-producing Research: A Community Development Approach*, Bristol: Policy Press, 49–68.

Marx, K. and Engels, F. (1968) 'Manifesto of the Communist Party' in K. Marx and F. Engels, *Marx and Engels Selected Works*, London: Lawrence and Wishart, 31–63.

Maslow, A. (1943) 'A theory of human motivation', *Psychological Review*, 50 (4): 370–96.

Maslow, A. (1954) *Motivation and Personality*, New York: Harper and Row.

Mayo, M. (1997) *Imagining Tomorrow*, Leicester: NIACE.

Mayo, M. (2017) *Changing Communities*, Bristol: Policy Press.

Mayo, M. (2019) 'The continuing relevance of Marxism for popular education today', *CONCEPT*, 10 (1).

Mayo, M and Annette, J. (eds) (2010) *Taking Part?*, Leicester: NIACE.

Mayo, M. and Rooke, A. (2006) *Active Learning for Active Citizenship*, London: Home Office.

Mayo, M., Mendiwelso-Bendek, Z. and Packham, C. (eds) (2013) *Community Research for Community Development*, Basingstoke: Palgrave Macmillan.

Mayo, M., Mendiwelso-Bendek, Z. and Packham, C. (2019) 'Promoting the "Take Part" approach', in H. Tam (ed), *Whose Government is it?*, Bristol: Policy Press, 213–28.

Mayo, P. (1999) *Gramsci, Freire and Adult Education*, London: Zed Books.

Mayo, P. (2004) *Liberating Praxis*, Rotterdam: Sense.

McIlroy, J. (1992) 'The triumph of technical training?' in B. Simon (ed) *The Search for Enlightenment*, Leicester: NIACE, 208–43.

McKenzie, L. (2015) *Getting By: Estates, Class and Cultures in Austerity Britain*, Bristol: Policy Press.

McMellon, C. (2018) 'What Freire means to me', *CONCEPT*, 9 (3): 52–3.

Meade, R. and Shaw, M. (2010) 'Community development and the arts: Sustaining the democratic imagination in lean and mean times', *Journal of Arts and Communities*, 2 (1): 65–80.

Melucci, A. (1996) *Challenging Codes*, Cambridge: Cambridge University Press.

Merrifield, J. (2010) 'Putting the learning into citizenship', in M. Mayo and J. Annette (eds), *Taking Part?*, Leicester: NIACE, 261–73.

Mezirow, J. (1991) *Transformative Dimensions of Adult Learning*, San Francisco: Jossey Bass.

Milbourne, L. (2013) *Voluntary Sector in Transition*, Bristol: Policy Press.

Milbourne, L. and Murray, U. (eds) (2017) *Civil Society Organizations in Turbulent Times*, London: UCL.

Miliband, R. (1972) *Parliamentary Socialism*, London: Merlin.

Miliband, R. (1977) *Marxism and Politics*, Oxford: Oxford University Press.

Miliband, R. (1994) *Socialism for a Sceptical Age*, Cambridge: Polity Press.

Monbiot, G. (2018) 'How US billionaires are fuelling the hard-right cause in Britain: Dark money is among the greatest threats to democracy', *The Guardian*, 7 December: 1.

Morris, P. (1979) 'Race, community and marginality: Spiralynx' in G. Craig, M. Mayo and N. Sharman (eds), *Jobs and Community Action*, London: Routledge and Kegan Paul, 100–12.

Mouffe, C. (2018) *For a Left Populism*, London: Verso.

Munck, R. and Waterman, P. (eds) (1999) *Labour Worldwide in the Era of Globalization*, London: Macmillan.

Murray, A. (2008) *The T and G Story*, London: Lawrence and Wishart.

Newham Docklands Forum and the GLC Popular Planning Unit (1983) *The People's Plan for the Royal Docks*, London: GLC.

Newman, M. (1979) *The Poor Cousin*, London: Allen and Unwin.

Newman, M. (2006) *Teaching Defiance*, San Francisco: Jossey-Bass.

Newman, M. (2014) 'Transformative learning: Mutinous thoughts revisited', *Studies in the Education of Adults*, 64 (5): 345–55.

Nussbaum, M. (2010) *Not for Profit*, Princeton: Princeton University Press.

O'Toole, F. (2018) *Heroic Failure: Brexit and the Politics of Pain*, London: Head Zeus.

Paik, A. (2017) 'Abolitionist futures and the US sanctuary movement', *Race and Class*, 59 (2): 3–25.

Panizza, F. (2005) 'Introduction: populism and the mirror of democracy' in F. Panizza (ed), *Populism and the Mirror of Democracy*, London: Verso, 1–31.

Patel, S. (1996) 'From a seed to a tree: building community organisation in India's cities' in S. Walters and L. Minicom (eds), *Gender in Popular Education*, London: Zed, 87–101.

Peters, J. and Bell, B. (1987) 'Horton of Highlander' in J. Fieldhouse (ed), *A History of Modern British Adult Education*, Leicester: NIACE, 243–64.

References

Player, J. (2013) 'Critical discourse analysis, adult education and "fitba"', *Studies in the Education of Adults*, 45: 57–66.

Pollins, H. (1984) *The History of Ruskin College*, Oxford: Ruskin College.

Popple, K. (2015) *Analysing Community Work*, Maidenhead: Open University Press.

Popple, K. (2018) 'Why Gramsci offers us a framework for understanding the work of Freire: And why their work is crucial at this time', *CONCEPT*, 9 (3): 84–9.

Poulantzas, N. (1973) *Political Power and Social Classes*, London: Sheed and Ward.

Raw, L. (2009) *Striking a Light: The Bryant and May Matchwomen and Their Place in Labour History*, London: Continuum UK.

Recknagel, G. with Holland, D. (2013) 'How inclusive and how empowering?' in M. Mayo, Z. Mendiwelso-Bendek and C. Packham (eds) (2013) *Community Research for Community Development*, Basingstoke: Palgrave, 19–39.

Rodgerson, C. (2018) *Routes, Executive Summary and Local Context*, Show Racism the Red Card.

Rooke, A. (2010) 'Learning from the ALAC hubs' in M. Mayo and J. Annette (eds), *Taking Part?*, Leicester: NIACE, 123–40.

Rooke, A. (2013) 'Contradiction, collaboration and criticality: Researching empowerment and citizenship in community-based arts' in M. Mayo, Z. Mendiwelso-Bendek and C. Packham (eds), *Community Research for Community Development*, Basingstoke: Palgrave Macmillan, 150–69.

Rosenberg, D. (2011) *Battle for the East End: Jewish Responses to Fascism in the 1930s*, London: Pluto.

Rosenberg, D. and Browne, C. (2015) *Rebel Footprints: A Guide to Uncovering London's Radical History*, London: Pluto.

Rowbottom, S. (1992) *Women in Movement: Feminism and Social Action*, London: Routledge.

Saunders, R. (2018) 'Cultures of resistance', *Jewish Socialist*, Autumn/Winter 2018/9: 10–11.

Scandrett, E. (2019) *Collective Learning in and from Social Movements: The Bhopal Disaster*, London: Routledge.

Schuller, T. and Watson, D. (2009) *Learning through Life*, Leicester: NIACE.

Seidler, V. (2018) *Making Sense of Brexit*, Bristol: Policy Press.

Sennett, R. and Cobb, J. (1993) *The Hidden Injuries of Class*, New York: Norton.

Shaw, M. and Martin, I. (2008) 'Community work, citizenship and democracy; remaking the connections' in G. Craig, K. Popple and M. Shaw (eds), *Community Development in Theory and Practice*, Nottingham: Spokesman, 296–308.

Shaw, M. and Mayo, M. (2016) 'Editorial introduction' in M. Shaw and M. Mayo (eds), *Class, Inequality and Community Development*, Bristol: Policy Press, 3–22.

Shildrick, T. (2018) *Poverty Propaganda*, Bristol: Policy Press.

Simon, B. (ed) (1992a) *The Search for Enlightenment*, Leicester: NIACE.

Simon, B. (1992b) 'The struggle for hegemony' in B. Simon (ed), *The Search for Enlightenment*, Leicester: NIACE, 15–70.

Sivanandum, A. (2006) 'Race, terror and civil society', *Race and Class*, 47 (3): 1–8.

Smith, G., Perez, E. and Smith, T. (2014) *Social Enquiry, Social Reform and Social Action*, Oxford: Department of Social Policy and Intervention.

Sng, P. (ed) (2019) *Invisible Britain: Portraits of Hope and Resilience*, Bristol: Policy Press.

Standing, G. (2011) *The Precariat*, London: Bloomsbury.

Stacey, M. (1969) 'The Myth of Community Studies', *British Journal of Sociology*, 20: 134.

Steele, T. (2010) 'Enlightenment public: Popular education movements in Europe, their legacy and promise', *Studies in the Education of Adults*, 42 (2): 107–23.

Steele, T. (2007) *Knowledge is Power*, Oxford: Peter Lang.

Sveinsson, K. (ed) (2009) *Who Cares About the White Working Class?*, London: Runnymede Trust.

Tandon, R. (ed) (2005) *Participatory Research*, New Delhi: Mosaic Books.

Tarrow, S. (2011) *Power in Movement: Social Movements, Collective Action and Politics*, Cambridge: Cambridge University Press.

Tawney, R. (1964) *Equality*, London: Unwin Books.

Taylor, M. (2011) *Public Policy in the Community*, 2nd edition, Basingstoke: Palgrave Macmillan.

Tett, L. (2018) 'What Freire means to me', *CONCEPT*, 9 (3): 43–8.

The Gold Paper (2018) *The Gold Paper*, London: Goldsmiths, University of London.

The Local Trust (2018) *The Future for Communities: Perspectives on Power*, London: IVAR.

The Russell Report (1973) *Adult Education: A Plan for Development*, London: HMSO.

The World Transformed (2018) 'The World Transformed programme', theworldtransformed.org

Thomas, D. (1983) *The Making of Community Work*, London: Allen and Unwin.

Thompson, E. (1970) *Warwick University Ltd*, Harmondsworth: Penguin

Thompson, J. (2007) 'Forward' in D. Clover and J. Stalker (eds), *The Arts and Social Justice*, Leicester: NIACE, xi–xii.

Tight, M. (ed) (1983) *Adult Learning and Education*, London: Routledge.

Tiller, C. (2013) 'Participatory arts and community development' in M. Mayo, Z. Mendiwelso-Bendek and C. Packham (eds), *Community Research for Community Development*, Basingstoke: Palgrave Macmillan, 133–49.

Touraine, A. (1981) *The Voice and the Eye*, Cambridge: Cambridge University Press.

Tower Hamlets, Southwark and West Ham Trades Councils (1981) *Employment in Docklands*, London: Joint Docklands Action Group.

Tyler, I. (2013) *Revolting Subjects: Social Abjection and Resistance in Neoliberal Britain*, London: Zed.

Wacquant, L. (2007) 'Territorial stigmatization in the age of advanced marginality', *Thesis Eleven*, 91: 66–77.

Waldman, L. (2010) 'Mobilization and political momentum: anti-asbestos struggles in South Africa and India' in J. Gaventa and R. Tandon (eds), *Globalizing Citizens*, London: Zed, 185–210.

Walters, S. and Manicom, L. (eds) (1996) *Gender in Popular Education*, London: Zed Books.

Ward, P., Banks, S. and Hart, A. (2019) 'Conclusion: Imagining different communities and making them happen' in S. Banks, A. Hart and P. Ward (eds), *Co-producing Research: A Community Development Approach*, Bristol: Policy Press, 203–9.

WEA (2018) *The Highway: The Magazine for Members of the WEA*, London: WEA.

Williams, R. (1973) *The Long Revolution*, Harmondsworth: Penguin Books.

Williams, R. (1976) *Keywords*, London: Fontana.

Williams, R. (1977) *Marxism and Literature*, Oxford: Oxford University Press.

Winlow, S., Hall, S. and Treadwell, J. (2017) *The Rise of the Far Right*, Bristol: Policy Press.

Wodak, R. (2015) *The Politics of Fear*, London: Sage.

Woodward, V. (2004) *Active Learning for Active Citizenship in the Voluntary and Community Sector*, London: Civil Renewal Unit/Home Office.

Woodward, V. (2010) 'Active Learning for Active Citizenship (ALAC): origins and approaches' in M. Mayo and J. Annette (eds), *Taking Part? Active Learning for Active Citizenship, and beyond*, Leicester: NIACE, 101–22.

Index

A

accreditation 64
active citizenship 51, 53, 58, 59–70
Active Learning for Active Citizenship (ALAC) 59–70
Agarwal, A. 97, 98, 99
Ahmed, S. 155–6
airport, Docklands 107–10
Alfred, D. 25
alienation 8, 163, 178
anti-racism
   and active learning for active citizenship 65–9
   and the arts 162
   guided walks 56, 100
   Hope Not Hate 163–7
   and Jewish communities 165–6, 168
   mayoral elections, London 129–31
   and Muslim communities 10, 166
   rising hate crime 175
   Rock against Racism (RAR) 100
   and sports 167–72
   see also black and minority ethnic communities
anti-Semitism 165–6, 168
anxiety 157–8, 160
Army Bureau of Current Affairs (ABCA) 44
Army School of Education 44
arts
   and community–university partnerships 147–51
   and emotions 161–3
   role of 70–1
   theatre projects 71–2, 161–3
asylum seekers 65, 67, 70
austerity 1, 7–8, 9, 12–13, 42, 44, 88, 178
Australia 55

B

Bachrach, P. 120
Bailey, M. 141
Banks, S. 147, 148–9, 150
Baratz, M. 120
Barcam, S. 86–7
Barnett House 48

Battle of Cable Street (1936) 100, 165
Bedford, J. 64
Bell, B. 34, 35, 36, 49, 95–6
Bell, D. 152
Benn, M. 141
Benn, Tony 170
Benwell, Newcastle 148, 149
Bhopal, India 96–9
Bhopal Survivors Movement 99
bias 121
Birmingham 166
black and minority ethnic communities
   Civil Rights Movement (US) 34, 35, 81, 96
   and urban regeneration 105–6
   and working conditions 102–3
   see also anti-racism; migrants
Boal, A. 72, 161
Boffo, M. 1
Boughton, B. 55
Brazil 29–30, 49, 85
Brexit 8–9, 160
British National Party (BNP) 129–31, 163
British Society for Social Responsibility in Science 88
Brookes, Peter 158
Brookfield, S. 41–2, 55, 58
Broughton, E. 97
Brownhill, S. 109
Buckner, J. 162
Butler, R.A. 44
Butterwick, S. 72

C

Cable Street, Battle of (1936) 100, 165
Canada 72
capitalism, and power 119
Center for Science and Environment (CSE) 97–8
Central Labour College 26
Centre for Crime and Justice Studies 91, 92–3
Chapman, Hugo 158
Chartist Movement 23
Chelsea FC 168
Christian Socialists 25

Chu, Clara 53
Citizenship Schools (US) 35
Civil Rights Movement (US) 34, 35, 81, 96
civil society and the state 42–7
claimed spaces 47, 49, 123, 124
class
　class politics 6–7
　and Marxism 176–7, 179
　and power 119
　and roots of popular education 23, 25–7
　working class 6, 7–8, 10–11, 23, 25–7, 54, 177
class politics 6–7
closed spaces 47, 123, 124
Clover, D. 72, 73
co-production of research/knowledge *see* community–university partnerships
Cobb, J. 158
Coelho, V. 45
Collini, S. 138–40
Colombia 21, 36, 37, 38, 53, 74
'common sense' 42, 119–20, 121, 123, 132, 133, 135, 181, 183
Communist Manifesto 119, 177
Community-Based Research and Social Responsibility in Higher Education 39, 50, 137
community, concept of 78–80
Community Development Projects (CDP) 101–3, 146, 148–9, 159
Community-Library Inter Action (CLIA) 53
Community Plan for Holloway 91, 93
community theatre 71–2
community–university partnerships 39, 48, 49–51, 137–53
　and active citizenship 59–60, 61, 63, 69–70
　challenges of 51, 140–1, 150, 151–2
　in Colombia 74
　Community Development Project (CDP) 101–2
　impact of research 140–1
　internal contradictions 140–1
　mobilisation of staff and students 141–6
　and public policy initiatives 146–52
　role of universities 138–40, 143
　see also universities

CONCEPT (journal) 176, 180, 181
Connected Communities programme 147
conscientisation 180, 183
consciousness raising groups 85
constructed conversations 63
Copsey, N. 10
Cornwall, A. 45, 47
created spaces 47, 49, 123, 124
Crick, B. 4–5
critical literacy skills 167
critical thinking/reflection 23, 41, 57, 58, 169, 176
Crowther, J. 19, 20, 49–50, 179–80, 181–2

D

David, M. 85
Davis, E. 7
de Figueiredo-Cowen, M. 30, 170
deconstructionism 6
Della Porta, D. 80, 81
Demertzis, N. 159–60
Democratic Football Lads Alliance 167
Demos 9
Dewey, John 28, 34
Dhaliwal, S. 79, 177
Diani, M. 80, 81
Docklands Community Poster Project 107
Docklands Forum 107, 109
Docklands Joint Committee (DJC) 104
Docklands, London 99–110
Docklands Strategic Plan 105
Dorling, D. 1, 11, 44
drama 71–2, 161–3

E

East London 99–110
East Midlands 63
Economic and Social Research Council 147
economic power 119
Edgar, D. 71
Ella Baker School of Transformative Community Organising 128–9
emotions 155–73
　and the arts 161–3
　emotional needs of educators 184–5
　Hope Not Hate 163–7
　'ressentiment' 158, 159
　and rise of populism 159–60

Index

and sports 163, 167–73
structures of feeling 156–61
tensions around 184
working with 155–6
employment/employers
and the arts 162
education of employees 23
and urban regeneration 99–110
see also trade unions; working conditions
Engels, F. 23, 119
English Defence League (EDL) 10–11, 163
environmental issues
Bhopal, India 96–9
campaigning 79, 86–8
Highlander Research and Education Center 35, 96–9
Ilva steel plant, Italy 86–8
pollution 86, 96–9
ethnic minority communities *see* anti-racism; black and minority ethnic communities
evaluation systems 60, 63
exhibitions 149, 151

F

Facer, K. 147
faith-based organisations 45
Fals Borda, O. 36–8, 137, 181
Fanon, F. 30, 31–2, 43
Far Right
British National Party (BNP) 129–31, 163
and emotions 159–60
English Defence League (EDL) 10–11, 163
and football 167, 169–70
Hope Not Hate 163, 164–5
Jewish communities 165–6, 168
and Marxist analyses 176, 177, 179
Muslim communities 10–11, 166
politicians 1
rise of 2, 159–60, 175
roots of 6, 9, 10–11
serious threat of 175
in United States 9
felt project 149
feminism
and active citizenship 63–4
approaches to learning 84–5
feminist critiques 33–4

quilting 72
second wave feminism 14, 84–5, 133
see also women
Fieldhouse, R. 23, 27
financial crisis 2008 1, 9, 13, 46, 54
Foley, G. 85
football 167–72
Forster, E.M. 155
Foucault, M. 121–2, 131
Fraser, N. 159, 168
free floating 'affects' 157, 160
Freedman, D. 141
Freire, P.
and active citizenship 70
approaches developed by 20, 29–33, 45, 70, 169
and class 176
and contested spaces 49
continuing relevance of 14, 179–82
and dreams and utopias 185
feminist critiques of 32, 33–4
and Gramsci, Antonio 30, 42, 121, 170
and Horton, Myles 35–6
learning styles 32, 74, 75
and Marxism 181
and oppression 31–2, 33, 121, 158
Pedagogy of Hope 181
Pedagogy of the Oppressed 49, 180, 181
and universities 39, 70, 137
Fryer, R. 58
Furniture Timber and Allied Trades Union (FTAT) 102–3

G

Galloway, V. 20, 49
Gastaldo, D. 30, 170
Gaventa, J. 37, 96–7, 98, 122–4
Giroux, H. 32, 58, 139–40
Gold Paper, The 141–2
Golders Green, London 166
Goldsmiths, University of London 141–6
Gorz, A. 6
Gott, R. 37
Gramsci, A. 30, 42–3, 119, 121, 170, 183
Grayson, J. 65–6, 67
Greater London Authority 129–31
Greater London Council (GLC) 106–10

Greece 160
guided walks 56

H
Hackney Gazette 129, 130–1
Hackney, London 129–31, 165
Hackney Trades Council 129–31
Hackney Unites 130–1
Hall, B. 37–9, 50, 86, 137, 181
Hall, S. 10, 11
Hall, Stuart 79, 159
Hartley, T. 65, 69
Harvey, D. 5–6
Hawley, G. 175
Heritage and Culture Partnership 149
hidden power 123, 124, 132–5
hierarchy of human needs 159, 168
Highlander Folk School 35
Highlander Research and Education Center 35, 37, 95–9
Hillfields, Coventry 150–1
histories and cultures, varying 77–94
  and concept of community 78–80
  and environmental issues 86–8
  and housing crisis 88–94
  and identities 79–80
  in practice 86–94
  within second wave feminism 84–5
  and social movements 80–2
  and trade unions 82–4
Hochschild, A. 9, 155
Hoggett, P. 156, 157, 159, 160–1, 184
Holloway prison, London 90, 91, 125–8
Holst, J. 41–2, 55
Homes for All 89, 90, 91, 93
hooks, b. 33–4
Hope Camps 163–5
Hope Not Hate 163–7
Horton, Myles 19, 29, 34–6, 37, 49, 96
House of Lords Select Committee on Docklands 105
Housing and Planning Bill (2015) 88
housing issues 88–94, 125–8, 143
Hughes, K. 22, 115
Hungary 68

I
identity politics 6, 7
Ilva steel plant, Taranto 86–7
Imagine Hillfields project 150–1
Imagine North East project 148–50
Imagine projects 147–52

immigration *see* migrants
IMPACT approach 64
India 38, 96–9
industrial action 26, 77, 100, 130, 141, 143–6
inequality 1
  and class 7, 177
  and emotions 158
  and football 167–72
  and popular education 20, 57–8, 61
  and power 122
  rising 5, 8, 12–13, 34, 44
  see also poverty
Inner London Education Authority 52
internalised power 121, 123, 124, 132–5
International Participatory Research Network (IPRN) 38
invisible power 123, 124, 132–5
invited spaces 47, 123, 124
Islington Hands Off Our Public Services (IHOOPS) 88, 89, 90, 91, 93
Italy 86–8

J
Jewish Chronicle, The 166
Jewish communities 165–6, 168
Johnson, A. 118
Joint Docklands Action Group (JDAG) 101, 104–7
Jones, Jack 21–2
Jones, Jonathan 157, 158
'Jungle, The' (play) 161–2
Justice for Cleaners 145–6

K
Kane, L. 21, 50, 182
Kick It Out 167–8
Kill the Housing Bill 89
knowledge
  and power 22, 121, 122, 135
  and roots of popular education 22–3
  valuing existing knowledge 183–4
  see also community–university partnerships
Knowledge for Change (K4C) 50–1, 137
Kotze, A. von 24, 50
Kumar, A. 141
Kyneswood, B. 150, 151

L
Labour Colleges 26, 83

Index

Labour Party
  New Labour 11, 51, 61
  political education 56
  The World Transformed (TWT) 13, 55, 74, 110–14
Laclau, E. 4
learning styles/approaches 32–3, 64, 74, 181–2
Ledwith, S. 27
legitimation of power 118–20
Lenin, V. 43
Leonardi, E. 86–7
Liberation Theology movement 30, 45
libraries 52–5
Lindeman, Eduard 28, 34
Lissard, K. 72
local history 147–9
(The) Local Trust 117–18
London Bubble Theatre Company 71–2
London City Airport 107–9
London, Docklands 99–110
London Docklands Development Corporation (LDDC) 105, 110
London Industrial Strategy 107
London mayoral elections 129–31
Lucio-Villegas, E. 182
Lukes, S. 118, 120–3, 135

M

Malik, K. 13
Manchester 70
Manicom, L. 33
Mansbridge, Albert 25, 28
marketisation 44–6, 49–50
  and planning 105–6
  and universities 49–50, 138–40, 142–3
Martin, I. 20, 49, 179–80, 181–2
Marx Memorial Library and Workers' School (MML) 54–5
Marx schools 55
Marxism 30, 54–5, 82–3, 119, 181
  continued relevance of 176–9
Maslow, A. 159, 168
Match Women's Strike (1888) 100
Mayo, P. 45
mayoral elections, London 129–31
McKay, G. 147
McMellon, C. 33–4
'Me? I just put British!' (play) 162
Meade, R. 73
Mechanics Institutes 23

Melucci, A. 80, 81
Merrifield, J. 96–7
Mezirow, J. 28–9
migrants
  negative attitudes to 5, 10, 160
  projects with 65–70, 161–3
Milbourne, L. 45
Miliband, R. 61
Miller, C. 156
Monbiot, G. 8
moral panics 160
Morris, P. 103
Mosley, Oswald 165
Munch, Edvard 157–8
Murray, A. 83
Murray, U. 45
Muslim communities 10, 166

N

National Council of Labour Colleges (NCLC) 26, 82, 83
neoliberalism 8, 11, 42, 44–7, 61, 182, 184
  see also marketisation
New Labour 11, 51, 61
Newham Docklands Forum 107–10
Newman, M. 52
North Shields 148–9
Northern College 65, 66–7
Nussbaum, M. 139

O

oppression 31–2, 42–3, 121, 123, 135, 158–9, 177, 179, 180–1
organic intellectual 183
O'Toole, F. 9

P

Packham, C. 70
Panizza, F. 5
Parks, Rosa 35
participatory action research (PAR)
  and active citizenship 69–70
  and the arts 71–2, 162–3
  community–university partnerships 148, 150
  concept of 36–7
  development of 36–8
  emotional needs of researchers 184–5
  and environmental issues 96–9
  and Freire, P. 180–1

participatory action research (PAR) (continued)
  and knowledge democracy 36–9
  remaining tensions and challenges 182–5
  spaces and places for 48, 49, 50–1
  and trade unions 54–5
  and urban regeneration 101, 104–5
  and working conditions 103
participatory democracy 41–2
Participatory Research in Asia (PRIA) 37–8, 96–9
People's Plan Centre 107
People's Plan for the Royal Docks (1983) 107–10
People's Tribunal 142
Peters, J. 34, 35
photography project 151
planning issues
  Docklands, London 101–10
  Holloway prison 90, 91, 125–8
Plebs League 47–8
politics/politicians
  alienation from 8, 11, 178
  British National Party (BNP) 129–31, 163
  New Labour 11, 51, 61
  polarisation 12
  political education 13, 52–6, 57, 74, 110–14
  and social movements 81–2
  see also trade unions
Pollins, H. 26
pollution 86, 96–9
Popple, K. 181, 183
popular education (general) 1–17
  continuing relevance of Paulo Freire 179–82
  definition of 19–22, 182–3
  emergence of initiatives 3–4
  emotional needs of educators 184–5
  remaining tensions and challenges 182–5
  scope for 12–14
Popular Education Network (PEN) 3, 19, 21
popular education, roots of 19–39
  definition of popular education 19–22, 182–3
  feminist critiques 33–4
  influence of early thinkers 28–9
  influence of Myles Horton 34–6
  influence of Paulo Freire 29–33
  participatory action research and knowledge democracy 36–9
  roots and tensions 22–8
  Ruskin College Oxford 25–7
  Workers' Educational Association (WEA) 25–7
popular education, spaces and places 41–56
  civil society and the state 42–7
  community–university partnerships 50–1
  in contemporary contexts 50–6
  contested spaces 48–9
  debates around 47–50
  libraries 52–5
  model of spaces 47
  and political parties 55–6
  role of the academic 47–50
  see also community-university partnerships
populism
  concept of 4–5
  and emotions 159–60
  rise of 1–2, 159–60
  roots of 5–12
  see also Far Right
postmodernism 5–7
poverty
  and class 7–8
  and lack of knowledge and power 30
  stigmatising 7–8, 44, 101, 149, 150, 158–9
  and urban regeneration 101–2
power and power analysis 117–35
  authority and influence within communities 131–5
  concept of power 118
  and consent 119–20
  dimensions of 120–2, 132–5
  imbalances 132–5
  and knowledge 121, 122, 135
  legitimacy and influence 117–20
  microphysics of 121–2
  power cube 122–4
  power mapping 124–9
  powerful communities 117–18
  and resistance 122, 135
  and social relations 121–2
  tools for analysis 122–9
power cube 122–4
power imbalances 132–5
power mapping 124–9
powerlessness 159

principles and practice of popular
    education 57–75
  Active Learning for Active
    Citizenship (ALAC) 59–70
  and the arts 70–3
  challenges of 74–5
  characteristics of 58
  tensions 58–9
  values 57–9
prisons 52, 90, 125
Professional Footballers' Association
    (PFA) 171
progressive social change 57–8
psycho-social approach 156
public consultation exercises 120–1

Q
quilting 72

R
racism *see* anti-racism; migrants
Refugee Charter for Manchester 70
Refugee Community Organisations
    (RCOs) 67
refugees 65–8, 70, 161–3
Research Excellence Framework (REF)
    140
resentment 158, 159
residential courses 66–7, 69, 83–4
ressentiment 158, 159
Robinson, Tommy 166, 167
Rock against Racism (RAR) 100
Rodgerson, C. 169
Rooke, A. 71
Rowbottom, S. 84
Royal Docks, London 107–10
Runnymede Trust 7
Ruskin College Oxford 25–7, 47, 82, 83
Russell Report (1973) 152–3

S
safe spaces 53, 69, 112, 117, 142, 185
Saunders, R. 100
Scream, The 157–8
second wave feminism 14, 84–5, 133
Seidler, V. 8, 12
Sennett, R. 158
Shaw, M. 73, 177
Sheffield 65–6
Shildrick, T. 44
Show Racism the Red Card 167,
    168–70

Simon, B. 26, 27, 83
Sivanandum, A. 65
Smith, G. 48
Sng, P. 8
social class *see* class
Society for Participatory Research in
    Asia (PRIA) 37–8, 96–9
Solent University, Southampton 168
South Africa 24, 49, 50, 52, 180
South Yorkshire 65–9
spaces, model of 47
sports 163, 167–73
Stalker, J. 73
state
  and civil society 42–7
  and power 117–19
Steele, T. 22–3
strikes 26, 77, 100, 130, 141, 143–6
structures of feeling 156–61
students, mobilisation of 141, 142–4
study visits 67, 68, 69
Sveinsson, K. 7
'Sweat' (play) 162
Sweden 67

T
Take Part Learning Framework for
    Active Citizenship Learning 53
Take Part programme (UK) 59–62, 74
Tandon, R. 37–9, 50, 98, 137, 181
Tanzania 37, 38
Tarrow, S. 80
Tawney, R.H. 25, 28
teach-ins 66
teachers, role of 32
territorial stigmatisation 149, 150
Tett, L. 33
theatre 71–2, 161–3
Thompson, E.P. 138
Thompson, J. 72–3
Together We Can programme (UK) 59
Touraine, A. 80, 81
trade unions
  anti-racism 169–72
  approaches to education 21–2, 82–4
  and austerity 88
  black workers 171
  contestation and struggle 45
  and discrimination 169–72
  and environmental campaigning 87
  Highlander Research and Education
    Center 35

trade unions (continued)
  history of 77
  Justice for the Cleaners 145–6
  mayoral elections, London 130
  participatory action research (PAR) 54–5
  strikes 26, 77, 100, 130, 141, 143–6
  and urban regeneration 104–7, 108
  and Workers' Educational Association (WEA) 25
  and working conditions 102–3
Transport and General Workers Union (T and G) 83
Treadwell, J. 10, 11
Trump, Donald, resistance to 12
Tyne and Wear 169

U
UK Arts and Humanities Research Council 147
UNESCO Chairs in Community-Based Research and Social Responsibility in Higher Education 50–1, 137
Union Carbide 97–9
United States
  and the arts 162
  Civil Rights Movement 34, 35, 81, 96
  Far Right 9
  Highlander Research and Education Center 35, 37, 95–9
  influence of thinkers 28, 34–6
  libraries 53
  and political education 55
  resistance to Trump 12
universities
  impact of research 140–1
  lecturers' strike 141, 143–5
  libraries 53
  marketisation 49–50, 138–40, 142–3
  popular political education 112
  role of 138–40, 143, 182
  Ruskin College Oxford 25–7, 47, 82, 83
  and Workers' Educational Association (WEA) 25–7
  see also community–university partnerships
Universities and College Union (UCU) 143

University of Illinois Mortenson Center 53
University of Lincoln 63
University of London 141–6
University of Manchester 70
University of Oxford 25–7, 47, 82, 83
urban regeneration 99–110
utopias 185

V
Vio Grossi, Francisco 29, 38
visible power 118, 123, 124, 132–5

W
Walters, S. 33
Ward, P. 152
Weber, M. 118
West, Don 34–5
West Midlands 63–4
white working class 7–8, 10–11
Williams, R. 156–7
Winlow, S. 10, 11, 179
Wodak, R. 6
women
  active citizenship 63–4
  quilting 72
  refugees 67
  second wave feminism 14, 84–5, 133
  and trade unions 83
  and urban regeneration 105–6
Women's Enterprise Development Agency 64
Woodward, V. 60–1, 62
Workers' Educational Association (WEA) 25–7, 48–9, 65, 67, 82–3
Workers' Educational Trade Union Committee (WETUC) 25, 83
working class 6, 7–8, 10–11, 23, 25–7, 54, 177
working conditions
  and Community Development Projects 102–3
  Ilva steel plant, Taranto 86–7
  Justice For Cleaners 145–6
  strikes 26, 77, 100, 130, 141, 143–6
World Transformed, The (TWT) 13, 55, 74, 110–14
Worley, M. 10

Y
Yuval-Davis, N. 79, 177